GERMAN SHORT STORIES 2

DEUTSCHE KURZGESCHICHTEN 2

Edited by David Constantine

PENGUIN BOOKS

PENGUIN BOOKS

Published by the Penguin Group
Penguin Books Ltd, 80 Strand, London WC2R 0RL, England
Penguin Putnam Inc., 375 Hudson Street, New York, New York 10014, USA
Penguin Books Australia Ltd, 250 Camberwell Road, Camberwell, Victoria 3124, Australia
Penguin Books Canada Ltd, 10 Alcorn Avenue, Toronto, Ontario, Canada M4V 3B2
Penguin Books India (P) Ltd, 11 Community Centre, Panchsheel Park, New Delhi – 110 017, India
Penguin Books (NZ) Ltd, Cnr Rosedale and Airborne Roads, Albany, Auckland, New Zealand
Penguin Books (South Africa) (Pty) Ltd, 24 Sturdee Avenue, Rosebank 2196, South Africa

Penguin Books Ltd, Registered Offices: 80 Strand, London WC2R 0RL, England

www.penguin.com

First published 1976
16

Printed in England by Clays Ltd, St Ives plc
Set in Monotype Bembo

ISBN-13: 978-0-140-04119-4
ISBN-10: 0-140-04119-2

CONTENTS

Acknowledgements are due to the following German publishers for permission to include German originals in this book: for Ernst Penzoldt and Thomas Bernhard to Suhrkamp Verlag; for Marie Luise Kaschnitz to Insel Verlag; for Günter de Bruyn to Mitteldeutscher Verlag; for Siegfried Lenz to Hoffmann und Kampe Verlag; for Ingeborg Bachmann and Alexander Kluge to Piper Verlag; for Johannes Bobrowski to Union Verlag.

INTRODUCTION

THE short story in Germany is a genre that writers seem happier about than critics. The *Novelle*, Germany's traditional form of shorter fiction, has been a critic's paradise; its highly contrived composition asks to be analysed and defined. But the short story, relatively new in Germany, has so far escaped definition; indeed, critics have only very recently recognized it as a serious genre at all.

There seems little point in discussing what a short story is or is not. The writers themselves are not anxious to define the form they are working in; rather, they think its indefiniteness of positive value.

This willingness to accept the open form, though nothing new in America and Britain, is new in Germany. It reflects the scepticism and modesty of much present-day writing. For various reasons works in the great nineteenth-century tradition, of the scope of Thomas Mann's *Buddenbrooks* or *Zauberberg*, are no longer thought possible. It may well be that no one of Mann's ability is writing today. But also, since the war, in part as a consequence of its horrors and as the dissolution of social norms and distinctions continues, human society and behaviour have seemed less and less tractable. Few writers nowadays, in the West at least, would think it proper to present a whole and coherent view of the world, whatever their ability. As Borges has said, we lack the nineteenth century's optimistic belief that the world can be captured 'in 500 pages'. The modern writer's experience, despite or because of the increase in communications and the vast surfeit of facts and information, is nothing like so large and whole as Mann's, to say

7

nothing of Dickens, Balzac or Goethe. For his partial and fragmented view other forms of fiction seem appropriate, ones more tentative, more sceptical, more honestly expressive of uncertainty and inconclusiveness. The *Novelle*, far more even than the novel, implied through its coherent composition a belief in the artist's duty and ability to order human experience; and thus a belief that there *was* an order, a moral order, in experience. The writer's job was to discern and affirm it. In the absence of such optimism the short story has come into its own.

Novelists have become less confident; omniscient narrators are fewer. In a sense writers have come to the short story as a *pis aller*, thinking the times not conducive to the production of anything more substantial. But having accepted the appropriateness of the genre they have soon discovered its potential richness too, and have been able to do a great deal with it.

'Short story' is nicely vague. In German it might be *Kurzgeschichte, Erzählung* or simply *Text* or *Prosa*; some writers wisely call their pieces nothing at all. I have not been concerned with definitions in compiling the anthology; the choice was determined by availability, by the consideration of what has already appeared in England, and on the grounds of interest and variety.

The most 'modern' of the authors are Kluge and Bernhard, the former in his montage technique and non-fictional manner, the latter in his oblique form of narrative. At this, the modern, experimental, end of the scale, I have, I suppose, been conservative in my choice. There are many stories, by writers such as Grass, Walser, Artmann or Arno Schmidt, that might have been included to illustrate innovation and experiment; works in which the 'story' has been reduced to vanishing point; in which reality has been confusingly deformed; in which complexity and obscurity are deliberate; others that are exercises in parody and self-irony. There is doubtless some chicanery here and some pomposity in the old German manner, but

if such stories are not included it is out of a wish that the anthology should be generally readable, and not to disparage experiment.

The subject most treated in modern German literature remains the Hitler years; inevitably, since nearly all those writing today, even the youngest, through their parents, were deeply affected. It is a subject that the short story, with its technique of setting the part for the whole, of working through exemplary instances, has approached again and again, with some success. The stories by de Bruyn and Lenz both work through allusion and understatement; they offer instances, from a deliberately limited perspective.

Das Gebell and *Anita G.* deal with the failure of human relationships and the consequent loneliness that have become common in urban society. And the recent past – the camps, the division of Germany – is seen continuing destructively in the characters' present lives. Bernhard, too, is concerned with isolation; but in *Der Zimmerer*, as in all his work, the situation itself, the sociological case, becomes an analogy of the deeper pessimism that all human existence is so.

Bobrowski's novels and stories, though modern in their language and narrative techniques, make use of milieu in a way reminiscent of the great nineteenth-century regional writers. He has, like them, the exact knowledge of a particular area, and the ability to treat widely significant topics in a limited context. The extreme north-east of Germany, now Russian and Polish, was perhaps the last region *intact* enough to inspire writing of that sort.

Finally, the two writers of an older generation: Penzoldt and Marie Luise Kaschnitz. Both, in their different styles, are first-rate storytellers. Both, like Penzoldt's 'wandering rhapsodist', have that essential gift, the ability 'to astound'. It may be something of a lost art, storytelling in the sovereign manner.

Each piece made its own demands on the translator; and each

translator responded in his or her own manner. But the general principle was, whilst accurately conveying the German, to produce English that would be readable for itself. These are not word-for-word translations but such, it is hoped, as do justice to both languages.

THE DOLPHIN

ERNST PENZOLDT

Translated by David Constantine

DER DELPHIN

Heut bedarf's der kleinsten Reise
zum vollgültigen Beweise,
daß wir mehr als Fische sind.

(FAUST II)[1]

«Ich sammle Kellner», sagte der mitteilsame Fremde, der sich unaufgefordert zu mir an den Tisch gesetzt hatte, «ich sammle sie mit Leidenschaft wie andere Leute Fayencen, Hinterglasbilder oder Geigenschnecken, was ich freilich immer als barbarisch empfunden habe. Denn sie sägen dazu doch wahrhaftig mir nichts dir nichts den herrlichsten Instrumenten den Hals ab und hängen die Schnecken in Glasschränken auf wie Skalps. Denn nur um sie ist es ihnen zu tun. Ich meinesteils sammle Kellner. Es sind sehr merkwürdige Menschen, obwohl, wie schließlich in jedem Beruf, ausgemachte Spitzbuben darunter sind. Ich kenne den Wiener Kellner so gut wie den Pariser, den von San Franzisko so gut wie den in Kapstadt oder Peking mit ihren landesüblichen Eigenheiten, aber, wo auch immer in der weiten Welt ich ihnen begegnete, alle waren unverwechselbar Kellner, ich meine, sie bilden innerhalb der Menschheit, ob sie nun weiß, gelb oder schwarz seien, eine besondere Gattung, eine Art Orden wie die Davidsbündler[2] oder Rosenkreuzer. Ich traf unter ihnen wahre Meister ihres Faches, Tänzernaturen, denen zuzusehen allein schon einen künstlerischen Genuß bereitet, Menschenkenner von hohen Graden und bedeutende Philosophen, wenn Sie wollen, auch Dichter. Machen Sie einmal den Versuch, Ihre Freunde oder bekannte Persönlichkeiten sich als Kellner vorzustellen. Das ist sehr lustig und aufschlußreich. Ich wurde nicht müde, mir von dem

THE DOLPHIN

But little distance need we go
Most conclusively to show
That we are more than fishes.
(FAUST II)

'I COLLECT waiters, said the talkative stranger who had sat down at my table uninvited. 'Waiters are my passion. I collect them as others do porcelain or *verres églomisés* or violin scrolls – and I must say I have always thought that barbaric, for they will quite cheerfully saw through the necks of the most splendid instruments and hang up the scrolls in cabinets like scalps. The scrolls are all they care about. But for my part I collect waiters. They are very remarkable people, although as in every profession there are some thorough scoundrels among them. The waiters of Vienna and Paris, San Francisco, Cape Town and Peking, all with their local peculiarities are equally well known to me; but wherever in the wide world I have encountered them they have all been unmistakably waiters, and white or yellow or black they seem a special breed among men, a sort of order like the League of David or the Rosicrucians. I have met real masters of their trade among them, some with the souls of dancers, whom simply to watch was an artistic treat; others great connoisseurs of human nature, notable philosophers if you like, and poets too. Try imagining your friends or well-known personalities as waiters. It is most amusing and instructive. I never wearied of having the small hunchbacked waiter in Vienna explain the menu to me. He could prepare the different dishes as he spoke, before my very eyes, deliciously – he extolled them in song; and what the

kleinen buckligen Kellner in Wien die Speisekarte erklären zu
lassen. Er wußte mit Worten die einzelnen Gerichte vor
meinen Augen köstlich zuzubereiten, er besang sie, und was
der Schenke in Perugia mir vom Wein erzählte, das kann ich
nur als orphisch bezeichnen. Einen anderen traf ich in Kairo,
der war ein Zauberer. Er setzte eine Terrine auf den Tisch und
ließ mich wünschen, was darinnen sein sollte. Ich riet aufs
Geratewohl: Schneehuhn mit Champignons in Burgunder-
soße. Er nahm seine Serviette – ich glaube, die Serviette ist die
materialisierte Seele des Kellners –, deckte sie darüber, murmelte Hokuspokus und hob den Deckel auf. Es war Schneehuhn! In Kairo! Aber die Zierde meiner Sammlung, eine
meiner frühesten Erwerbungen übrigens, fand ich auf der
Insel Anthos. Hören Sie zu. Ich schenke Ihnen die Geschichte.
Aber: ein Drittel Wein, ein Drittel Tabak, ein Drittel Phantasie, das ist mein Rezept.»

Also ließ ich ihm ein Glas bringen, schenkte ein und schob
ihm meine Zigaretten hin. Denn ich hatte, noch ehe der Ober,
einer von der tänzerischen Art übrigens, mit einem vielsagen-
den, warnenden Blick über die Natur meines Gastes mich ins
Bild gesetzt hatte, erraten, daß der Fremde von seinen
Geschichten lebte. Ein hartes Brot fürwahr. Denn nicht immer
mochte er ein so williges Ohr finden wie bei mir, obwohl er
durch lange Übung einen Blick dafür gewonnen hatte, wem
er sich zumuten dürfe. Sonst hätte er sich ganz gewiß nicht
zu mir gesetzt.

Mir fiel damals gerade wieder mal gar nichts ein, so daß ich
froh sein mußte, wenn mir jemand eine Geschichte schenkte.
Man wird sich fragen, warum der wandernde Rhapsode sie
nicht selber zu Papier brachte. Aber das war eben sein Ver-
hängnis, daß er es nicht vermochte. Er erfand sie im Augenblick und hatte, wenn er begann, wahrscheinlich noch keine
Ahnung, wie sie enden werde. Ich bedeutete dem besorgten
Ober, daß ich im Bilde sei und daß es mir nicht darauf an-

wine-waiter in Perugia told me concerning his wine I can only describe as Orphic. Another I met in Cairo: a magician. He placed a tureen on the table and said I should wish what I liked in it. At random I suggested ptarmigan with mushrooms in Burgundy sauce. He took his napkin – I do believe the napkin is a waiter's visible soul – draped it over the dish, muttered abracadabra and lifted the lid. It was ptarmigan! In Cairo! But the jewel of my collection, and incidentally one of my earliest acquisitions, I found on the island of Anthos. Listen. I'll make you a present of the story. But: one part wine, one part tobacco, one part fancy, that is my recipe.'

And so I had a glass brought; I poured out, and pushed my cigarettes towards him. For even before the waiter, one of the dancing kind incidentally, had enlightened me with a meaningful warning look as to the nature of my companion, I had guessed that the stranger lived from his stories. A hard living indeed. He would not always find such a willing listener as myself, although through long practice he had an eye for the sort of person he might approach. Otherwise he would quite certainly not have sat down by me.

At that time I was again rather short of ideas and was glad enough to have a story given me. You might ask why the wandering rhapsodist hadn't written it down himself. But that was precisely his destiny: not to be able to. He made it up on the spur of the moment, and when he began probably had no idea how it would end. I indicated to the worried waiter that I knew how things stood and that I didn't really mind being fleeced a little. For my *vis-à-vis*, as was obvious from his

kommen sollte, ein wenig gerupft zu werden. Denn mein Gegenüber, das sah man ihm an, war ein durstiger Erzähler. Er brauchte den Wein, um fabulieren zu können, und mußte fabulieren, um zu seinem Wein zu kommen.

«Also, hören Sie zu», begann er, nachdem er die Flasche behutsam mit beiden Händen zum Licht gehoben, die Legende auf der Etikette mit Jahrgang und Wachstum kennerisch betrachtet, ihr zugenickt und mit einem prüfenden Schluck die Lippen gefeuchtet hatte, «von Anthos will ich erzählen, der blonden kleinen Insel, der göttlichen, von der dortzulande die Sage geht, sie sei vom Monde gefallen – man könnte es wahrhaftig meinen, daß sie nicht von dieser Erde sei – und von dem kummervollen Kellner Apollo und von der merkwürdigen Sache mit dem Fisch.»

«Apollo», unterbrach ich ihn ungläubig, um ihm anzudeuten, daß ich wohl merkte, wie bedenkenlos er in der Wahl seiner Namen sei, «hieß er wirklich so?»

«Doch, doch», beharrte der Fremde, leicht verstimmt, «ich kann's nicht ändern, er hieß tatsächlich Apollo, obwohl er durchaus nichts an sich hatte von dem lichten, leuchtenden Musageten, dem heilenden, reinigenden delphinischen[3] Gott. Er glich vielmehr dem unglücklichen Marsyas, wenn er auch kein Flötenspieler war, kein Künstler jedenfalls wie jener, der sich vermaß, mit einer Gottheit in musikalischen Wettstreit zu treten. Welch ein Unrecht! Ich meine von dem Gott der Leier, daß er darauf einging. Welche Göttergrausamkeit! Mein Mitgefühl stand immer auf des armen, geschundenen Marsyas' Seite, des großen Künstlers. Ist es Ihnen schon aufgefallen, daß viele Künstler und Weise sein Antlitz tragen, daß sie Satyrgesichter haben wie Sokrates oder Verlaine? Der Kellner von Anthos glich einem Satyr. Sie kennen den Marsyas des Myron, so etwa sah er aus, oder aber wie der tote Zentaur auf der Schale in München. Ich werde sein Gesicht nie vergessen.

appearance, was a thirsty storyteller. He needed the wine to tell his tale, and had to tell his tale to get his wine.

'Listen, then,' he began, having held the bottle up carefully in both hands to the light, and given the label with the year and provenance an expert look and a nod, and sampled a mouthful to wet his lips – 'it is Anthos I shall tell of, the small fair island, island of the gods, that fell from the moon the local legend says – and truly one could believe it to be not of this earth – and of the unhappy waiter Apollo, and the curious business of the fish.'

'Apollo,' I interrupted disbelievingly, to show I had noticed how heedless he was in his choice of names, 'was he really called that?'

'Yes, yes,' the stranger insisted slightly aggrieved, 'I can't alter it, he was really called Apollo, although in his person he had nothing at all of the light and shining Leader of the Muses, the healing, cleansing, Delphinian god. He resembled much more the unfortunate Marsyas, though not a flute-player, not an artist as *he* was who dared compete in music with a god. Such an injustice! I mean on the part of the God of the Lyre, that he entered into it. A divine cruelty. My sympathies were always with the poor flayed Marsyas, the great artist. Have you ever noticed that many artists and sages wear his face? that they have the faces of satyrs, like Socrates or Verlaine? The waiter of Anthos looked like a satyr. You know the Marsyas done by Myron – he looked something like that, or like the dead centaur on the bowl in Munich. I shall never forget his face.

Die Insel mit dem reizenden Städtchen gleichen Namens kannte dazumal kein Mensch, als ich sie zum ersten Male besuchte aus purer Neugier. Denn ich war jung und hatte es mir in den Kopf gesetzt, die ganze Welt sehen zu müssen. Heute weiß ich, daß das gar nicht nötig ist. Es genügt, an einer Ecke des Lebens zu stehen, wenn man sich nur Zeit läßt und nicht ungeduldig wird. Ungeduld ist ein gefährliches Laster. Die Welt kommt ganz von selbst zu einem, ob man will oder nicht. In meines Großvaters Haus (er hatte die Gegend nie verlassen und konnte weder lesen noch schreiben) saß eines Tages Goethe am Tische, von einem Ritte rastend, und auch Napoleon kam mit seinem Schlitten vorüber von Rußland. Ein Bekannter von mir, auch ein Kellner übrigens, ein lieber, geduldiger Mensch, ist aus seinem idyllischen Heimatort im Thüringer Wald nie herausgekommen und wurde daselbst am hellichten Tage von einem Berberlöwen gefressen, der aus einer wandernden Menagerie ausgebrochen war. Doch das ist eine andere Geschichte.»

Mein Erzähler schien von dem schauerlichen Ereignis ehrlich bewegt, obwohl er es doch eben erst erfunden hatte. Er spülte die traurige Erinnerung mit einem Schluck Wein hinunter. Ich meinesteils hatte ihn jedoch in hinreichendem Verdacht, daß er selber auch nicht viel weiter in der Welt herumgekommen war als sein beklagenswerter Freund, obwohl er es mich glauben machen wollte. Auch zeigte er eine unausstehliche Sucht, sein akademisches Wissen an den Mann zu bringen. «Wo war ich bloß stehengeblieben», fuhr er fort, nachdem er sich über die Augen gewischt, «Insel, Meer, Kellner Apollo, ganz recht! Wie kam ich dorthin? Ich bereiste damals als Berichterstatter der *Frankfurter Zeitung*[4] den Süden und hatte zufällig in der Bahn ein seltsames Gerücht gehört, eine unwahrscheinliche Geschichte, so unglaubwürdig, daß ich mir sofort sagte: Da mußt du hin.

In der Bucht von Anthos, sagten meine Gewährsleute, wo

No one knew the island in those days, with its charming town of the same name, when I first visited it out of pure curiosity. For I was young and had got it into my head that I must see the whole world. I realize now that is quite unnecessary. It is enough to stand in one corner of life, if you will only give yourself time and not get impatient. Impatience is a dangerous vice. The world comes to you of its own accord, whether you will or no. In my grandfather's house (my grandfather who had never left the district and could neither read nor write) Goethe sat at table one day, resting from a ride, and Napoleon too passed by with his sledge from Russia. An acquaintance of mine, another waiter incidentally, a good-natured, patient fellow, never left his idyllic home in the Thuringian Forest and in that very spot, in broad daylight, was eaten by a Barbary lion which had escaped from a travelling zoo. But that's another story.'

My storyteller seemed genuinely moved by this frightful occurrence, even though he had just invented it. He washed down the unhappy memory with a drink of wine. For my part I strongly suspected that he himself had not seen much more of the world than his unfortunate friend, though he wanted me to think he had. He was also insufferably eager to parade his academic learning.

'Where was I?' he continued, wiping his eyes, 'island, sea, the waiter Apollo, ah yes ... How did I get there? At that time I was travelling in the south as journalist for the *Frankfurter Zeitung* and had happened to hear a strange tale on the train, an improbable story, so incredible that I told myself at once I should have to go and see.

In the bay of Anthos, my sources said, where the young

die jungen Burschen der Insel zu baden pflegen, gibt es Delphine, die, wie Sie wissen werden, sehr kluge, gesellige, zärtlich verspielte Tiere sind. Einer von ihnen nun habe sich nach anfänglicher Scheu mit einem beherzten Jüngling namens Chorillo – der Name ist spanisch und bedeutet Wasserstrählchen – so befreundet, sei alsbald so zutraulich geworden, daß er den ungleichen Gespielen auf seinen Rücken reiten lasse und ihn durch die Brandung trage. Er komme auf Chorillos Ruf hurtig herbeigeschwommen. Denn: er ist neugierig wie ein Fisch,[5] Faust Zwo. ‹Simo, Simo›, muß man rufen, darauf hören die Delphine, wenn man dem Plinius glauben darf, bei dem Sie einen ähnlichen Bericht nachlesen können.

Der Delphin, sagten die Leute in der Bahn, bringe seinen Freund sogar auf dem Wasserwege zu den Fischerdörfern ringsum, seinen Dienstgang abzukürzen; denn Chorillo ist der Postbote von Anthos.

Dies also hörte ich, aber ich glaubte natürlich kein Wort von der Geschichte, obwohl die Leute das anmutige Schauspiel mit eigenen Augen vom Dampfer aus gesehen haben wollten. Entweder, so sagte ich mir, hat ein Spaßvogel das Märchen des jüngeren Plinius aufgewärmt, was in den Hundstagen zuweilen vorkommt, wie die berühmte Seeschlange zeigt, oder Chorillo ritt auf einem Balken oder einem Gummidelphin, wie man sie überall in den Seebädern kaufen kann. Genug, ich beschloß, der Sache an Ort und Stelle nachzugehen.

Die Insel Anthos ist mit dem besagten Dampfer zu erreichen, der bei Bedarf einmal in der Woche vor der Bucht vor Anker geht. Natürlich hielt ich während der Fahrt fleißig Ausschau.»

Nun, dachte ich bei mir, während der Erzähler sich neu einschenkte, nun wird gleich das Wort: *Reling* kommen – denn er erging sich in den ausgefahrenen Gleisen der Sprache. Wirklich, es kam!

men of the island came to bathe, there were dolphins, which, as you will know, are very intelligent, sociable, affectionate and playful creatures. One of them, after some initial shyness, had become such good friends with a spirited youth by the name of Chorillo – the name is Spanish and means little water-spout – and had soon grown so familiar, that he let his odd playfellow ride on his back and carried him through the surf. At Chorillo's call he would come swimming swiftly along. For: "he is as curious as a fish", (*Faust II*). "Simo, Simo", is what you must call, and the dolphins heed it, if we may believe Pliny, in whose works you may read up a similar account.

The dolphin, said the people on the train, would even carry his friend over the water to the neighbouring fishing villages and shorten his round; for Chorillo was the postman of Anthos.

This then was what I heard, but of course I did not believe a word of the story, although the people claimed to have wit-nessed the agreeable spectacle with their own eyes from the steamer. Either, I said to myself, some joker has warmed up the fairy-tale from the younger Pliny, which happens some-times in the dog-days, as the great sea-serpent proves, or Chorillo was riding on a plank of wood or a rubber dolphin of the kind one can buy anywhere in the seaside resorts. Anyway, I decided to investigate the matter on the spot.

The island of Anthos is reached by the said steamer, which anchors once a week, if required to, off the bay. Of course I kept a diligent look-out during the voyage.'

'Now,' I thought, while the storyteller poured himself another glass, 'any moment now the phrase "leaning over the rail" will come,' for he was proceeding along well-worn tracks of language. And sure enough it did come.

«Ich lehnte mich über die Reling. Die Delphine stimmten jedenfalls, die sich aus Meereswogen, so scheint es, in Tiere verwandelt haben. Sie begleiteten unser Schiff. Es war das übliche kurzweilige Bild, an dem man sich freilich nicht satt sehen kann. Aber der Delphin-Reiter war nicht dabei.

Ein Boot mit zwei großen Augen am Bug, wie man sie auf griechischen Augenschalen findet, brachte mich an Land zu dem einzigen Hotel am Platze, denn Hotel nennt sich im Süden jede elende Herberge. Allein das Hotelchen in Anthos (ich habe seinen Namen vergessen, und er tut auch nichts zur Sache) sah ganz vertrauenerweckend aus, hatte eine bezaubernde Lage, und vom Fenster meines bescheidenen Zimmers, das mir der satyrgesichtige Kellner Apollo anwies, konnte ich die ganze Bucht überschauen, den orangefarbenen Strand mit den an Land gezogenen bunten Fischerbooten und die den Hafen umarmenden Höhen. Die Vorgebirge glichen den Häuptern gewaltiger Löwen, die sich zur Tränke lagern.»

Die poetische Gedankenverbindung gab meinem Gast willkommene Gelegenheit, selbst zu trinken, ehe er fortfuhr.

«Sie zweifelten vorhin an dem Namen Apollo. Ich hatte einmal einen schwarzen Diener, der sogar Jupiter hieß. Der Kellner Apollo begegnete mir anfangs mit unverhohlenem Mißtrauen, er war bildhäßlich von Angesicht, eine Herausforderung an alle Schönheit, ihr tragischer Kontrapunkt sozusagen. Man konnte erschrecken, panisch erschrecken, wenn er einen so ansah, mit seinen schrägstehenden, bernsteinfarbenen Ziegenaugen und der aufgeschnupften Nase. Denn auch sie schien einen anzustaunen aus runden Nüstern. Sein Mund, wenn man es als Mund bezeichnen darf, war groß und wulstig, gleichsam ein Urmund, groß seine Ohren, hinter deren einem der abgekaute Stummel eines Bleistiftes stak. Er hatte dazu eine zarte rosige Haut, die dem Gesicht etwas Nacktes, leicht Verwundbares gab, und das rötliche, dünne, feuchte Haar hing ihm schlaff in die kummervolle Stirn. Wehe

'I was leaning over the rail. It was true about the dolphins at least – waves of the sea, one might think, that have turned into creatures. They were accompanying our ship. It was the usual pleasing scene, that one can never see enough of, admittedly. But the dolphin-rider was not there.

A boat with two great eyes on the prow, as they are to be found on Greek eye-bowls, brought me ashore to the only hotel in the place – for in the south every wretched tavern calls itself a hotel. But the little hotel in Anthos (I've forgotten the name, and it is of no importance) was most reassuring in its appearance, was enchantingly situated, and from the window of my modest room, which the satyr-faced waiter Apollo showed me to, I could look out over the whole bay, the orange-coloured beach with the bright fishing-boats drawn up on shore and the mountains embracing the harbour. The promontories were like the heads of mighty lions settling down to drink.'

The poetical association of ideas gave my companion a welcome opportunity to drink himself, before continuing.

'You were dubious earlier about the name Apollo. I even had a black servant once called Jupiter. The waiter Apollo met me at first with undisguised mistrust. His face was the very picture of ugliness, a challenge to all beauty, Beauty's tragic opposite, so to speak. It was frightening, you felt a sort of panic when he looked at you with his slant, amber-coloured goat's eyes and his wrinkled-up nose. For that too seemed to be staring at you from its round nostrils. His mouth, if it could be called a mouth, was large and swollen, like the father of all mouths, and his ears, too, were large, with a chewed stub of pencil stuck behind one of them. He had moreover a delicate pink skin which made the face seem naked and easily vulnerable, and his reddish, thin, damp hair hung limply over his pathetic brow. Woe unto this poor soul should he ever fall in love. For who could have loved him in return? He seemed

diesem Armen, wenn er je Liebe empfand. Denn ihn zu lieben, wer hätte es vermocht? Seine Gestalt wirkte verwachsen, er hinkte ein wenig. Sie werden verstehen, daß er sofort meine Sammelleidenschaft erregte.

Ich setzte mich, vorsorglich mit Fernglas und Fotoapparat bewaffnet, auf die Terrasse vor das Hotel auf einen der üblichen weißen Metallstühle an einen runden Tisch mit der ebenfalls in den Cafés der ganzen Welt gebräuchlichen weißen Marmorplatte, bestellte mir Wein und genoß die Aussicht, das rot-weiße Sonnensegel über mir.

Apollo, die Serviette – seine Seele – unter die Achselhöhle geklemmt, brachte das Gewünschte. Seine Serviette hatte er immer bei sich. Über den Arm gelegt, über die Schulter geworfen, in die Tasche gesteckt, daraus ihre Zipfel hervorhingen, oder in den Schürzenlatz geschoben. Ich glaube, er hatte sie nachts unter dem Kopfkissen und schlief mit ihr. Er trug eine weiße Schürze und ein nachtfarbenes Lüsterjäckchen darüber.

Meine Anwesenheit schien ihn zu beunruhigen.

‹Sie kommen wegen des Fisches, mein Herr›, fragte er ganz nebenbei, während er auf meinen Wunsch aus der blauen Syphonflasche einen Strahl Sodawasser in meinen Wein zischen ließ.

‹Ein Delphin ist kein Fisch›, antwortete ich.

‹Ganz recht. – Vom Festland?›

‹Ja. Man hat dort davon gehört.›

Apollo machte eine bedauernde Handbewegung.

‹Polizei?›

‹Nicht ganz. Zeitung.›

‹Oh›, sagte Apollo abschätzig, ‹Sie sind Journalist?›

‹Erschreckt Sie das?›

‹Offen gestanden, ja. Wenn es keine Journalisten gäbe, wäre weniger Unglück in der Welt.›

‹Sie verwechseln Ursache und Wirkung, mein Bester. Es

deformed, and limped a little. You will appreciate that he aroused my collector's passion at once.

I armed myself with binoculars and camera and sat down on the terrace in front of the hotel, on one of the usual white metal chairs at a round table with the white marble surface also customary in cafés throughout the world, ordered some wine and enjoyed the view, the red and white awning above me.

Apollo, the napkin – his soul – tucked under his arm, brought me what I had asked. He always had his napkin with him. Laid over one arm, thrown over his shoulder, thrust into his pocket, with the corners hanging out, or shoved into the front of his apron. I dare say he had it under his pillow at nights and slept with it. He wore a white apron and a lustre jacket the colour of night.

My presence seemed to disturb him.

"You're here on account of the fish, are you?" he asked quite by the way whilst squirting a jet of soda-water into my wine from the blue siphon, as I had requested him to.

"A dolphin isn't a fish," I answered.

"Quite right. From the mainland?"

"Yes. They've heard about it over there."

Apollo made a gesture of regret.

"Police?"

"Not quite. Newspaper."

"Oh," said Apollo disparagingly, "you're a journalist?"

"Does that frighten you?"

"To be honest, yes. If there were no journalists there'd be less misery in the world."

"You are confusing cause and effect, my dear fellow. Some-

ereignet sich etwas irgendwo, und wir schreiben darüber. Das ist alles.›

Apollo bedachte sich einen Augenblick, indem er seine Serviette ansah, die in seinen Händen wirklich einem beseelten Wesen glich.

‹Verzeihung›, sagte er dann, ‹aber haben Sie noch nicht bemerkt, daß, sobald irgendwo ein Journalist erscheint, ein Unglück passiert? Ich übertreibe.›

‹Sie überschätzen uns›, warf ich ein, während ich ihn zum Sitzen einlud.

‹Danke, mein Herr, ich sitze nie. Sie sind von Berufs wegen natürlich darauf erpicht, den Lesern Ihres Blattes etwas Interessantes berichten zu können. Sie rechnen mit der Eitelkeit des Unglücks. Sie kitzeln es. Es gefällt sich in seiner Rolle. Es will beachtet sein und liefert Ihnen bereitwillig Stoff.›

Sein gescheites Gesicht nahm einen flehenden Ausdruck an. ‹Lassen Sie uns doch hier in Frieden! Ich bitte Sie darum.›

‹Aber, lieber Freund, ich kann doch schließlich nichts dafür, wenn auf dieser schönen Insel, in dieser herrlichen Bucht sich so erstaunliche Dinge begeben. Ich glaube nebenbei kein Wort davon, ehe ich es nicht mit meinen eigenen Augen gesehen habe.›

‹Das ist es ja›, jammerte der Kellner. ‹Würden Sie es einfach glauben, es hinnehmen, dann kämen Sie gar nicht auf den Gedanken, hierher zu kommen. Es geht Sie doch eigentlich gar nichts an.›

‹Aber, erlauben Sie›, erwiderte ich und suchte mit meinem Fernglas die Bucht ab, ‹es ist doch schließlich nichts Alltägliches, wenn man sich erzählt, daß ein Delphin – kein Fisch übrigens, ein Warmblütler, er bringt lebendige Junge zur Welt – ich meine, wenn ein Delphin innige Freundschaft mit einem jungen Manne schließt, auf seinen Ruf an den Strand geschwommen kommt, ganz zahm, gefügig wie ein Hund,

thing happens somewhere, and we write about it. That's all."

Apollo thought for a moment, and looked at his napkin which in his hands really did seem an animate being.

"Pardon me," he said then, "but have you never noticed that as soon as a journalist appears anywhere some misfortune occurs. But perhaps I'm exaggerating."

"You think too highly of us," I objected, inviting him to be seated.

"Thank you, no, I never sit. For professional reasons you are naturally bent on being able to report something interesting to the readers of your paper. You count on the vanity of misfortune. You flatter it. It likes the role you give it. It wants to be noticed, and gladly supplies you with material."

His shrewd face took on an expression of pleading.

"Leave us in peace here. I beg you."

"But my dear chap, I really cannot help it if on this beautiful island, in this splendid bay, such extraordinary things happen. Not that I'll believe a word of it, by the way, until I've seen it with my own eyes."

"That's just it," the waiter lamented. "If you'd simply believe it, accept it, you'd never think of coming here. Really it's no concern of yours."

"But, begging your pardon," I replied, scanning the bay with my binoculars, "it is after all not every day we hear of a dolphin – not a fish, incidentally, but a warm-blooded animal, the young are brought forth alive – of a dolphin becoming close friends with a young man, and swimming to the beach

und den Jüngling auf seinen Rücken nimmt, nur ihn, wie man behauptet.›

‹Nur ihn›, sagte der Kellner und nickte.

Ich muß hier erwähnen, daß unser Gespräch nicht fortlaufend geführt wurde. Apollo hatte zu tun. Er bediente noch andere Gäste, Einheimische, die drinnen im kühlen Hause ihren schwarzen Wein tranken, nicht in der Sonne wie ich, der Fremdling. Aber er kam zwischendurch immer wieder zu mir. Ich ließ nicht locker.

‹Eine reizende Erfindung ohne Zweifel, aber ich glaube es nicht.›

‹Sie scheinen wenig Phantasie zu haben›, erwiderte Apollo, der es offenbar darauf anzulegen schien, mich zu kränken.

‹Dachte, ich's doch! es ist also ein Märchen. Unser Delphin ist eine Ente. Bitte zahlen!›

Apollo nahm überhaupt keine Notiz von meinem Wunsch. Wieder beschäftigte er sich angelegentlich mit seiner Serviette, die er krüppelte, an der er zupfte und ihr allerlei faltige Gestalten gab, daß sie wirklich einem lebenden Wesen glich, bald einer Möwe, bald einer Blume oder einem Engel oder einem Fisch. Was er dann sagte, war sehr merkwürdig. Es hatte eigentlich nichts mit dem Delphin zu tun, so dachte ich wenigstens.

‹Die Wissenschaft behauptet›, brachte er zögernd vor, ‹sie hat es sogar einwandfrei nachgewiesen, so widernünftig es auch erscheint, daß gewisse kleinste Körper die Eigenschaft besitzen, gleichzeitig an verschiedenen Orten im Raum zu sein.›

‹Ganz recht. Sie tun es eben›, erwiderte ich.

‹Ich glaube es nicht, ehe ich es nicht mit eigenen Augen gesehen habe. Sie, mein Herr, haben es gesehen?›

‹Nein. Natürlich nicht.›

‹Aber Sie glauben es?›

‹Natürlich ja.›

when he calls, quite tame, amenable like a dog, and taking the youth on his back, only him, they claim."

"Only him," said the waiter and nodded.

I should mention that our conversation did not proceed without interruption. Apollo was busy. He was serving other customers, locals, drinking their black wine inside in the cool indoors, not in the sun like myself, the stranger. But between times he came out again and again to me. I kept at him.

"A charming invention, doubtless, but I don't believe it."

"You don't seem to have much imagination," Apollo replied, evidently out to offend me.

"Just as I thought, it's a fairy-tale. Our dolphin's a duck. Let me have the bill, please."

Apollo took absolutely no notice of my request. He was again very busy with his napkin, twisting and tugging at it and giving it all sorts of creased shapes, until it really did look like a living creature, now a seagull, now a flower or an angel or a fish. What he said next was very remarkable. It actually had nothing to do with the dolphin, or so I thought.

"Science asserts," he began hesitantly, "and has even proved beyond doubt, unreasonable though it appears, that certain minute particles have the property of being simultaneously at different points in space."

"Quite right," I replied. "They do have that property."

"I shan't believe it until I've seen it with my own eyes. You already have?"

"No, of course not."

"But you believe it?"

"Yes, of course."

‹Natürlich!›

Ich hatte keine Ahnung, wo er hinaus wollte. Zudem fesselte jetzt etwas anderes meine Aufmerksamkeit. Ein Mädchen hatte den Schauplatz betreten, eine Hirtin mit ihren Ziegen. Sie warf mir einen scheuen feindseligen Blick zu und blickte sich suchend um. Dann setzte sie sich auf die Mauer gegen das Meer und wartete. Sie trug eine gelbe Bluse, sie hatte etwas von einer Zigarrenschachtelbilderschönheit.

‹Chorillo ist nicht hier, Moira›, bemerkte Apollo nebenhin.

‹Nicht hier?› sagte Moira traurig.

‹Du siehst es doch›, antwortete Apollo gereizt. ‹Vielleicht ist er im Wasser.›

‹Im Wasser?› Sie sprang erregt auf und stand nun auf der Mauer, mit der Hand die Augen beschattend, und schaute auf die Bucht. Zur gleichen Zeit vernahm ich einen klagenden Ruf nicht von Menschenmund, sondern von einem sehnsüchtigen Tier. Auch ich war aufgestanden.

‹Hörst du es?› sagte Apollo, ‹da ist er wieder.›

‹Der Fisch›, flüsterte Moira schaudernd.

Also doch. Wahrhaftig, er war es. Ich konnte ihn mit bloßen Augen erkennen, auch das Wasserstrählchen über seiner Schnauze. Er schwamm ganz nahe am Strand auf und ab, unruhig schnaubend hin und her. Die Schwanzflosse tauchte auf für einen Augenblick wie die Mondsichel aus den schäumenden Wolken der Wogen.

‹Nein, sehen Sie bloß einmal an›, sagte ich voller Entzücken zu dem Mädchen.

‹Ich will ihn gar nicht sehen›, stieß sie giftig hervor. Sie zitterte am ganzen Leibe vor Zorn und Leidenschaft.

Der nasse Rücken des Delphins glänzte wie nachtblaue Seide, sein Bauch schimmerte silberweiß, wie die Samenscheide der Mondviole mit einem Hauch von Rosa. «Welch ein herrliches, welch ein klassisches Tier!» unterbrach sich mein Gast. «Eine echt griechische Erfindung möchte man sagen, aber es ist

"Of course!"

I had no idea what he was getting at. Moreover my attention was now drawn elsewhere. A girl had come on the scene, a girl herding her goats. She gave me a shy, hostile glance and looked round in search of something. Then she sat down on the wall facing the sea and waited. She wore a yellow smock; she was beautiful, but somewhat in the manner of the girls on cigar boxes.

"Chorillo isn't here, Moira," Apollo remarked casually.

"Not here?" Moira said sadly.

"You can see he isn't," Apollo answered in an impatient tone. "Perhaps he's in the water."

"In the water?" She sprang up excitedly and stood on the wall, shading her eyes with her hand, and looked out over the bay. And at that moment I heard a plaintive cry – not from any human mouth but from some yearning animal. I too had stood up.

"Do you hear?" said Apollo, "he's back."

"The fish," Moira whispered with a shiver.

Well, well. It was really him. I could see him with my naked eyes, and the small jet of water above his snout. He swam quite close to the beach, restlessly up and down and to and fro, blowing through his nose. The tail fin emerged for a moment like the moon's crescent from among the billowing clouds of the waves.

"Just look at him," I said in complete delight to the girl.

"I don't want to," she said venomously. Her whole body was trembling with anger and passion.

The dolphin's wet back shone like blue-black silk, his belly shimmered silver-white, like honesty pennies, with a tinge of pink. 'What a splendid creature!' my friend broke off to say, 'how classical! A truly Greek discovery one might almost say, but of course it's the other way round. Look at this shell: the

natürlich umgekehrt. Betrachten Sie diese Muschel. Es ist die gemeine Herzmuschel. Ich trage immer eine mit mir. Sie ist das Sinnbild des Meeres, die Quintessenz des Wellenschlages. Aus dieser Form hat sich die griechische Kunst entwickelt. Griechenland! denkt man unwillkürlich, nicht wahr? Oder hier, der Delphin auf der Münze. Welch ein Geld! Welche Würde des Geldes – das Wort stammt nicht von mir –, welch ein Volk, das solche Münzen hatte! Sie trugen sie im Mund, wenn sie zum Markte gingen! Und wir? Doch ich schweife ab.

‹Ist es derjenige welcher?› fragte ich den Kellner.

‹Derjenige welcher›, antwortete Apollo wie im Traume.

Er hatte die Serviette in den Brustlatz seiner weißen Schürze geschoben und stand, die Hände hinter seinem Lüsterjäckchen verschränkt, anscheinend ganz unbeteiligt in den Hoteleingang gelehnt.

Währenddem kam ein junger Bursche von höchstens siebzehn Jahren munter des Weges geschritten, nur in Hose und Hemd, die schwarze Ledertasche mit dem silbernen Posthörnlein, das einer Brezel glich, lässig umgehängt, die Amtsmütze flott ins wirre Haar gesetzt. Übers ganze Gesicht, ja, mit dem ganzen Körper lachend, kam er dahergeschlendert, ab und zu in eine pralle, dunkle Traube beißend, daß ihm der Saft von den Lippen troff, Häute und Kerne über die Schulter spuckend.

Moira saß wieder auf der Mauer, zusammengekauert. Sie spielte, als beachte sie ihn nicht, mit ihrem offenen Haar und sah nach ihren Ziegen.

‹Der tägliche Brief›, sagte Chorillo, ‹und immer die gleiche Schrift.›

Er befühlte ihn und hielt ihn gegen die Sonne.

‹Und stets nur ein leerer Umschlag.›

Er warf ihn dem Mädchen zu. Sie fing ihn auf und zerriß ihn, ohne ihn zu öffnen, in kleine Stücke.

Ich durchschaute den Vorgang. Ich kannte einmal in Prag

common cockle. I always have one on me. It is the symbol of the sea, the quintessence of the surf. Out of this form Greek art developed. Greece! one can't help thinking, isn't that so? Or here, the dolphin on the coin. Such money! What dignity – I quote – such money has; what a people, to have coins like this. They carried them to market in their mouths. And nowadays . . . ? But I digress.

"Is that the one that . . . ?" I asked the waiter.

"The one that . . ." Apollo answered, as if in a dream.

He had thrust the napkin down the front of his white apron and stood with arms folded under his jacket, leaning in the hotel doorway apparently quite unconcerned.

Meanwhile a boy of at most seventeen came striding cheerfully along. He was wearing only trousers and shirt, the black leather bag with its silver posthorn like a pretzel slung casually over his shoulder and his postman's cap set jauntily in his tangled hair. He strolled towards us, laughing all over his face, indeed with his whole body, now and then biting into large, dark grapes and spitting the skins and pips behind him, the juice trickling from his lips.

Moira was back sitting on the wall, huddled up. She was playing with her loose hair, as though taking no notice of him, and watching her goats.

"The daily letter," said Chorillo, "and always the same writing." He felt the letter and held it up to the sun.

"And never anything but an empty envelope."

He threw it to the girl. She caught it, and without opening it tore it into pieces.

I saw through the performance. I knew a girl in Prague once

ein Mädchen, das schrieb sich selber Briefe, schickte sich Blumen und Pralinieren ins Haus, damit man denken sollte, sie hätte einen Freund. Und am Ende heiratete sie den Postboten.

Sosehr ich es Moira nachfühlen konnte, daß sie in den Burschen vernarrt war, sowenig wollte es mir gefallen, daß er sie so unzart vor uns bloßstellte.

‹Wie geht's, alte Fratze›, wandte sich Chorillo nun an den Kellner, ‹wie häßlich du doch bist, beinah zum Verlieben häßlich.›

‹Chorillo, horch›, sagte Apollo, ohne seine Haltung zu verändern.

Wieder hörte ich den klagenden, sehnsüchtigen Ton vom Meere her. Der Delphin brauste noch immer den Strand entlang, wendete, sich überschlagend, daß man den weißen Bauch mit dem zartrosa Schimmer sah, und noch immer stieß er den Strahl zwischen den klugen Augen hervor.

Chorillo lauschte und sah nach dem Meer wie verzaubert. Dann rief er durch die Muschel seiner Hände, langgezogen: ‹Siiimo, Simo, ich komme.›

‹Geh nicht baden, Chorillo›, bat Moira, ‹heute nicht! Mir zuliebe!›

‹Laß ihn doch, schöne Hirtin›, warf ich ein, ‹schau, ich bin eigens von weither gekommen, um es zu sehen. Es wäre doch schade, wenn ich umsonst ...›

‹Da hörst du es›, sagte Chorillo unwirsch, ‹ich muß ja nun wohl. Ehrenhalber.›

‹Der Herr glaubt nur, was er sieht›, murmelte anzüglich Apollo.

‹Und ich sehe nur, was ich glaube›, antwortete Chorillo wieder lachend, nahm seine Postmütze ab und setzte sie dem Kellner auf, der sehr lächerlich damit aussah, hängte ihm auch die Tasche mit dem Hörnlein um, als wäre er ein Kleiderständer. Apollo ließ sich's gleichmütig gefallen. Aber ehe Chorillo sich zum Gehen wandte, nahm der Kellner rasch die

who wrote herself letters and sent flowers and chocolates to her own home so that people would think she had a boyfriend. And in the end she married the postman.

It was all too apparent that Moira was hopelessly in love with the boy, and his cruel humiliation of her in front of us was all the more distasteful.

"How do, ugly mug," now Chorillo turned to the waiter, "my word you're ugly – nearly lovable, you're that bad."

"Chorillo, listen," said Apollo, without altering his manner.

Again I heard those tones of lament and longing from the sea. The dolphin was still coursing along parallel to the beach, turning and diving so that we saw the white belly with its delicate shimmer of pink, and still the water spurted up from between the knowing eyes.

Chorillo listened and looked towards the sea as if enchanted. Then he cupped his hands and gave a long drawn-out cry: "Siiimo, Simo, I'm coming."

"Don't go swimming, Chorillo," Moira begged, "not to-day, just for me."

"Let him go," I put in. "I've come a long way to see this. It would be a pity if it were all for nothing."

"You hear that?" said Chorillo brusquely, "I'll have to now, won't I? Matter of honour."

"The gentleman only believes what he sees," Apollo murmured pointedly.

"And I only see what I believe," Chorillo replied, laughing again. He took off his postman's cap and put it on the waiter, who then looked very ridiculous, and hung the bag with the little horn on round him as though he were a hat and coat stand. Apollo bore it patiently; but as Chorillo turned to go he seized the soda-siphon from the table and squirted the boy in

Siphonflasche vom Tisch und spritzte dem Burschen einen Strahl ins Gesicht. Der machte-ihm eine lange Nase und lief hurtig zum Strand. Im Laufen schon begann er sich seiner Kleider zu entledigen. ‹Chorillo›, rief ihm das Mädchen drohend nach, ‹du wirst dich noch erkälten, du wirst dir dabei noch den Tod holen, hörst du, den Tod! Ganz bestimmt!›

Sie wünschte es so sehr nicht, daß es fast klang, als wünsche sie es ihm. ‹Halt den Mund, du Hexe›, herrschte Apollo sie an, schneeweiß im Gesicht, ‹scher dich zum Teufel!›

Er ging ins Haus, Chorillos Sachen zu verwahren. Der aber plätscherte gerade ins Wasser. Aufjauchzend warf er sich in die Brandung.

‹Simo›, rief er, ‹komm, da bin ich, fang mich!›

Der Fisch, will sagen der Delphin, rauschte heran. Ich nahm meine Kamera und rannte zur Bucht hinunter, wo inzwischen sich noch andere Burschen eingefunden hatten. Oh, es war wunderbar. Ich verknipste einen ganzen Film. Simo schlug vor Freuden förmlich Purzelbäume um Chorillo, er lockte ihn mit Äolsharfentönen, lustig quirlte das Strählchen vor seiner gewölbten Stirn. Dann tauchte er unter dem Jüngling weg und hob ihn empor. Nun ritt er durch die Wogen. Sie scherzten miteinander.

Ich sah mich nach Moira um. Sie saß mit angezogenen Knien, das Kinn auf die Fäuste gestützt, auf eine Strähne ihres Haares beißend und schaute nach ihrem braunen Geliebten, Unheil im Blick, totenblaß. Der Kellner Apollo stand hinter ihr, vorgeneigt, seine Serviette wringend.

Nun zischte der Delphin seinem Reiter einen Strahl mitten ins Gesicht. Der Fisch lachte. Ich lüge nicht. Es sah wirklich so aus. Er lachte übermütig wie ein Mensch.

Auch der Kellner lachte von Herzen. Er bog sich vor Vergnügen und drückte die Serviette vor den Mund. Sein runder Rücken schütterte. Dann schob er das Tuch in den Schürzenbund, machte ein paar Schritte vorwärts, ein paar Schritte

the face. Chorillo thumbed his nose at Apollo and ran quickly down to the beach. And even as he ran he began taking off his clothes.

"Chorillo," the girl called after him threateningly, "you'll catch cold, you'll catch your death of cold, do you hear, your death. For sure."

She so much didn't want it to happen that it almost sounded as though she wished it would.

Apollo turned on her, white as a sheet: "Shut your mouth, you witch. Get to the devil."

He went inside to put Chorillo's things away. Chorillo meanwhile splashed straight into the water. Shouting for joy he threw himself into the waves.

"Simo," he cried, "here I am, come and get me."

The fish, that is to say the dolphin, rushed forward. I took my camera and ran down to the shore, where in the meantime other youths had gathered. Oh, it was wonderful! I snapped a whole film. Simo fairly somersaulted for joy around Chorillo, called to him in the tones of an aeolian harp, and the plume of water turned merrily on the dolphin's domed forehead. Then he dived under the boy and lifted him up. Now he rode through the waves. They joked with one another.

I looked round for Moira. She sat with drawn-up knees, her chin resting on her fists, biting a strand of her hair and gazing after her brown lover with ominous eyes, deadly pale. The waiter Apollo stood behind her, leaning forward, wringing his napkin.

Now the dolphin squirted a jet of water into the rider's face. The fish was laughing. I swear it. It really did appear so. The fish was laughing boldly like a man.

The waiter too was laughing for all he was worth. He was doubled up with delight and pressing the napkin to his mouth. His round back shook. Then he thrust the cloth into the belt of his apron and did a few steps forward, a few steps back, with

zurück, die Arme gekrümmt, mit gehobenen Ellenbogen, er tanzte, ein grotesker Anblick fürwahr, täppisch, serviettengeschwänzt, satyrhaft.

Moira war wütend. Sie stand nun wieder und stampfte heftig mit dem Fuß auf. Sie drohte mit geballter Faust nach dem Meere.

Wenn ich eben sagte, der Delphin lachte wie ein Mensch, so blieb er doch in allem ein Tier. Doch sagt man, daß ja auch die Menschen von Fischen abstammen. Beim Embryo sind die Kiemenspalten noch nachweisbar.

Chorillo und der Delphin waren inzwischen hinter der Düne verschwunden, die der Bucht vorgelagert ist. Ich trat zu Apollo, der wieder zur Terrasse zurückgekehrt war, der Gäste im Hause wegen. Er sagte bitter: ‹Sie werden nun darüber in Ihrer Zeitung schreiben, und alle Menschen werden es lesen und werden es nicht glauben, ehe sie es mit eigenen Augen gesehen haben. Sie werden in Scharen auf die Insel kommen.›

‹Ich bringe ja die Bilder.›

‹Ach, es gibt ja bekanntlich Gummitiere zum Aufblasen. Sehr naturgetreu, mit schwarzem Rücken und weißem Bauch›. Er berührte obenhin Röckchen und Schürze.

Ich war noch ganz aufgeregt von dem anmutigen Schauspiel in der Bucht und lobte es laut.

‹Ich bitte Sie, lieber Herr›, meinte Apollo finster, ‹schreiben Sie nichts davon in der Zeitung. Wenn es nicht wahr gewesen wäre, hätten Sie doch auch nichts berichten können, ich bitte Sie!›

Er hob die Hände mit der Serviette zu einer rührenden Gebärde. Er hatte Tränen in den Augen.

‹Man könnte doch›, versetzte ich, ‹gerade aus einer Nichtwahrheit eine sehr hübsche Glosse machen.›

Nun kam der Delphin mit Chorillo an Bord wieder hinter der Insel hervor, die sie unseren Blicken für eine Weile entzogen hatte. Sie waren sichtlich des Spieles müde geworden

bent arms and elbows raised he danced, awkward and satyr-like with the napkin for a tail, a most grotesque spectacle.

Moira was furious. She stood up again and stamped her foot violently. She waved her clenched fist threateningly at the sea.

I may have just said the dolphin laughed like a man, but he remained a beast in everything. But then they say men are descended from fish. In the embryo the gill-slits are still detectable.

Meanwhile Chorillo and the dolphin had disappeared behind the sandbank that lies across the mouth of the bay. I went over to Apollo who had gone back on to the terrace to see to the customers indoors. He said bitterly: "Now you'll write about it in your newspaper and everyone will read it and won't believe it until they've seen it with their own eyes. They'll come to the island in droves."

"I'll have the photos, don't forget."

"But there are those rubber animals, the kind you blow up, they're very lifelike, with black backs and white bellies."

He kept touching his jacket and apron.

I was still excited by the agreeable spectacle in the bay, and extolled it loudly.

"Sir, I entreat you," Apollo said gloomily, "don't write anything about it in your newspaper. If it hadn't been true you wouldn't have been able to report anything either – so please don't."

He raised his hands holding the napkin in a moving gesture. There were tears in his eyes.

"On the contrary," I replied, "one could do a nice little piece on an untruth."

Now the dolphin, with Chorillo on board, re-appeared from behind the island that had hidden them from our view for a time. They had clearly become tired of their game, and

und sahen abgekämpft aus. Ganz langsam schwamm der Delphin. Chorillo, vornübergesunken, umschlief ihn. Der Fisch trug ihn behutsam an Land. Chorillo stieg ab. Er streichelte die Flanken des Tieres wie ein Reiter sein Pferd. Auf dem Wege zu uns durch die Brandung plätschernd, wandte er sich noch oft nach dem Freunde um und winkte ihm zum Abschied. Simo, das Wasser mit der mondförmigen Schwanzflosse peitschend, entfernte sich in großen Schleifen dem offenen Meere zu.

Es war vorüber, so bildete ich mir wenigstens ein.

Frohgelaunt und unbefangen, wenn auch etwas weniger lebhaft als vorher und leicht fröstelnd von dem langen Bad, trat der Postjunge von Anthos zu uns auf die Terrasse des Hotels, um Mütze und Tasche zu holen. Apollo, die Serviette im Brustlatz, humpelte diensteifrig mit den Sachen herbei, aber es ritt ihn der Teufel, denn er begann nun den Burschen zu narren, er hielt ihm freundlich die Mütze hin, zog sie aber, als der arglos danach griff, zurück und lief damit um den Tisch herum davon, unbeholfen wie er war. Chorillo tat mit. Er wußte, wie er den Kellner am besten ärgern konnte. Er entriß ihm mit raschem Griff das Tuch, die Seele riß er ihm gleichsam aus dem Herzen, ließ es vor Apollos Nase flattern, der aufgeschnupften, und trotzte seinerseits dem alten Kindskopf.

Mit verzerrtem Gesicht schaute Moira zu. Ich hatte Apollo nicht soviel Behendigkeit zugetraut. Er erhaschte Chorillo, dem es gerade noch gelang, die Serviette zwischen die lachenden Zähne zu nehmen. Apollo aber war nun am Ende seiner Kraft, er mußte arg schnaufen. Er mußte sich setzen. Er legte die Hand auf sein Herz.

‹Ätsch›, machte Chorillo und warf ihm die Serviette zu, während er ihm die Zunge herausstreckte.

In diesem Augenblick sprang Moira dazwischen, fing das Tuch aus der Luft und riß es, wie ein Blitz die Wolke, mitten entzwei.

‹Seid verflucht›, schrie sie, die Hände krallend, als wollte sie

looked worn out. The dolphin was swimming very slowly.
Chorillo had sunk forward as though asleep, his arms round
the dolphin's neck. The fish carried him carefully ashore.
Chorillo dismounted. He stroked the flanks of the creature as a
rider does his horse. Splashing towards us through the surf he
turned round several times still to his friend and waved him
good-bye. Simo, slapping the water with his crescent tail,
withdrew in great loops towards the sea.

It was over, or so I imagined at least.

Good-humoured and at ease, if somewhat less lively than
before and shivering slightly from the long bathe, the young
postman of Anthos came over to us on the hotel terrace to
collect his cap and bag. Apollo, the napkin down the front of
his apron, hobbled eagerly forward with Chorillo's things –
but for a sudden devilment he began teasing the boy, amicably
holding out the cap to him and taking it back when the un-
suspecting Chorillo reached for it, and running away round
the table in his clumsy fashion. Chorillo played along. He
knew how best to annoy the waiter. With a quick grab he tore
the cloth from him, tore the soul out of his heart, so to speak,
and flapped it in front of Apollo's snub nose, and got his own
back on the old simpleton.

Moira watched, her features twisted. I should not have
expected Apollo to be so agile. He caught Chorillo, who just
managed to bite hold of the napkin between his laughing
teeth. But by now Apollo was exhausted, and was puffing
badly. He had to sit down. He put his hand on his heart.

"There you are, then," Chorillo jeered, and threw him the
napkin, sticking his tongue out.

At that moment Moira sprang between them, caught the
cloth in mid-air, and tore it in two, as lightning does a
cloud.

"Curse you," she cried, clawing with her hands, as if to

41

ihnen die Augen auskratzen, ‹seid verflucht, dreimal verflucht!› Dabei warf sie jedbeiden einen Fetzen vor die Füße.

Jetzt war es Zeit, daß ich mich ins Mittel legte. ‹Aber, aber›, sagte ich begütigend, ‹wer wird denn gleich so eifersüchtig sein.› Auch Chorillo trat gutherzig auf sie zu, um ihr schönzutun. Sie stieß ihn zurück.

‹Geh weg, du riechst nach Fisch›, rief sie nun völlig außer sich, ‹sei verflucht!›

Da wurde es dem Apollo zu dumm. Mit einem Glas Wein in der Hand ging er langsam auf Moira zu. Dann sagte er bedrohlich leise: ‹Nimm es zurück, Moira, nimm den Fluch zurück, sofort, hörst du!›

Sie verachtete ihn. ‹Nie!› rief sie, ‹du Schweinsfisch, du Plattnase. Nie! Nie! Nie!› Da schwappte ihr Apollo den Wein ins Gesicht. Ohne ihn abzuwischen flüsterte sie: ‹. . . und du mit.› Dann ging sie ohne sich umzusehen zwischen ihren Ziegen davon.

Apollo blickte mich vorwurfsvoll an, als wollte er sagen, sehen Sie, nun ist es passiert. Habe ich es nicht gleich gesagt! Er war völlig erschöpft. Er sah zum Sterben müde und alt aus, während er den einen Fetzen der Serviette auf dem Knie glattstrich. Er tat mir in der Seele leid. Aber plötzlich nahm er sich zusammen. ‹Chorillo›, stieß er hervor, mit einem Klagelaut nicht von Menschenmund, ‹Chorillo, was ist dir?›

Chorillo hustete. Sein Gesicht und seine Hände waren mondenbleich. ‹Ich weiß nicht›, sagte er, mühsam atmend, mit einem Versuch zu lächeln, ‹mir wird so komisch auf einmal.› Er hüstelte wieder und führte den anderen Fetzen der Serviette zum Munde. ‹Ich habe mich wohl etwas überanstrengt. Es ist Blut, fürchte ich.› Er betrachtete verwundert das Tuch. Das Fieber schüttelte ihn.

Ich lief ins Haus, meinen Mantel zu holen.

‹Er muß sofort ins Bett›, rief ich, als ich wiederkam. ‹Er braucht einen Arzt.›

scratch out their eyes, "curse you, triple-curse you."

It was time I intervened.

"Come, come," I said soothingly, "why be so jealous?" And Chorillo came forward to be nice to her. She pushed him back.

"Go away, you smell of fish," she shouted, quite beside herself by now, "curse you both."

That was going too far for Apollo. He advanced slowly on Moira with a glass of wine in his hand. Then he said, in menacingly quiet tones: "Take it back, Moira, take the curse back at once, d'you hear?"

She scorned him. "Never!" she cried, "swine of a fish, flat-nosed thing. Never! Never! Never!" Apollo splashed the wine into her face. Without wiping it off she whispered: "And you too." Then without looking round she went off among her goats.

Apollo glanced at me reproachfully, as much as to say "there now, it's happened. Didn't I tell you it would?" He was utterly exhausted. He looked dead tired and old smoothing out one piece of the napkin on his knee. I was deeply sorry for him. But suddenly he pulled himself together. "Chorillo," he gasped, with such a sound of grief as no human mouth might make, "Chorillo, what's the matter?"

Chorillo coughed. His face and hands were pale as the moon.

"I don't know," he said, breathing with difficulty, and trying to smile, "I feel funny suddenly." He coughed again and put the other piece of napkin to his mouth. "I think I must have strained myself. I'm afraid it's blood." He looked wonderingly at the cloth. The fever shook him.

I ran indoors to fetch my coat. "He must go to bed at once," I cried when I came back. "He needs a doctor."

‹Auf Anthos gibt es keinen Arzt›, sagte Apollo und nahm Chorillo ohne weiters auf den Rücken. Der Kranke ließ sich's willig gefallen. Ich konnte und wollte es nicht hindern. Auf dem Rücken trug ihn Apollo ins Haus.»

Der Erzähler machte eine nachdenkliche Pause, nicht allein um zu trinken, denn das tat er auch, wenn nicht gerade vom Wein die Rede war, aber dann immer, sondern wohl um seinen Zuhörer in Spannung zu halten, wie die Geschichte enden würde. Während er sprach, nahm er unbewußt das Aussehen seiner Gestalten an, ähnelte dem Kellner Apollo, ja sogar dem Delphin, sah bald alt, bald jung, bald gut oder böse aus, darin dem Proteus verwandt, dem sterblich geborenen Seegreis des griechischen Mythos, dem Zauberer, Wahrsager und Tausendkünstler, der sich in allerlei Gestalten, in Tiere, Bäume, ja selbst in Feuer und Wasser zu verwandeln wußte. Der Sage nach soll er seinen Söhnen Tmolos und Telogenes, zweien Riesen von unerhörter Grausamkeit, im Spiegel erschienen sein und sie so in Erstaunen gesetzt haben, daß sie künftig von ihrer Barbarei geheilt waren, der Sage nach.

In Erstaunen setzen, ist das nicht die Natur des Poeten und also auch des sonderbaren Fremden Auftrag?

«Ich pflege», fuhr dieser nach einer Weile mit schwerer Zunge fort, «auf meinen Reisen eine wohlassortierte Taschenapotheke mit mir zu führen und verstehe mich ein wenig darauf, sie mit Erfolg anzuwenden. Schlaf, Ruhe schienen mir in Chorillos Fall zunächst die besten Heilmittel, und auch Apollo brauchte etwas für sein krankes Herz. Zu Bett gebracht erholte sich unser junger Patient sichtlich und schlief bald ein. –

Da es Abend geworden war, gelüstete es mich, noch etwas ans Meer zu gehen. Ich fand es aufgeregter als am Tage, unheimlich schwarz auf einmal und immer wieder vergeblich bemüht, aufs Land zu kommen. Wo mochte der Delphin sein? Ich hörte ihn. Bald nah, bald fern vernahm ich seinen klagenden Ruf, aber ich konnte ihn nicht sehen. Also kehrte

"There isn't a doctor on Anthos," said Apollo, and without more ado he took Chorillo on his back. The sick boy let him willingly. I could not prevent it, nor did I wish to. He was carried indoors on Apollo's back.'

The storyteller paused reflectively, not only to drink, for he did that even when wine was not mentioned, but always then, but rather to keep his listener in suspense as to how the story would end. While he spoke he unwittingly took on the appearances of his characters, and resembled the waiter Apollo, or even the dolphin, now old, now young, now good, now evil; and in this he was kin to Proteus, the mortal-born Old Man of the Sea of Greek mythology, the magician, the sooth-sayer, the conjurer, who could transform himself into all shapes, into animals, trees, even into fire and water. Legend says he once appeared in the mirror to his sons Tmolos and Telogenes, two giants of unspeakable cruelty, and so astounded them that they were cured in future of their barbarity, the legend says. Is not that the nature of poets, to astound? and thus also the task of my curious stranger?

After a while he continued, rather thickly: 'I normally carry a well-stocked first-aid kit with me on my journeys, and have some small skill in putting it to use. Sleep and quiet seemed to me the best remedies in Chorillo's case, for the present, and Apollo too needed something for his poorly heart. Once put to bed our young patient visibly recovered and soon fell asleep.

It was now evening; I wanted to go down to the sea again. I found it more agitated than by day, uncannily black of a sudden, and straining again and again, in vain, to come up on to the land. Where might the dolphin be? I could hear him. I heard his plaintive call, now close in, now far off, but I could not see him. So I turned and strolled through the little town,

ich um und schlenderte durch die kleine Stadt, mich ein bißchen umzuhören. Ich erfuhr, daß nach anfänglichem Entzücken der Bevölkerung über das Wunder von der Freundschaft des Delphins mit dem Jünglingsknaben[6] – diesen Ausdruck gebraucht Goethe irgendwo, der ja auch einmal von diesem gesegneten Alter sagt: sie duften Jugend![7] – die Stimmung allmählich umgeschlagen war. Man nahm Ärgernis. Ich begegnete dem Priester des Ortes, der sich bemüßigt fühlte, mit Rauchfäßchen und Weihwasserwedel eine kleine Prozession zum Strand zu veranstalten, um das Meerungeheuer, so nannte er den unschuldigen Fisch, zu beschwören und dem heidnischen Treiben in der Bucht ein frommes Ende zu machen. Das mußte ich sehen. Ich schloß mich dem Zuge an. Aber wir kamen zu spät. Das Unheil war bereits geschehen. Der Delphin mußte, ich kann mir's nicht anders denken, gespürt haben, daß sein Spielgefährte krank sei. Er wollte zu ihm und war auf Strand gelaufen. Wir hörten ihn stöhnen und fanden ihn hilflos im noch heißen Sande liegen, ein Messer in seinem Herzen, sich verblutend, sterbend fanden wir ihn, nicht anders als ein Mensch stirbt. Und ich sah etwas, in jener Nacht, was ich meiner Lebtage nie vergessen werde, ich sah den Fisch unter Schluchzen reichlich Tränen vergießen, ehe er mit einem Seufzer verschied. Unsere Tränen, mein Herr, sind eine Erinnerung an das Meer, aus dem auch wir stammen.

Als der Fisch tot war, machten sich sofort Leute aus Anthos daran, ihn auszuschlachten. Die Leber des Delphins gilt dort zu Lande als Heilmittel gegen die Schwindsucht. Angewidert verließ ich den Strand. Was würde geschehen, wenn Chorillo den Tod des Gespielen erfuhr, und der Kellner Apollo? Es war nicht auszudenken.

Da ich im Hause alles still fand, begab ich mich auf mein Zimmer. Was hatte sich in diesen wenigen Stunden meines Aufenthaltes auf der Insel ereignet! Ich machte mir ernstliche Gedanken, ob nicht am Ende doch meine sträfliche Neugier

to see what I could find out. I learned that after the people's initial delight at the miracle of the friendship between the dolphin and the "youthful boy" – Goethe uses the expression somewhere, and also says, does he not, of that blessed age: "they scent of youth" – the mood had gradually changed. Offence was taken. I met the priest of the place who felt it incumbent upon him to stage a small procession down to the beach with censer and aspergillum, to exorcise the sea-monster, as he called the innocent fish, and put a pious stop to the heathen goings-on in the bay. I had to see it. I joined the procession. But we were too late. The calamity had already happened. The dolphin must have sensed that his playmate was ill, I can't think any other, and had wanted to come to him and had stranded himself on the beach. We heard him groaning and found him lying helpless in the still warm sand, a knife in his heart, bleeding to death, we found him dying, no differently than a man dies. And I saw something that night I shall never forget so long as I live, I saw the fish sobbing and weeping copious tears, before he died with a sigh. Our tears, my dear sir, are a reminder of the sea from whence we came.

When the fish was dead people from the town of Anthos immediately began cutting it up. In those parts dolphin's liver is held to be a remedy against consumption. I left the beach in disgust. What would happen when Chorillo heard of his companion's death, and the waiter Apollo? I did not dare think.

Finding everything quiet in the hotel I went to my room. So much had happened on the island in the few hours of my stay, I began seriously wondering whether my reprehensible

sollte schuld gewesen sein, das Unheil heraufzubeschwören. Ich konnte keine Ruhe finden.

Inzwischen war der Mond heraufgekommen. Ich sah aus dem Fenster über den nun wieder menschenleeren Strand zum Meer, das mir ärmer geworden schien ohne den Fisch mit seiner sonderlichen Liebe zu einem Menschen, und der dafür gestorben war.

Vielleicht war ich doch ein wenig eingenickt, gleichviel, ich hörte plötzlich Stimmen, Chorillos Stimme meinte ich zu vernehmen und die des Kellners Apollo, wenn mich nicht die Sinne täuschten.

‹Du bist noch gar nicht braun›, hörte ich den Jüngling sagen, ‹du warst wohl noch nicht viel in der Sonne?›

‹Oh, ich denke doch›, antwortete er freundlich, ‹ziemlich viel. Wollen wir nicht baden gehen?›

‹Jetzt, mitten in der Nacht?› fragte Chorillo mit einem Schauder.

‹Bei Mondenschein ist es am schönsten›, entgegnete der andere.

Ich beugte mich aus dem Fenster. Ich gewahrte Chorillo in Begleitung eines fremden Mannes. Sie waren beide nackt, Chorillo braun, der andere weiß, leuchtend wie Marmor und herrlich wie ein Gott.

‹Wie heißt du›, fragte der Postbote zutraulich.

‹Delphinios heiße ich›, antwortete der Fremde.

Sie schritten selbfreund dem Meere zu.» – – –

«Dies also», schloß mein trunkener Gast, «dies wäre meine Geschichte von Chorillo und dem Fisch. Ich schenke sie Ihnen, wie gesagt», lallte er. Dann sank sein weinschweres Haupt ihm auf den Arm, wobei er die Hand öffnete zu einer Schale, wie Bettler tun, wenn sie um eine milde Gabe bitten. Er lebte ja schließlich von seinen Geschichten.

THE DOLPHIN

curiosity might not after all have been to blame in conjuring up the misfortune. I could find no rest.

In the meanwhile the moon had risen. I looked out of my window across the beach, now once more empty of people, to the sea that seemed to me the poorer now without the fish and its strange and fatal love for a human being.

Perhaps I did nod off. All the same, I suddenly heard voices, Chorillo's voice I thought I heard and the waiter Apollo's, unless my senses were deceiving me.

"You're not at all brown," I heard the boy saying, "you haven't been in the sun much yet?"

"Oh I think I have," came the friendly reply, "quite a lot. Shall we not go and bathe?"

"Now, in the middle of the night?" Chorillo asked, with a shudder.

"It's best by moonlight," the other replied.

I leaned out of the window. I saw Chorillo in the company of a strange man. They were both naked. Chorillo brown, the other white, shining like marble and splendid as a god.

"What are you called?" the postboy asked trustingly.

"I'm called Delphinios," the stranger answered.

They strode as friends to one another towards the sea.'

'That, then,' my drunken companion concluded, 'that, if you like, is my story of Chorillo and the fish. I'll make you a present of it, as I said,' he slurred. Then his wine-heavy head sank down on to his arm, and he opened his hand as beggars do asking for alms. After all, he lived from his stories.

JENNIFER'S DREAMS

MARIE LUISE KASCHNITZ

Translated by Helen Taylor

JENNIFERS TRÄUME

Am 2. April wird Jennifers achter Geburtstag gefeiert. Sie bekommt eine Torte, die ihre Mutter selbst gebacken und mit silbernen Zuckerperlen verziert hat, und darf ihre Freundinnen einladen. Am Abend verbringt sie eine Stunde im Zimmer ihres Vaters, eines Rechtsanwalts, der sich in seiner Freizeit mit dem Aufnehmen und Abhören von Tonbändern beschäftigt. Um Jennifer Vergnügen zu machen, steht Herr Andrew an diesem Abend bei einer Sinfonie von Schostakowitsch auf und dirigiert, und Jennifer, die glaubt, daß alle diese Töne wirklich auf sein Geheiß erklingen, sieht ihn bewundernd an.

Am 3. April erzählt Jennifer ihrer Mutter gleich nach dem Aufwachen einen Traum. Sie ist über eine gewölbte Brücke gegangen, sie hat einen Teich voll Seerosen gesehen. In dem schlammigen Teich haben Kühe bis zum Bauch im Wasser gestanden, ein kleines rotes Auto ist über den Hof gefahren, und der Kies hat geknirscht. Frau Andrew findet das alles nicht besonders aufregend, schon gar nicht komisch, aber Jennifer lacht noch in der Erinnerung über das ganze Gesicht.

Am 4. April erwacht Jennifer mit derselben strahlenden Miene wie am Morgen vorher. Sie erzählt von jungen Schwänen und von einem Spiegelzimmer, in dem sie Spinnweben von den erblindeten Scheiben gewischt hat. Frau Andrew muß über Jennifers Begeisterung lachen, weil das Kind im wachen Zustand zur Hilfe im Haushalt nur schwer zu bewegen ist.

Am 5. April sieht Frau Andrew, die einmal gehört hat, daß in Träumen die Erfahrungen des vergangenen Tages lebendig werden, in Jennifers Bilderbüchern, auch in ihren Schul-

JENNIFER'S DREAMS

On 2nd April Jennifer celebrated her eighth birthday. Her mother gave her a cake that she had baked herself and decorated with silver balls. She was allowed to invite her friends to tea. In the evening she spent an hour in her father's study. A lawyer by profession, her father's hobby was his tape-recorder and he spent his spare time recording and listening to tapes. That evening, to please Jennifer, Mr Andrew put on a symphony by Shostakovitch and stood up to conduct the orchestra. Jennifer looked at him in admiration believing that the notes really did sound at his command.

On 3rd April Jennifer described a dream to her mother when she woke up. She was walking over a hump-backed bridge. She saw a pond full of water lilies. Cows were standing up to their stomachs in the muddy water. A small red car was driven into the farmyard and the gravel crunched. Mrs Andrew was not particularly surprised and certainly not amused by all this, but Jennifer's face lit up and she laughed as she remembered her dream.

On 4th April Jennifer woke up with the same beaming expression as on the previous morning. She talked about cygnets and a room lined with mirrors where she wiped cobwebs from the misty glass. Mrs Andrew had to laugh at Jennifer's enthusiasm for it was a hard job getting the child to help with the housework in her waking hours.

On 5th April, having once heard that daytime experiences are re-lived in dreams, Mrs Andrew examined Jennifer's picture books and school books. But she found nothing that she

büchern nach. Sie findet aber nichts, das den Traumbildern ihrer Tochter entspricht. Am Abend dieses Tages berichtet sie ihrem Mann von der sonderbaren Verzückung, in der sich Jennifer befindet, wenn sie von ihren Träumen erzählt. Sie erwähnt auch, daß Jennifer ihre nächtlichen Erlebnisse als Träume nie bezeichnet. Ich war, sagte sie, da und dort, ich habe dies und jenes getan. Herr Andrew wundert sich darüber nicht.

Am 7. April wacht Jennifer in derselben Glückseligkeit auf wie alle Tage vorher. Sie sagt aber nichts, und Frau Andrew fängt an, ihr Fragen zu stellen. Hast du wieder etwas Schönes geträumt, will mein Mäuschen mir heute gar nichts erzählen, heraus mit der Sprache, flink, flink. Woraufhin das Strahlen in Jennifers Augen erlischt und sie auf ihrem Marmeladebrot herumkaut mit mürrischem Gesicht.

Am 8. April stellt Frau Andrew fest, daß Jennifer blaß aussieht und Ringe um die Augen hat. Sie läßt den Stuhlgang des Kindes auf Würmer untersuchen, obwohl sie davon überzeugt ist, daß die Ursache von Jennifers schlechtem Aussehen nur ihre Träume sind.

Nach dem 10. April redet Jennifer wieder, ist guter Laune, ich war in einem Heckengarten, ich habe mich verlaufen und dann doch zurechtgefunden, ich bin auf einem Pferd mit schwarzer Mähne geritten, ich war im Gewölbe. Über dieses «Gewölbe» versucht Frau Andrew vergebens Näheres zu erfahren. Sie hört aber nur, daß Jennifer dort nicht allein war, sondern mit einer Frau, die ihr mit einem großen Taschentuch die Tränen abgewischt hat. Du weinst also, fragt Frau Andrew überrascht. Jennifer antwortet, es weint aus mir, aber nicht, weil ich traurig bin.

Am Abend des 13. April beklagt sich Frau Andrew bei ihrem Mann über Jennifer, die ihre Mutter jetzt manchmal lange ansieht, kritisch und kalt. Laß das Kind in Ruhe, sagt Herr Andrew, frag nicht mehr, sag nichts mehr, auch diese

could identify with her daughter's dreams. In the evening she told her husband about Jennifer's strange excitement whenever she talked about her dreams. She also mentioned that Jennifer never described her experiences as if they were dreams. She said, 'I was here and I was there, I did this and I did that.' None of this surprised Mr Andrew in the least.

On 7th April Jennifer woke up as cheerful as on all the previous days. But she said nothing, and Mrs Andrew began to ask her questions. 'Did you have another beautiful dream, doesn't my little mouse want to tell me anything at all today, come on, tell me.' Whereupon the excitement suddenly died in Jennifer's eyes and she chewed on her bread and jam with a sullen face.

On 8th April Mrs Andrew noticed that Jennifer looked pale and had rings round her eyes. She had her stool examined for worms, although she was convinced that Jennifer's sickly appearance was only due to her dreams.

By 10th April Jennifer was talking again and in a cheerful mood. 'I was in a garden with a hedge round it. I got lost but then I found my way. I rode a horse with a black mane. I was in a vault.' Mrs Andrew tried unsuccessfully to find out more about this 'vault'. But she heard only that Jennifer was not there alone, but with a woman, who dried her tears with a large handkerchief. 'You were crying then,' asked Mrs Andrew, surprised. Jennifer replied, 'tears were running down my face, but not because I was unhappy.'

On the evening of 13th April Mrs Andrew grumbled to her husband about Jennifer who would often fix her mother with a long, cold critical stare. 'Leave the child in peace,' said Mr Andrew, 'don't ask her any more questions, don't talk to her

Zeit geht vorüber und vielleicht schon bald. Frau Andrew, die vor ihrem Mann, vielleicht gerade wegen seines ernsten und einsiedlerischen Wesens, großen Respekt hat, nimmt sich vor, nicht mehr nach Jennifers Träumen zu fragen. Sie ahnt aber schon, daß sie ihrem Vorsatz nicht treu bleiben wird.

Am 15. April geht Frau Andrew bei strömendem Regen in die Stadt, um einen Film abzuholen, den sie zum Entwickeln gegeben hat. Sie hat die Aufnahmen erst vor kurzem gemacht. Mehrere zeigen das Vorstadthäuschen in der Märzsonne, eine ihren Mann im Garten, ein Beet umgrabend, eine Jennifer, wie sie vor der Haustür auf der Treppe sitzt und auf eine unbeschreiblich beunruhigende Weise nirgendwohin schaut. Diese Aufnahme zerreißt Frau Andrew in ganz kleine Fetzen, die sie im Abfalleimer unter Kohlstrünken und Teeblättern vergräbt.

Am 17. April erzählt Jennifer am Morgen wieder von der fremden Frau. Die Frau hat Kaninchenfleisch in einer Schüssel gewaschen, und ihre Hände waren voll Blut. Jennifer hat es gegraust, und sie hat sogar weglaufen wollen. Die Frau hat nicht gescholten, sie hat ihre Hände unter viel strömendem Wasser gewaschen, und am Ende war kein Blut mehr zu sehen. Die Frau ist mit Jennifer in den Garten gegangen und hat sie umarmt. Küßt sie dich auch, fragt Frau Andrew argwöhnisch. Jennifer sagt nicht ja nicht nein, macht aber ein Gesicht, als ob mit dem Wort küssen die Seligkeit dieser Berührung gar nicht auszudrücken sei. Frau Andrew empfindet eine so heftige Eifersucht, daß sie sie nicht einmal ihrem Mann einzugestehen wagt.

Am 21. April bleibt Frau Andrew, die bemerkt hat, daß Jennifer neuerdings statt wie früher vor dem Schlafengehen endlos herumzutrödeln, gleich nach dem Abendessen ins Bett verlangt, auf dem Bettrand der Tochter eine volle Stunde sitzen. Sie erzählt aus ihrer Kindheit, liest vor, singt Lieder, deren Texte sie nicht richtig auswendig weiß. Wie ging das

about it any more. This phase will pass too, perhaps quite soon.' Possibly precisely because of his serious and solitary nature, Mrs Andrew had great respect for her husband and she resolved not to ask Jennifer any more about her dreams. But she realized already that she would not abide by her resolution.

On 15th April Mrs Andrew went into town in the pouring rain to pick up a film that she had left to be developed. She had taken the pictures only recently. Several of them showed the little suburban house in the March sunshine; one of her husband in the garden digging the flower bed; one of Jennifer sitting on the front doorstep and staring into space in an indescribably disturbing manner. Mrs Andrew tore this last picture into small pieces and buried them in the dustbin under cabbage stalks and tea leaves.

On the morning of 17th April Jennifer talked again about the strange woman. The woman was washing rabbit meat in a dish and her hands were covered in blood. Jennifer was horrified and even wanted to run away. The woman did not scold her. She rinsed her hands thoroughly under running water and eventually there was no trace of blood left on them. The woman took Jennifer into the garden and put her arms around her. 'Did she kiss you too,' asked Mrs Andrew suspiciously. Jennifer did not say yes or no, but pulled a face as if the word kiss could not possibly describe the blissful nature of the contact. Mrs Andrew felt such a violent pang of jealousy that she did not dare admit it even to her husband.

On 21st April, having noticed that recently Jennifer had wanted to go straight to bed after supper, rather than dawdling around endlessly as before, Mrs Andrew sat at her daughter's bedside for a full hour. She told stories about her childhood, read aloud and sang songs, the words of which she could not fully remember. 'How does it go on,' she asked, 'can you

weiter, fragt sie, erinnerst du dich? Aber Jennifer hat schon lange nicht mehr zugehört. Sie dreht das Gesicht zur Wand.

Am 23. April spielt Frau Andrew, die ihre Tochter verhext glaubt, mit dem Gedanken, einen jener Priester zu rufen, die in der Stadt London mit allerlei frommem Hokuspokus die Poltergeister vertreiben. Weil aber von nächtlicher Ruhestörung nicht die Rede ist, und auch weil Frau Andrew fürchtet, ihren Mann durch solchen Aberglauben zu erzürnen, führt sie diesen Gedanken nicht aus.

Am 25. April dringt Frau Andrew in die Tochter, ihr mehr von der fremden Frau zu erzählen. Wie sieht sie aus, wie sind ihre Haare, wie alt ist sie, was für Kleider trägt sie, schläfst du bei ihr und in was für einem Zimmer, in was für einem Bett. Jennifer antwortet nicht, sie erbricht ihr Frühstück und kann erst eine Stunde später in die Schule gehen.

Am 30. April erbricht Jennifer wieder ihr Frühstück, obwohl von ihren Träumen diesmal die Rede nicht war. Frau Andrew läßt den Hausarzt kommen, der mit Jennifer Späße macht, sie ah sagen läßt und ihr das Augenlid herunterzieht. Als Frau Andrew sieht, daß ihm nichts anderes einfällt, schickt sie ihn ungeduldig weg. An der Tür dreht der Arzt sich noch einmal um und sagt, und Sie, Frau Andrew, und sieht ihr aufmerksam ins Gesicht. Frau Andrew, die genau weiß, daß sie schlecht aussieht und fahrige Bewegungen hat, sagt zornig, mir fehlt nichts, mir geht es gut, ich mache mir nur Sorgen um Jennifer, und an meinem Mann habe ich keine Stütze, der kümmert sich um nichts.

Am 3. Mai ist Frau Andrew nicht mehr so sicher, daß ihr Mann von Jennifers Träumen nichts wissen will und auch nichts anderes weiß, als was er von ihr selbst erfahren hat. Als sie gegen Abend in sein Zimmer tritt, sitzt Jennifer auf einem Schemel zu seinen Füßen, und er spielt mit ihren langen Haaren. Frau Andrew kommt es vor, als hätten die beiden leise miteinander gesprochen und schwiegen nun, wie Verschwörer, die man beim Pläneschmieden ertappt. In der Nacht

remember?' But Jennifer had stopped listening some time ago. She turned her face to the wall.

On 23rd April Mrs Andrew, who believed her daughter was bewitched, was toying with the idea of summoning one of those London priests who drive out evil spirits with all sorts of religious hocus-pocus. But she did not carry out her idea as it was not a case of disturbed sleep and also because she was afraid she would infuriate her husband with such superstitions.

On 25th April Mrs Andrew urged her daughter to tell her more about the strange woman. 'What does she look like, what's her hair like, how old is she, what clothes does she wear, do you sleep with her, and in what sort of room, what sort of bed?' Jennifer did not answer. She brought up her breakfast and could not leave for school for another hour.

On 30th April Jennifer brought up her breakfast again, although no one had mentioned her dreams this time. Mrs Andrew called the doctor who joked with Jennifer, made her say 'ah' and pulled back her eyelids. When Mrs Andrew saw that he couldn't think what else to do she impatiently sent him away. On the doorstep the doctor turned once more to Mrs Andrew and said, 'and what about you, Mrs Andrew?' and looked searchingly at her face. Mrs Andrew, who knew very well that she looked ill and jittery, said angrily, 'there's nothing wrong with me, I'm fine, I'm just worried about Jennifer, and I don't get any support from my husband, he doesn't bother about anything.'

On 3rd May Mrs Andrew was no longer sure that her husband had no wish to know about Jennifer's dreams, nor that he knew no more about them than she herself had told him. Towards evening, when she went into his room, Jennifer was sitting on a stool at his feet and he was playing with her long hair. It seemed to Mrs Andrew that the pair had been talking quietly to each other and were now silent like conspirators surprised in the act of making their plans. During the night

setzt sich Frau Andrew im Bett auf und sagt schluchzend, du und Jennifer, Jennifer und die Frau, um mich kümmert sich niemand, ich bin allein. Herr Andrew beruhigt sie, er hat nie mit Jennifer über ihre Träume gesprochen, sie kommt manchmal abends in sein Zimmer, meistens wenn er Musik macht, aber gelegentlich auch so.

Am 10. Mai erzählt Jennifer ihrer Mutter am Morgen wieder bereitwilliger, aber nun immer nur von der fremden Frau, ihren weichen Händen, ihrem tiefen Lachen, ihrem hellen Haar. Sie ist schöner als du, sie ist lieber als du, und zum ersten Mal kommt Frau Andrew auf den Gedanken, daß Jennifer gar nicht träumt, nie geträumt hat, sondern das alles nur erfindet, um ihr weh zu tun. Sie versucht sich an jede Einzelheit von Jennifers angeblichen Geschichten zu erinnern. Gab es da nicht viel zuwenig Irrationales, traf Jennifer nicht immer an denselben Orten dieselbe Frau? So träumt man nicht, denkt Frau Andrew, so erfindet man, und in bestimmter Absicht, in böser Absicht gewiß.

Am 13. Mai kommt Frau Andrew beim Bettenmachen, beim Einkaufen, beim Kochen, beim Bügeln, von diesem Gedanken nicht los. Sie geht vor dem Schlafengehen zu ihrem Mann und sagt außer sich, jetzt weiß ich es, es gibt keine Träume, nur ein halbverrücktes, gehässiges Kind. Herr Andrew erschrickt, er schiebt seiner Frau einen Stuhl hin und streicht ihr mit der Hand über das Haar. Dann fängt er wieder an, zum Guten zu reden, sie sind alle überreizt und sollten ausspannen, er schlägt eine gemeinsame Reise, dann, weil die Ferien noch in weiter Ferne liegen, einen Wochenendausflug vor. Andrews haben auf dem Land keine Verwandten und wenig Bekannte, schließlich erinnert sich Frau Andrew eines Ehepaars, das einmal neben ihnen gewohnt hat, das aber, vor etwa neun Jahren, aufs Land gezogen ist. Zwischen den beiden jungen Paaren hatte sich damals ein freundschaftliches Verhältnis entwickelt, noch jetzt werden Neujahrsgrüße ausge-

Mrs Andrew sat up in bed sobbing and said, 'you and Jennifer, Jennifer and this woman, nobody cares about me, I'm quite alone'. Mr Andrew comforted her. He had never spoken to Jennifer about her dreams, she sometimes came into his room in the evening, mostly when he was playing music, but now and then for no particular reason.

On the morning of 10th May Jennifer talked to her mother again, more eagerly, but now it was only about the strange woman, her soft hands, her deep laugh, her fair hair. 'She is more beautiful than you. She is nicer than you.' And for the first time it occurred to Mrs Andrew that Jennifer was not dreaming at all, had never had these dreams, but was only inventing it all in order to hurt her. She tried to remember every detail of Jennifer's alleged stories. Wasn't there far too little that was irrational, didn't Jennifer continually meet the same woman in the same places? People don't dream like that, thought Mrs Andrew, that is how they make up stories, and for a particular purpose, an evil purpose no doubt.

On 13th May Mrs Andrew busied herself making the beds, shopping, cooking and ironing, but she could not shake off these thoughts. She was quite beside herself when she went to her husband before going to bed and said, 'I'm certain now that there haven't been any dreams, she's just a half-crazy, spiteful child.' Mr Andrew was alarmed. He pushed a chair towards his wife and smoothed her hair with his hand. Then he spoke soothingly to her again. They were all overwrought and needed to relax. He suggested a family trip, or rather, as the holidays were still a long way off, a week-end outing. The Andrews had no relatives and few friends who lived in the country. Finally Mrs Andrew remembered a couple who had once lived next door, but had moved to the country about nine years ago. The two young couples had become friendly in those days and they still exchanged New Year's greetings which always included a sincere invitation to visit. 'The

tauscht, die jedesmal auch eine herzliche Einladung enthalten.
Die Fergussons, sagt Frau Andrew, und freut sich, daß sie auf
den Gedanken gekommen ist. Ihr Mann stimmt ihrem Vorschlag, wenn auch ein wenig zögernd, zu.

Am 16. Mai, einem Donnerstag, melden sich Andrews bei
ihren alten Freunden Eddie und Liz Fergusson telefonisch an.
An diesem und am nächsten Tag bereiten sie ihren Ausflug vor.
Jennifer, die in der Aussicht auf die kleine Reise ganz die alte
ist, packt ihr Krämchen; sie bleibt am Abend bei den Eltern
sitzen, die auf der Landkarte die Straßen heraussuchen, welche
zu dem recht abgelegenen Besitz der Freunde führen. Frau
Andrew näht Jennifer ein schottisches Röckchen, schließlich
waschen alle drei zusammen den Wagen und freuen sich, daß
er glänzt wie neu.

Am 18. Mai um 8 Uhr früh, als die Andrews losfahren, ist
zwar diesiges Wetter, aber es steht auch in den Vorstadtgärten
vieles in Blüte, Flieder, Schneeballen und tränendes Herz. Die
kleine Familie hat sich auf den Vordersitzen zusammenge-
drängt, wenn der gutgelaunte Vater schalten will, sagt er,
verzeihen Sie, meine Dame, und Jennifer rutscht kichernd ein
Stückchen weg. Frau Andrew legt ihren Arm um die Tochter,
das hätten wir längst tun sollen, denkt sie, einmal heraus aus
dem Alltag, und alles wird gut. Jennifer, die sich zuerst mit
blanken Augen umgesehen hat, wird bald schläfrig, schläft
auch ein bißchen, um 11 Uhr, als sie aufwacht, sind keine
Straßen und Häuser mehr um sie, sondern Wiesen und Wald.

Am 18. Mai um 11 Uhr steht der Wagen am Straßenrand
still. Herr und Frau Andrew haben die Karte ausgebreitet, sie
sind sich nicht einig über den bei der nächsten Kreuzung ein-
zuschlagenden Weg. Nach links, sagt Jennifer ruhig. Die
Eltern lachen, fahren dann aber wirklich nach links auf eine
kleine Ortschaft zu. Beim Dorfausgang gibt es noch einmal
eine kleine Meinungsverschiedenheit, über die Jennifer den
Kopf schüttelt, nach rechts, sagt sie, an der Eiche vorbei, und

Fergussons,' said Mrs Andrew, pleased that she had thought of them. Her husband agreed with her suggestion, if a little hesitantly.

On 16th May, a Thursday, the Andrews rang up their old friends Eddie and Liz. That day and the next were spent preparing for the outing. Jennifer packed her bits and pieces, acting quite her old self at the prospect of the short trip; she stayed up in the evening and sat with her parents as they traced the route on the map which would take them to their friends' isolated farm. Mrs Andrew made Jennifer a little kilt and finally they all washed the car together and were delighted to see it shining like new.

On 18th May as the Andrews set off at eight o'clock in the morning the weather was rather misty, nevertheless many flowers were in bloom in the suburban gardens, lilacs, viburnum and bleeding hearts. The small family had squashed up together on the front seats. Whenever the good-humoured father wanted to change gear, he said, 'excuse me, ladies,' and Jennifer giggled and slid along a little. Mrs Andrew put her arm round her daughter. 'We should have done this long ago,' she thought. 'Once we get away from the daily routine, everything will be all right again.' At first Jennifer looked about her, her eyes shining, then she soon became sleepy and even fell asleep for a while. When she woke up at about eleven, the streets and houses had gone and there were fields and woods around her.

On 18th May at eleven o'clock the car had stopped at the side of the road. Mr and Mrs Andrew had spread the map out. They did not agree which road they should take at the next cross-roads. 'Left,' said Jennifer calmly. The parents laughed, but then did turn left and drove on to a small village. At the end of the village they had another small difference of opinion at which Jennifer shook her head. 'Turn right,' she said, 'past the oak tree', and as a cyclist coming the other way gave the

weil ein entgegenkommender Radfahrer denselben Bescheid
gibt, fährt Herr Andrew nach rechts an der Eiche vorbei. Und
wohin nun, kleine Hellseherin, fragt er lustig, als sich mitten
im Sumpfwald der Weg noch einmal verzweigt. Jennifer sagt,
nachdem sie ihre Umgebung gründlich ins Auge gefaßt hat,
jetzt wieder nach links durch den Hohlweg, wenn wir da
herauskommen, ist schon die Brücke zu sehen. Ihr Gesicht
glänzt plötzlich vor Freude, sie rutscht aufgeregt auf ihrem Sitz
hin und her. So kann Daddy nicht fahren, sagt Frau Andrew
streng, während ihr Mann Jennifer von der Seite verwundert
betrachtet. Im Hohlweg schlagen die Zweige an die Wagen-
fenster, es riecht nach Schnecken und Pilzen, beim Herauskommen sieht man eine gewölbte Brücke und einige Stall-
gebäude, Kühe stehen bis zum Bauch in einem schlammigen
Teich. Es ist plötzlich heiß, fast schwül, und Frau Andrew reißt
sich das Seidentuch vom Hals. Zum Haus geht es bergauf, sagt
Jennifer jetzt eifrig, um die Ställe herum. Was weißt denn du,
gar nichts weißt du, sagt Frau Andrew, deren gute Laune
plötzlich verflogen ist. Aber es stimmt, als sie den Hügel
hinaufgefahren sind, sehen die Andrews das Wohnhaus, einen
eher bescheidenen Bau, dem aber einige weißblühende Mag-
nolien großen Glanz verleihen. Auf der Treppe steht Liz
Fergusson und kommt auch schon die Treppe herunter und
über den Hof gelaufen, und die Andrews wundern sich, wie
jung sie aussieht, fast jünger als in der vergangenen gemeinsamen Zeit. Und das ist Jennifer, sagt Frau Andrew nach der
ersten Begrüßung, und wendet sich nach dem Kinde um. Da
hat aber das sonst so scheue Mädchen bereits seine Arme um
Liz Fergussons Hals gelegt und sie geküßt.

Am 18. Mai um 12 Uhr gehen, weil auf den Hausherrn noch
gewartet wird, die Andrews mit ihrer alten Freundin noch
nicht ins Haus, sondern auf dem Anwesen umher. Sie sehen
einen Heckengarten, junge Schwäne, einen Jährling mit
schwarzer Mähne und stehen noch einmal auf der gewölbten

same advice, Mr Andrew turned right and drove past the oak tree. 'And where now, little clairvoyant?' he asked cheerfully, when the road forked again in the middle of a damp forest. After she had examined her surroundings in detail, Jennifer said, 'Now go left again down the sunken lane. When we're out of there, we'll be able to see the bridge.' Her face suddenly shone with happiness and she slid excitedly backwards and forwards on her seat. 'Daddy can't drive like that,' said Mrs Andrew sharply, whilst her husband looked sideways at Jennifer in amazement. In the lane twigs hit the car windows. It smelt of snails and fungi. As they came out they saw a hump-backed bridge and a few stables. Cows stood up to their stomachs in a muddy pond. It was suddenly hot, almost oppressive, and Mrs Andrew pulled her silk scarf from her neck. 'We go up the hill to the house and round the stables,' said Jennifer, eagerly now. 'What would you know about it then, you know absolutely nothing,' said Mrs Andrew, who had suddenly lost her good humour. But it was correct. As they drove up the hill, the Andrews saw the house, rather a modest building, but given great distinction by some white magnolias. Liz Fergusson was standing on the steps and she now came running down across the yard. The Andrews were surprised to see how young she looked, almost younger than when they had known her in the past. 'And this is Jennifer,' said Mrs Andrew, after she had greeted her, and she turned round to the child. But the normally shy little girl had already put her arms round Liz Fergusson's neck and kissed her.

On 18th May at twelve o'clock the Andrews were walking around outside. They had not yet gone into the house with their old friend because they were still waiting for her husband. They saw a garden enclosed by a hedge, young swans and a colt with a black mane, and they stood on the same

Brücke, über die sie hergefahren sind. Auf der Brücke nun beugt sich Liz Fergusson zu Jennifer und sagt leise, aber doch laut genug, daß Frau Andrew ihre Worte verstehen kann, dir brauche ich ja nichts zu erklären, du kennst alles, du bist immer hier, und Jennifer freut sich und nickt. Sie gehen danach noch durch einen halbverfallenen unterirdischen Gang, und dort fürchtet sich Jennifer ein bißchen, und die Freundin Liz umfaßt ihre Schultern und zieht sie an sich wie zum Schutz. Frau Andrew ist beklommen zumute, sie nimmt ihren Mann beiseite und fragt, ob sie nicht am Abend schon wegfahren könnten. Herr Andrew hat nichts dagegen, es ist ihm recht.

Am 18. Mai fährt in einem roten Wagen Eddie Fergusson auf den Hof. Er winkt und ruft schon von weitem und sobald er ausgestiegen ist, stellt sich das heiternachbarliche Verhältnis von einst wieder her. Beim Essen, das in einer Art von Spiegelzimmer eingenommen wird, beim Spaziergang und später beim Tee werden Erinnerungen ausgetauscht und Späße gemacht. Frau Andrew ist jetzt guter Dinge, sie gibt sich Mühe zu übersehen, daß Jennifer die Hand der alten Freundin nicht losgelassen hat und nicht aufhört, sie anzustarren. Auch ein paar Blicke, die zwischen ihrem Mann und Liz Fergusson hin und her gehen, will Frau Andrew nicht bemerken, obwohl diese Blicke recht seltsam sind, nämlich wortlos und tief und von einem fast ungehörigen Ernst.

Am 18. Mai um 18 Uhr brechen die Andrews auf, obwohl sie zum Übernachten mehrmals herzlich aufgefordert worden sind. Auf dem Heimweg schläft Jennifer an der Brust des Vaters, während Frau Andrew fährt. Um das Kind nicht zu wecken, sprechen sie nicht. Als sie zu Hause angelangt sind, bringt Frau Andrew Jennifer sofort zu Bett. Dann sucht sie, was sie sehr lange nicht getan hat, ihren Mann in seinem Arbeitszimmer auf und hört zu, wie er eines seiner Tonbänder ablaufen läßt. Das Fenster steht offen, und es riecht nach feuchten Gartenwegen und jungem Laub. Frau Andrew sitzt in dem

hump-backed bridge that they had driven over on their way. On the bridge Liz Fergusson bent down to Jennifer and said quietly, though loudly enough for Mrs Andrew to understand what she was saying, 'I don't have to explain anything to you, you know it all, you're always coming here', and Jennifer nodded happily. Next, they went through a crumbling underground passage. Jennifer was a little afraid in there and Liz grasped her shoulders and pulled her to her as if to protect her. Mrs Andrew was uneasy. She took her husband on one side and asked if they could drive back that evening. Mr Andrew had no objections, that would be fine by him.

On 18th May Eddie Fergusson drove into the yard in a red car. He was waving and shouting from a distance, and as soon as he got out, the happy neighbourly friendship started again from where it had left off. They had lunch in a kind of hall of mirrors and exchanged memories and cracked jokes over their meal and afterwards while they went for a walk and had their tea. Mrs Andrew was now in high spirits and she made an effort to ignore the fact that Jennifer had not let go of her old friend's hand and had not stopped gazing at her. She also chose not to notice a few glances between her husband and Liz Fergusson, although they were very strange looks; silent and deep and of an almost indecent intensity.

On 18th May at six o'clock the Andrews left, although they had been eagerly invited to stay the night many times. On the way home Jennifer slept against her father's chest, whilst Mrs Andrew drove. They did not talk, so as not to wake the child. When they reached home Mrs Andrew took Jennifer straight to bed. Then she did something she had not done for a long time; she went to see her husband in his study and listened while he played one of his tapes. The window was open and the air smelt of damp garden paths and new leaves. Mrs Andrew sat on the child's seat that Jennifer normally used. She

Kinderstuhl, den sonst Jennifer benützt. Sie sieht aus wie manchmal in ihrer Mädchenzeit, verwundert und leer. Wir dürfen morgen nicht vergessen, den Klempner zu bestellen, sagt sie, als das Klavierstück zu Ende ist. Nein, das dürfen wir nicht vergessen, sagt ihr Mann und sieht sie liebevoll an.

Am 19. Mai und an allen folgenden Tagen trödelt Jennifer beim Zubettgehen und läßt sich von ihrer Mutter eine Geschichte nach der andern erzählen. Eines Morgens sagt sie, ich habe geträumt und berichtet Kunterbuntes – von der Brücke, den Kühen im Wasser, dem unterirdischen Gang und der fremden Frau ist die Rede nie mehr.

looked bewildered and vacant as she had sometimes looked in her girlhood. 'We mustn't forget to ring for a plumber to-morrow,' she said, when the piano piece had ended. 'No, we mustn't,' said her husband, giving her a loving glance.

On 19th May, and from that day forward, Jennifer dawdled at bedtime and let her mother tell her one story after another. One morning she said, 'I had a dream,' and she related some nonsense. There was no more talk of the bridge, the cows in the water, the underground passage and the strange woman.

FEDEZEEN

GÜNTER DE BRUYN

Translated by Peter Anthony

FEDEZEEN

DER Weg zu Großvater war weit, anstrengend und oft gefährlich, die Kekse aus der Blechbüchse schmeckten muffig, und abends fürchtete ich mich in dem alten Mietshaus; trotzdem ging ich gern zu ihm, um von den verzauberten Teichen zu hören.

Immer, wenn ich zu ihm kam, saß er am Fenster neben der Nähmaschine und sah hinaus auf die Brandmauer des zweiten Hinterhauses, deren graues Putzkleid bei jedem Regen mehr zerschliß und die scheußliche Nacktheit nachlässig gemauerter Ziegel sehen ließ. Er hielt den Kopf wie einer, der am fernen Horizont etwas zu erkennen versucht, und erst wenn er mir sein knochiges Gesicht mit den stumpfen, milchigblauen Augen zuwandte, wußte ich wieder, daß er fast blind war.

«Tach ok, min Jung», sagte er, erhob sich langsam aus dem leise ächzenden Korbstuhl, schlurfte zum Kleiderschrank, nahm die Keksbüchse herunter und trug sie zur Nähmaschine, auf der ich bereits saß und darauf wartete, daß er zu erzählen begann. Meist aber dauerte es lange, bis er sein Schweigen brach. Im Sommer summten Fliegen an der Scheibe auf und ab, im Winter trieben verirrte Windstöße Schneewirbel gegen die Fenster, im Hofschacht unten klapperten Müllkästen, weit entfernt, von der Yorck- oder Belle-Alliance-Straße her, erklangen Marschmusik und Autogehupe. Mein Gesäß schmerzte vom harten Sitzen, manchmal fielen mir, wenn ich auf das eintönige Ticken des Regulators hörte, die Augen zu, aber nicht eine Minute bereute ich es, gekommen zu sein.

«Kannst du schwimmen?» Völlig munter war ich, wenn er mit dieser Frage begann.

FEDEZEEN

IT was a long walk to grandfather's, tiring and often dangerous, there was a stale taste to the biscuits in the tin box, and at night the old tenement made me feel scared; all the same I liked going to see him – to hear about the magic pools.

Whenever I came he would be sitting at the window, next to the sewing machine, gazing at the fire wall of the second block of rear tenements, the grey plaster coat of which was being worn increasingly away with each fall of rain, revealing beneath the ugly nakedness of slovenly brickwork. He held his head like someone trying to distinguish something on the far horizon, and only when he turned his gaunt face with its blank, milk blue eyes towards me would I remember that he was almost blind.

'A good day to you, my lad,' he would say, get up slowly from the faintly creaking wicker chair, shuffle over to the wardrobe, take out the biscuit tin and carry it to the sewing machine on which I would already be sitting, waiting for him to start speaking. But it usually took a long time for him to break his silence. In the summer flies would be buzzing their way up and down the window pane, in the winter stray gusts of wind would drive flurries of snow against the windows, in the well of the courtyard dustbins clattered, far away, from Yorck St or Belle-Alliance St, march music rang out and the hooting of car horns. The hard seat made my bottom sore, and sometimes, if I listened to the monotonous tick of the pendulum-clock, I would nod off, but never for a moment did I regret having come.

'Can you swim?' At this first question I would be wide awake again.

«Ja, Großvater, ein bißchen.»

«Dat's gaut; ohne Schwimmen helpt dat nicht so veel!»

Das Stückchen Himmel, das man sehen konnte, wenn man den Kopf auf die Fensterbank legte und steil nach oben blickte, war meist schon grau wie der Mauerputz geworden, wenn Großvater zu sprechen begann. Er redete mit leiser Verschwörerstimme, bei deren Klang sich die Haut auf meinen Armen in angenehmer Erregung zusammenzog.

«Hest du wedder wat?»

«Ja, Großvater», sagte ich und breitete auf der Fensterbank die Pfennige und Sechser und Groschen aus, um die ich seit Stunden meine Faust gepreßt hatte. Großvater betastete jedes der handwarmen Geldstücke und rechnete leise dabei. Auf einen Wink von ihm lief ich zum Bett und zog unter dem Keilkissen das großkarierte Tuch hervor, in das er die neuerworbenen Schätze einwickelte. Wieder rechnete er mit aufgeregt flatternden Lippen. Ich schlich zur Tür und legte den Riegel um; Großvater öffnete den Nähmaschinenkasten. Unter Lappen und Garnrollen versteckt, lag unsere Kassette, eine Tabakschachtel mit dem knallbunten Bild eines pfeiferauchenden Robinson; trotz der Kratzspuren waren die Felljacke, der Sonnenschirm und der im Hintergrund arbeitende schwarze Freitag noch gut zu erkennen. Verräterisch schepperte das Blech, wenn das Geld hineinfiel. Großvater feuchtete den kurzen Stift mit der Zunge an und gab ihn mir. Vor Aufregung zitternd, trug ich die neue Summe auf der beiliegenden Schreibheftseite ein. Dann wurde Robinson wieder unter Tuch, Zwirn und Stecknadelkissen begraben. Die Tür wurde entriegelt; nun erst konnte ich mich richtig freuen.

«Wie lange noch, Großvater?»

«Iher, as du di denkst, Jung!»

Wir sparten seit Jahren. Ich drängte mich den Nachbarn als

'Yes, grandfather, a little.'

'That's my boy; it doesn't do you as much good if you can't swim.'

The little patch of sky that could be seen by laying your head on the window ledge and looking straight up had usually turned as grey as the plaster by the time grandfather began speaking. He would talk in a hushed, conspiratorial voice, the sound of which made the skin of my arms tense with pleasurable excitement.

'Did you bring something?'

'Yes, grandfather,' I said, and spread out on the window ledge the farthings, halfpennies and pennies that I had been clutching tightly in my hand for hours. Grandfather fingered each of the coins, still warm from my hand, calculating softly to himself as he did so. At a sign from him I ran to the bed and drew out from under the bolster the broad-checked cloth in which he wrapped up the newly acquired treasures. Again he calculated, his lips quivering with excitement. I crept to the door and slid the bolt; grandfather opened the sewing machine box. Concealed beneath scraps of cloth and reels of cotton lay our cashbox, a tobacco tin on which, painted in garish colours, Robinson Crusoe was smoking his pipe; despite the scratches, the fur jacket, the parasol and the black figure of Man Friday at work in the background were all still easily recognizable. There was a tell-tale clatter as the money dropped into the tin. Grandfather moistened the pencil stub with his tongue and passed it to me. With a shiver of excitement I entered the new total on the accompanying sheet of notebook paper. Then Robinson Crusoe was reburied under cloth, cotton and pincushion. The door was unbolted; only now could I feel really happy.

'How much longer, grandfather?'

'Sooner than you think, lad!'

We had been saving for years. I pestered the neighbours

Einholer auf; ich hackte beim Kohlenhändler Holz, zählte Briketts in die Kästen; ich bettelte den Jungen aus unserer Straße, die als Lehrlinge ihr erstes Geld verdienten, die Pfennige ab; ich kramte leere Flaschen aus Mülltonnen, hütete gegen Bezahlung Kleinkinder in Buddelkästen, erpreßte meinen älteren Bruder, den ich mit einem Mädchen im Park gesehen hatte; ich hangelte mit Magneten Münzen aus Kellergittern, verkaufte Weihnachts- und Ostersüßigkeiten an Schulkameraden; ich suchte vor Kinokassen, Theken, Ladentischen und auf Rummelplätzen nach heruntergefallenen Geldstücken und versuchte auch manchmal den Bäcker oder Milchhändler zu betrügen. Großvater aber sparte am Essen, an Strom und an Gas. War er allein, ging er mit der Sonne zu Bett, mit mir saß er im Dunkeln, kam meine Mutter, drehte er oft die Sicherungen heraus, und wir aßen das mitgebrachte Abendbrot bei Kerzenschein. Tee brühte er sich für Tage im voraus und trank ihn kalt; zum Mittag aß er nur Gerichte mit kurzer Kochzeit, Haferflocken-, Grieß- und Maggisuppen, Eierkuchen oder Blutwurst. Manchmal ging angeblich sein Kocher entzwei, und er ließ sich Erbswurstsuppen von der mitleidigen Nachbarin kochen. Sein Versuch, den sonntäglich gestimmten Spaziergängern neben dem künstlichen Wasserfall am Kreuzberg[1] mit demütig gezogener Mütze und frisch gewaschener gelbschwarzer Armbinde Groschen zu entlocken, endete zwar schnell auf einer Bank im Polizeirevier, aber auch ohne das füllte sich langsam unsere Kasse, und der ersehnte Tag rückte näher.

Zweimal glaubten wir uns schon nahe am Ziel und wurden enttäuscht. Das war, als Großvater von der Fahrpreiserhöhung erfuhr, die irgendwann in den grauen Jahren seines Stadtlebens einmal erfolgt war, und dann, als ich zehn Jahre alt wurde und damit die Kinderermäßigung für mich wegfiel. Aber wir gaben nicht auf, sparten weiter und hüteten unser Geheimnis.

into sending me on errands; I chopped wood for the coal merchant, or counted the coal briquettes into the boxes; I begged pennies from the boys in our street who were earning their first wages as apprentices; I ferreted empty bottles out of dustbins, took money for watching over small children in sand pits, blackmailed my elder brother whom I had seen with a girl in the park; with magnets I fished for coins that had fallen down grilles in the pavement; I sold sweets to schoolfellows at Christmas and Easter; I searched in front of cinema ticket-offices, bars, shop counters and at fairgrounds for lost coins, and sometimes even tried to cheat the baker or milkman. For his part grandfather economized on food, electricity and gas. If he was on his own, he went to bed at dusk; if I was there, he would sit in the dark; if my mother came, he would often remove the fuses and we would eat the supper she had brought by candlelight. He brewed tea for days in advance and drank it cold; for his midday meal he ate only those dishes that require a minimum of cooking: porridge, semolina, dried soups, pancakes or black sausage. Sometimes he pretended that his cooker had broken down, and he would ask the sympathetic woman next door to make him some pea and ham soup. His attempt to exploit the good humour of the Sunday afternoon strollers and cadge coins from them near the artificial waterfall on the Kreuzberg by humbly holding out his cap and showing his freshly laundered yellow and black invalid's armband, did, indeed, end rather quickly on the bench of the local police-station, but even so our savings slowly grew and the longed for day drew nearer.

Twice we thought we were near our goal, and twice we were disappointed. That was when grandfather learnt of the fare increase which had occurred sometime during the drab years of his life in the city, and again when I reached the age of ten and we could no longer claim the reduced rates for children. But we didn't give in, continued saving and kept our secret safe.

77

Die Versuchung, Freunde einzuweihen und zu Großvater mitzunehmen, war groß; denn der Weg war langweilig und manchmal, wenn in den Schluchten der Nebenstraßen uniformierte Jungenhorden lauerten, auch gefährlich; aber obwohl Großvater es mir nicht ausdrücklich verboten hatte, tat ich es nie, weil ich ahnte, daß niemand den Zauber unserer Teiche würde begreifen können, und weil ich Angst vor ihrem Lachen hatte. Schon der Name der Straße, in der Großvater wohnte, reizte sie dazu. Fidizin war für sie ein komisches Wort; ich verstand es nicht, wußte es aber aus bitterer Erfahrung. Es verführte sie zu albernen Witzen; sie machten Medizin daraus oder hängten weitere Silben mit i an. Für mich hatte das Wort einen überaus schönen Klang: So surrten die vielfarbig glitzernden Libellen über die Teiche. Und wenn an den schularbeitsfreien Mittwochnachmittagen, während die anderen ihren «Dienst» hatten, auf dem Weg zu Großvater die ermüdend vielen steinernen Rechtecke des Pflasters, die aussahen wie traumhaft-endlose Hopsefelder, unter meinen schwächer werdenden Schritten vorbeizogen, übte auch ich mich in Fidizin-Wortspielen, aber in ernsten. Fodozoon, das war die Sonne über den Feldern, Fadazaan der Dufthauch des Kalmus, der Flug des Milans, Fuduzuun der Ruf der Unken, das Hämmern des Spechts, der nächtliche Schrei der Eulen. Nur das Fedezeen hielt ich zurück; es erinnerte an das «Nee» des Großvaters, an leere Kassen und trostlose, gelbe Sandberge. Aber auch darüber hätten sie gelacht, die anderen, mehr aber noch, wenn sie nach mühevollem Treppensteigen im Kirchenlicht der buntbemalten Flurfenster den in kunstvoll verschnörkelten Buchstaben auf glänzendes Messing gemalten Namen des Großvaters, Wilhelm Rosinchen,[2] entziffert hätten. Nein, man konnte sie nicht einweihen; man konnte sie nicht mitnehmen.

It was a great temptation to let my friends into the secret and take them along to grandfather's, for the way there was boring and sometimes, when gangs of uniformed youths were prowling in the depths of the side streets, dangerous as well; but although grandfather had not expressly forbidden it, I never gave way because I suspected that nobody would be able to understand the magic of our pools, and because I was afraid of their laughter. Even the name of the street where grandfather lived was enough to start them off. For them 'Fidizin' was a funny word; I didn't understand why, but bitter experience had taught me that it was so. It inspired them to make silly jokes, they made 'medicine' out of it, or tacked on additional syllables with 'i'. For me the word possessed a most beautiful sound: thus the glossy, iridescent dragon-flies hummed over the pools. While walking to grandfather's on Wednesday afternoons when there was no homework to be done and the other boys had their 'duty', while the arid expanse of paving stones passed by under my flagging feet like a dream of an endless game of hopscotch, I, too, would experiment with 'Fidizin' variations, but not just flippantly. 'Fodozoon' was the sun above the fields, 'Fadazaan' the breeze laden with the fragrance of the calamus, the flight of the kite, 'Fuduzuun' the croak of the toad, the hammering of the woodpecker, the screech of the owls at night. But 'Fedezeen' I avoided, for that rhymed with grandfather's 'Nay' and brought to mind empty cash-boxes and desolate yellow sand-hills.

Even that would have made them laugh, and they would have laughed still louder when, after the exertion of climbing the stairs, they reached the landing on which the brightly coloured glass of the windows cast the dim light of a church interior, and managed to decipher my grandfather's name, painted with ornately flowing letters on gleaming brass: William Littlecherry. No, it was impossible to let them into the secret, impossible to take them with me.

Daß Großvater schwieg, ist sicher. Großmutter hatte alles gewußt; aber sie lag schon länger, als ich denken konnte, mit ihrem schneeweißen Papierhemd im Sarg und wartete auf ihn, der ihr aber erst folgen wollte, wenn er mir die Teiche gezeigt hatte. Wenn er von ihnen redete und meine Mutter die Stube betrat, schwieg er sofort oder brabbelte sinnloses Zeug vor sich hin. Einmal hatte ich Kitty, das Mädchen mit den vorstehenden Zähnen, das zweimal wöchentlich Brot und Maggisuppen für ihn einkaufte, im Verdacht der Mitwisserei; aber auf meine eifersüchtige Frage erzählte er mir, daß sie ihm vorgeschlagen hatte, die Nähmaschine, Großmutters Nähmaschine, zu verkaufen, und da wußte ich, daß sie unwürdig war.

2

Unsere Teiche lagen in der Gegend, in der Großmutter geboren war. Sie hatten keinen Namen, da niemand sie kannte; nur ein Köhler hatte von ihnen gewußt und vor seinem Tode Großvater davon erzählt. Vielleicht waren sie auch zu klein für einen richtigen Namen. Großvater nannte sie manchmal Waldaugen, manchmal Glücksteiche, meist aber kamen wir ohne Namen aus.

Sie lagen tief in den Wäldern, die so trocken waren, daß niemand sie in ihnen vermuten konnte. Daß sie auch in den heißesten Sommern nicht austrockneten, daß Fische in ihnen lebten und Laubbäume, die es sonst in der Gegend nirgendwo gab, sie umstanden, konnte Großvater erklären; unerklärlich aber war auch ihm, daß sie im Winter nicht zufroren. Lag es an den Unmengen vielfarbenen Laubs, das im Herbst die winzigen Wasserspiegel wärmend bedeckte? Brachten Quellen aus dem Erdinnern heiße Wasser herauf? Man wußte es nicht, auch wenn man erfuhr, wie die Teiche

That grandfather kept it secret is certain. Grandmother had known all about it, but for longer than I could remember she had been lying in her coffin, wrapped in her snow-white paper shroud, and waiting for him. But he wanted to show me the pools first before he followed her. If he was talking about them and my mother came into the room, he would immediately fall silent or begin to mumble gibberish to himself. I had once suspected Kitty, the girl with the buck teeth who went to buy bread and dried soups for him twice a week, of having been made a confidante, but he answered my jealous questions by telling me that she had suggested selling the sewing machine, grandmother's sewing machine, and then I knew that she was unworthy.

2

Our pools lay in the region in which grandmother was born. They had no name, since nobody knew of their existence except for one charcoal burner who had told grandfather of them just before he died. Perhaps they were even too small to have a proper name. Grandfather sometimes called them the eyes of the wood, sometimes the pools of good fortune, but usually we managed to get along without names.

They lay deep in the woods which were so dry that nobody could possibly suspect their presence. That they never dried up, not even in the hottest of summers, that fish lived in them and that deciduous trees, which were not to be found anywhere else in the district, surrounded them, grandfather could explain; but even he could not explain why they never froze over in winter. Was it due to the profusion of multi-coloured leaves, which in autumn provided the tiny pools with a layer of warming insulation? Did springs bring hot waters up from the depths of the earth? It remained a mystery even when the

entstanden waren; aber doch schien einem dann einiges klarer
zu sein.

Da stand einmal, vor unvorstellbar vielen Jahren, als Groß-
vater noch nicht lebte und dessen Großvater auch noch nicht,
dort, wo unsere Teiche jetzt durch Astgewirr zum Himmel
sahen, ein Berg und auf dem Berg ein Schloß von glänzendem
Weiß, im Umkreis von vielen Meilen sichtbar, und auf dem
Schloß wohnte eine Prinzessin, die schön war wie das erste
Schilf im Frühjahr und spröde wie das braune Rohr im Frost.
Bewerber strömten aus allen Himmelsrichtungen herbei, füll-
ten Straßen und Wirtshäuser, standen Schlange vor dem
Schloß, schöne Jünglinge und weise Greise, von nah und fern,
Schwarze, Gelbe selbst dabei, Ritter und Schriftgelehrte,
Clowns und andere Künstler, Gnomen und Riesen; jeder
wollte sie besitzen, sie aber wollte niemandes Besitz werden,
weil sie besessen war vom Traumbild eines Jünglings, der
nicht kam. Ein großer Zauberer schließlich, der übers Meer
gekommen war, um sie zu freien, und wie die anderen abge-
schlagen wurde, verfluchte sie. Ein Erdbeben erschütterte das
Land, ein gähnend schwarzer Abgrund tat sich auf, und Berg
und Schloß und Jungfrau stürzten in die Tiefe. Von der
Tränenflut der Prinzessin aber blieben die Teiche zurück.
Einmal in hundert Jahren zur Johannisnacht steigt sie empor,
Glühwürmchen umschweben sie, die gelben Mummeln auf
den Teichen verneigen sich vor ihr, sie sitzt am Ufer, weint,
flicht weiße Seerosen zu einem Kranz und wartet auf den
reinen, unbescholtenen Jüngling, das Sonntagskind, das sie
erlösen kann.

Immer wieder verlangte ich von Großvater diese Schöp-
fungsgeschichte zu hören, und er erzählte, und sie wurde
immer schöner und länger und detailreicher dabei. Beim Auf-
tritt der Prinzessin in der Johannisnacht spielten bald nicht nur
die Seerosen mit, auch die Libellen und Frösche, die Binsen
und Enten bekamen ihre Aufgaben. Nie aber versäumte er,

story of how the pools came into being was known; yet things did then seem a little clearer.

Once a upon a time, an unimaginably long time ago, before grandfather, or even his grandfather, was born, there stood on the spot where our pools now looked up towards the sky through the maze of branches, a hill, and on the hill a shining white castle, visible for many miles around, and in the castle there lived a princess who was as beautiful as the first rushes in spring and as cold as the brown reeds in the chill of winter. Suitors flocked thither from all corners of the globe, filled the streets and inns, queued up in front of the castle, handsome youths and venerable sages, from far and near, black men, even yellow men were there, knights and scholars, clowns and other performers, gnomes and giants; each wanted to make her his own, but she didn't want to be anybody's possession because she was already possessed by the vision of a young man who did not come. Finally, a great sorcerer who had come from across the sea to seek her hand and had, like the others, met with refusal, laid a curse on her. The land was convulsed by an earthquake, a black yawning abyss gaped wide and hill, castle and maiden plunged into its depths. From the princess's floods of tears there remained the pools. Once in every hundred years, on the night of midsummer, she rises up, glow-worms hover in attendance around her, the yellow water-lilies bow down their heads, she sits on the bank, weeps, plaits white water-lilies into a garland and waits for the pure and blameless youth, Sunday's child, who can break the spell.

Over and over again I asked grandfather to let me hear this story of the pools' creation, and he would tell it, and at each telling it grew more and more beautiful, ever longer and more detailed. In the scene where the princess appears on midsummer night, it was soon not only the water-lilies that participated; the dragonflies and frogs, the rushes and the ducks were also given roles to play. But to forestall disappointment,

Enttäuschungen vorwegnehmend, zu betonen, daß ich an einem Sonnabend geboren und also nicht bestimmt sei, sie zu erlösen. Aber er wußte auch, daß sie sich über jeden freute, der ihre Teiche fand und darin badete, und diese überschüttete sie dann mit Glück, mit größerem die, die bis zur Mitte schwimmen konnten.

Großvater hatte auch gebadet in den Tränen der Prinzessin, aber nur am Rand, da er nicht schwimmen konnte. Trotzdem: kaum war er anderentags aus dem Walde heraus, sah er zum erstenmal die Großmutter, sie hütete am Wegrain Ziegen, und sie nur anzusehen schien ihm schon Glück genug. Jedoch der Zauber der Prinzessin wirkte weiter; Großmutter sagte ja auf seine Frage, obwohl er weder Geld noch Arbeit hatte und die Polizei ihn suchte; sie küßte ihn und ging mit ihm nach Berlin. Und nicht genug damit. Als in der fremden, grauen Stadt sich nichts zu beißen und zu brechen für sie fand, nahm die alte Frau sie auf, die bald darauf verstarb und ihnen die Nähmaschine hinterließ, die sie und meine winzig kleine Mutter, die in der Fidizinstraße, zwei Treppen rechts, zur Welt gekommen war, vorm Hungertod bewahrte. Und dabei hatte Großvater nur am Rand gebadet, nicht einmal sein Kopf war naß geworden dabei.

Ich aber konnte schwimmen und sogar tauchen, was wohl noch mehr bedeuten mußte, doch kümmerte mich die Glücksverheißung erstaunlich wenig. Mir war vorstellbares Glück so eng mit der Fahrt zu den Teichen verbunden; der erste Schritt an ihren Ufern, der erste Blick zu den Ulmen, das erste Bad auch so sehr Endpunkt, so sehr Erfüllung, daß mir zukünftiges Glück ganz und gar unwichtig erschien.

Ich sagte es Großvater, und er freute sich darüber, denn er fühlte ebenso. Glück war das Leben an den Teichen, fern der Stadt, fern ihrem Lärm aus Lautsprechern und Fanfaren, ihren Häuserschluchten mit uniformierten Horden, fern von Schule, Benzingestank und Kommandos. Großvater wußte: Viele

he never failed to stress that I was born on a Saturday and thus not destined to be her deliverer. But he also knew that she delighted in anyone who found her pools and bathed in them; upon these she would heap good fortune, and even greater good fortune upon those who could swim to the middle.

Grandfather had also bathed in the tears of the princess, but only at the edge because he could not swim. Nevertheless, he had hardly left the forest the following day when he saw my grandmother for the first time, she was tending goats on the raised path between the fields and in his eyes merely looking at her seemed good fortune enough. Yet the magic of the princess continued to work; grandmother said yes to his question, even though he had neither money nor a job and was wanted by the police; she kissed him and went with him to Berlin. And it didn't end there, either. When in the grey and alien city they couldn't find two pennies to rub together, the old woman took them in and, dying shortly afterwards, left them the sewing machine which kept from starvation both them and my tiny baby mother who had seen the light of day in Fidizin St, second floor on the right. And yet grandfather had only bathed at the edge, had not even got his head wet.

But I could swim, and even dive, which must surely mean more, and yet the promised happiness bothered me surprisingly little. Happiness I could imagine was so closely linked with the journey to the pools; the first step on their banks, the first glance at the elms, my first dip – all seemed so very much to be the ultimate, the fulfilment, that future happiness seemed wholly unimportant.

I told grandfather so, and he was pleased for he felt the same way. Happiness was living by the pools, far away from the city, far from its din of loudspeakers and fanfares, from the dark clefts between buildings where the uniformed gangs lurked, far from school, the stench of petrol and the voice of authority. Grandfather knew: many were suffering as we

litten wie wir, aber keiner außer uns beiden kannte den Ausweg ins Glück, die Wälder, die Teiche.

3

Nicht nur an Fahrgeld war zu denken, auch an das Gepäck. Immer fiel uns zuerst ein, was wir nicht brauchten, Essen zum Beispiel. Auf der Bahnfahrt würde die freudige Erregung jeden Hunger ersticken. In entsetzlicher Ungeduld vergehen die ersten Stunden, ich lese Großvater die Namen der Stationen vor, er schüttelt den Kopf, wieder und wieder, dann aber auf einem elenden Bahnhof, nur Gleis und einsames Wartehäuschen, richtet er sich auf, seine Lippen zittern wie immer vor den ersten Worten, er preßt die Nase an der Scheibe platt, dann brabbelt er los: Hier ist Großmutter mal in Stellung gewesen. Auf der nächsten Station, einer kleinen Stadt mit der einen kopfsteingepflasterten Straße, an deren Anfang der Bahnhof und an deren Ende die Kaserne liegt, hatte Großvater einrücken müssen zur Artillerie, weil er mit Pferden umgehen konnte. Nun brauche ich nicht mehr vorzulesen, Großvater weiß die Reihenfolge der Dörfer. Wir stehen schon auf, schnallen den Rucksack über, nehmen Großmutters Hutschachtel aus dem Gepäcknetz, obwohl wir wissen, daß wir erst auf der vierten Station aussteigen. Dann ist es soweit, wir stehen auf dem Bahnsteig, allein, hoffentlich allein, atmen tief und gehen los, durch blühende Rapsfelder, Großvater frisch wie nie, ohne Rast dem Walde zu. Würden wir bis dahin ans Essen denken können? Und unter den Kiefern dann, zu Beginn der großen Waldtour würden wir finden, was wir brauchten: Beeren, vielleicht auch Kräheneier, bestimmt aber Pilze, die gibt es immer, sogar im Winter den Schneepilz mit weißgrauem Hut, Großvater wußte Bescheid.

Das Geld für Brot und Wurst also konnten wir sparen, aber zu trinken würden wir etwas mitnehmen, Tee am besten, in

were, but none except us two knew of the escape route to happiness: the forests, the pools.

3

It was not just the fare-money that had to be thought of, but the luggage as well. We always thought of things we wouldn't need first. Food, for instance. On the train the exhilaration and excitement would stifle any hunger pangs. We spend the first hours in a state of terrible impatience, I read out the names of the stations for grandfather, he shakes his head again and again, but finally, at a miserable little station, just the track and a small, solitary waiting room, he straightens up, his lips tremble as they always do before he speaks, he presses his nose flat against the window, then he gabbles away about how grandmother was once in service here. At the next station, a small town with one cobbled street, at one end of which lies the station and at the far end the barracks, grandfather had been drafted into the artillery because he knew how to handle horses. From now on I don't need to read out the names, grandfather knows the order of the villages. Although we realize that our station is four stops further on, we start getting ready, buckle on the rucksack and take grandmother's hat-box down from the rack. Then we are there, we are standing alone, we hope we are alone, on the platform, we take a deep breath and start off across fields of rape in full bloom. Grandfather feels fitter than ever before and, without resting, we make for the forest. Until we reached it, would there be time to think about food? And then, among the pine trees, at the beginning of the great forest excursion, we would find what we needed: berries, perhaps crows' eggs too, but certainly mushrooms, for they are always there, even in winter there is the boletus with its greyish-white cap, grandfather knew all about that.

Großvaters alter Kaffeeflasche; denn der Wald, den wir stundenweit durchqueren würden, war trocken und sandig; Mahlheide nennen ihn die Leute aus Großvaters Dorf. Grau und pulvrig ist der Sand auf den Hügeln, wir stapfen lautlos hindurch; dann geht es über schwärzliches Moos, das knistert, wenn man drauf tritt; Äste knacken unter unseren Stiefeln, heiser krächzend, flattern Eichelhäher vor uns her. Kein Lufthauch lindert die Hitze, die zwischen den dürftigen Kiefernstämmen steht. Selbst wenn es geregnet hat, ist der Wald wieder trocken, bevor der letzte Tropfen von den Ästen gefallen ist. Die Kaffeeflasche wäre leer, ehe Großvater stehenbliebe und aufgeregt die Nase in die Luft streckte. Nun rieche auch ich es. Duft von feuchtem Moos, von dicksaftigen Blättern, von Wasser weht uns entgegen wie der kühle Atem des Morgens. Noch einen mahlsandigen Hügel müssen wir hinauf, höher und steiler als die zuvor, dann sehen wir unter uns den Teppich der Laubbaumkronen.

Die Frage, ob Decken nötig wären, beschäftigte uns lange. Auch Laub und Moos waren warm und weich, aus Binsen konnte man Matten weben, ein Wetterdach aus jungen Buchenstämmen war schnell errichtet. Und doch entschieden wir uns schließlich für die Decken. Am Spätnachmittag erst könnten wir durch dichte Farne zu den Teichen hinunterlaufen, ich voran bis zu der kleinen, baumlosen Kanzel mit dem Findlingsblock, von dem aus man die Teiche zuerst sieht, vier tellerrunde schwarze Spiegel in schattenüberspieltem Grün. Schwer schnaufend, den schweißnassen Schnurrbart zerzaust, tastet Großvater sich mir nach. Ich schäme mich, ihn vergessen zu haben, und laufe zurück. Dann stehen wir dicht beieinander, das Ziel endlich vor Augen. Seine von Adern überzogene Hand mit den zerstörten Nägeln liegt auf meiner Schulter. Ich will ihm erklären, was alles zu sehen ist, aber er schüttelt den Kopf. Er weiß es auch so. Als wir uns langsam den Teichen nähern, beginnen Bläßhühner zu kreischen. Bei

So we could save the money for bread and sausage, but we would take something to drink, tea would be best, in grandfather's old thermos flask, since the forest which we would be crossing for hours was dry and sandy; the people from grandfather's village call it 'Powder Heath'. The sand on the hills is grey and powdery. We trudge silently through it; next comes a stretch of blackish moss which crackles as we walk on it; branches crack under our boots; with hoarse croaks jays flutter away in front of us. Not a breath of wind relieves the heat which hangs between the scrawny pine trunks. Even after it has rained, the forest is dry again before the last drop has fallen from the branches. The thermos would be empty before grandfather halted and sniffed excitedly at the air. Now I can smell it, too. The odour of moist moss, of rich, succulent leaves, of water blows towards us like the cool breath of morning. One more hill of powdery sand has to be climbed, higher and steeper than all its predecessors, then beneath us we see the green carpet of the deciduous trees.

Whether we needed blankets or not was a question that occupied us for a long time. Leaves and moss were warm and soft, mats could be woven from rushes, a shelter could be speedily erected using beech saplings. And yet we did finally decide to take blankets with us. It would be late afternoon before we were able to run down through the dense ferns to the pools; I would be in front, running up to the small treeless promontory with its drift boulder, from which the first sight of the pools was to be had: four round, black mirrors amid green leaves and shifting shadows. Panting heavily, his moustache beaded with sweat and in disarray, grandfather gropes his way after me. I feel ashamed for having forgotten him and run back. We stand close together, our goal at last in sight. His hand with its protruding veins and cracked nails rests on my shoulder. I want to explain to him all that there is to see, but he shakes his head. He knows anyway. As we slowly

jedem Schritt bergab ändert sich die Färbung des Wassers; aus Schwarz wird blendendes Silber, aus Silber Grün, aus Grün Blau; dann stehen wir am Ufer, beugen uns vor und sehen, daß das Wassser klar und durchsichtig ist wie frisch geputzte Fensterscheiben. Jede Windung des spitzen, gedrehten Hauses einer Wasserschnecke ist deutlich zu erkennen. Schade würde es sein, in diesen ersten Stunden an die Arbeit für ein Nachtlager denken zu müssen. Deshalb ist es gut, Decken zu haben; ich werde Großvater in seine einwickeln, wenn die Dämmerung von den Zweigen fällt; ich schlüpfe in meine, und dann liegen wir im schweren Geruch des Kalmus, der seine schwertartigen Blätter vor uns zum Himmel reckt, und lassen kein Auge von unseren Teichen, die jetzt rosenfarbig geworden sind. Von irgendwoher fällt ein Wind in das Tal und läßt das Rohr sirren und zittern. Sumpfgasblasen perlen empor und zerplatzen lautlos. Zwei Enten erschrecken uns mit hastigen Flügelschlägen, sie fallen ein und reißen die stille Wasserfläche auf. Die Dunkelheit füllt das Tal mit feuchter, kalter Luft.

Die Decken mußten mit wie auch die Werkzeuge und Angelgeräte, die gleich am ersten Morgen ausgepackt werden würden. Von diesem ersten Morgen sprach Großvater am liebsten. Er versuchte das Knarren des Drosselrohrsängers und die Lockrufe der Entenmutter nachzuahmen, beschrieb mir das Flügelknistern der stahlblauen Libellen, die Blütenfarbe der Sumpflilien und das Flugbild des Milans, der vielleicht noch immer in der Eiche nistet. In den Wipfeln ist schon heller Tag. Finster steht das Binsengebüsch vor dem Schilfgürtel. Scharen kleiner Fische beginnen zu springen und bringen das Wasser stellenweise zum Brodeln. Während ich nach dem ersten prickelnd-kalten Glücksbad die Angel auswerfe, watet Großvater durchs Schilf und bringt eine Handvoll Frühstückseier mit, weiße und graugesprenkelte. Die Fische beißen, als hätten sie seit der Verwünschung der Prinzessin auf unsere

approach the pools, coots begin to screech. At each step down-hill the water changes its hue; from black to a dazzling silver, from silver to green, from green to blue; then we are standing at the edge, we lean forwards and see that the water is as clear and transparent as freshly washed window panes. Each whorl of the pointed, spiral shell of a water-snail can be clearly distinguished. It would be a pity to have to think about making a bed for the night during these first few hours. That is why it is nice having the blankets; I shall wrap grandfather up in his when dusk falls from the branches; I slip beneath mine, and then we lie there, the air heavy with the fragrance of the calamus which at our feet raises up its sword-shaped leaves towards the sky, and we keep our eyes fixed on the now rose-coloured pools. From somewhere or other a wind descends into the valley, making the reeds sigh and shiver. Bubbles of marsh gas rise to the surface and silently burst. Two ducks make us start with the rapid beating of their wings, they alight, ruffling the tranquil surface of the water. Darkness fills the valley with damp, cold air.

The blankets had to be taken with us – like the tools and fishing tackle which would be unpacked first thing the following morning. Grandfather liked to talk of this first morning most of all. He would try to imitate the harsh cry of the great reed warbler and the calls of the duck to her brood, he would describe to me the rustling wings of the steel-blue dragonflies, the colour of the yellow flag in bloom, and the flight silhouette of the kite which perhaps still nests in the oak tree. In the tree tops above it is already bright daylight. The clumps of rushes are dark and gloomy against the encircling reeds. Shoals of small fish begin to jump and in places make the water bubble. Having taken my first dip in the tingling cold waters which are to make my fortune, I cast out my line, while grandfather wades through the reeds and brings back a handful of white and grey-speckled eggs for breakfast. The fish are

Köder gewartet. Silberweiße Plötzen, goldglänzende Rotfedern, bleifarbene Brassen, schwarzstreifige, spitzflossige Barsche, schleimige Schleie fliegen an Land, zappeln zwischen den mit Kuckucksspucke verzierten Lichtnelken. Dann reißt die Schnur unter den wasseraufwirbelnden Schwanzschlägen eines gelbbäuchigen, breitmäuligen Hechts. Großvater lacht so über mein schafsdummes Gesicht, daß ihm der Speichel über das unrasierte Kinn tropft. Angelschnüre wollten wir reichlich mitnehmen. Der Hecht war uns sicher; einmal würde er sich an dem der Länge nach durch ihn getriebenen Spieß über dem Holzfeuer drehen. Auch Zündhölzer mußten wir mitnehmen, mehrere Pakete. Bis der Frost kam, mußten sie reichen; dann würde unser Feuer im Blockhaus nicht mehr ausgehen.

Mehr als das sagte Großvater nie über den Winter. Mich fröstelte manchmal beim Gedanken daran. Auch fragte ich mich, ob es genug Schneepilze geben würde. Aber wir hatten ja die Fische aus den immer offenen Teichen.

Von einer Heimkehr in die Stadt war nie die Rede.

4

In den Wochen vor den Sommerferien lebte ich wie ein gehetztes Wild. Fast täglich klingelte es an unserer Wohnungstür, und vor meiner Mutter strammstehende Jungen brachten Befehle, zum «Dienst» zu kommen. Ich versteckte mich, meine Mutter bot den Boten Bonbons an, die sie stolz ablehnten, und suchte nach Entschuldigungsgründen. Nachdem der Klassenlehrer mich öffentlich gerügt hatte, hielten auch meine Freunde nicht mehr zu mir. Auf einen amtlichen Brief hin ging meine Mutter in das Büro des Stammführers, eines netten jungen Mannes mit Abitur. Er machte einen so guten Eindruck auf sie, daß sie mich danach zum erstenmal scharf verhörte. Auch sie verriet mich, indem sie mein Schweigen nicht verstand. Es hätte auch nichts genutzt, ihr zu sagen, daß ich mich

biting as though they have just been waiting for our bait since the curse was laid on the princess. Silvery-white roach, gleaming gold rudd, leaden bream, black-striped, sharp-finned perch, slimy tench fly on to land and wriggle among the ragged robin, to which white beads of cuckoo-spit add their lustre. Then the line parts as a yellow-bellied, broad-jawed pike whips up the water with blows from its tail. Grandfather laughs so much at my asinine expression that spittle dribbles down his unshaven chin. We planned on taking plenty of fishing lines with us. The pike would not escape us; one day he would be revolving over our wood fire, the spit driven through the length of his body. We would have to take matches as well, several boxes of them. They would have to last until the first frosts came; from then on our fire in the log-cabin would never go out.

Grandfather never said any more about the winter than that. A cold shiver would sometimes come over me when I thought of it. I also wondered whether there would be enough boletus. But, after all, we would have the fish from the pools which never freeze over.

There was never any word of a return to the city.

4

In the weeks before the summer holidays I lived like a hunted animal. Practically every day the doorbell would ring and when my mother answered, boys, standing stiffly to attention, brought orders for me to report for 'duty'. I hid, and my mother offered the messengers sweets which they haughtily refused, and tried to find excuses for me. After my form-master had reprimanded me in front of the class, even my friends began to desert me. Following an official letter, my mother paid a visit to the office of the troop leader, a nice young man who had passed his matriculation. He made such

vor dem Sohn unseres Gemüsehändlers, der Mittwoch nachmittags eine grünweiße Kordel trug, nicht auf eine Handbewegung hin in den Dreck fallen lassen konnte. Anscheinend
konnten es alle außer mir; ich wußte nicht, warum.

Mutter brachte mich zu einem Arzt. Auch er war nett und
verständnisvoll, aber auf den Zettel für den Stammführer
schrieb er, daß ein Aufenthalt im Zeltlager meiner schwachen
Konstitution gut bekommen würde. Dem Zettel glaubte
meine Mutter mehr als meinem Schweigen. Am zweiten
Ferientag sollte ich fahren. Am ersten machte ich mich auf den
Weg zur Fidizinstraße, fünfundneunzig schwerverdiente
Pfennige in der Faust. Ich hatte nicht einmal geweint in dieser
Zeit. Wie gut, daß ich keinem von unseren Teichen erzählt
hatte.

Bei Großvater gingen zwei Männer auf und ab, die aussahen, als ob sie mit zehn Jahren auch Kordel und Koppel
getragen hatten. Großvater sollte in ein Veteranenheim
umsiedeln. Sie wechselten sich ab im Reden, sprachen von der
Bombenverpflegung, dem schneidigen alten Heimvater, der
auch eine Stimmungskanone sein konnte, von den Kameraden,
die sie Pfundskerle nannten, und von der stolzen Freude an
Kriegserinnerungen, und dann sagten sie immer gleichzeitig:
«Wahrhaftig ein würdiger Abschluß eines deutschen Front-
kämpferlebens!» Sie wollten Großvater aus dem Haus haben,
weil seine Einzimmerwohnung vom Blockwart[3] als Lager-
raum für Helme, Sandsäcke, Wassertonnen und Feuerpat-
schen gebraucht wurde.

Großvater hatte sein dämlichstes Gesicht aufgesetzt. Seine
halbgeschlossenen Augen blickten blöde ins Leere, und unaufhörlich kaute er sabbernd an seinem schlohweißen Schnurrbart. Wenn nach dem gemeinsamen Spruch über das Front-
kämpferleben eine kurze Pause eintrat, brabbelte er nicht zur
Sache gehörendes Zeug vor sich hin, das die Männer nicht
verstanden. «Koppweih hadd de oll Korporal kregen, as dat

a good impression on my mother that afterwards she interrogated me closely for the first time. By not understanding why I did not answer, she, too, betrayed me. And it would have been pointless telling her that I could not prostrate myself at a signal from the son of our greengrocer, who wore a green and white shoulder-cord on Wednesday afternoons. They could all do it except me, apparently; I did not know why.

Mother took me to a doctor. He, too, was friendly and understanding, but on the note for the troop-leader he wrote that a stay at camp would be beneficial to my weak constitution. My mother had more faith in this note than in my silence. I was to depart on the second day of the holidays. On the first day I made my way to Fidizin St, in my hand ninety-five hard-earned pennies. I had not cried once during this time. How glad I was that I hadn't told anybody about our pools.

At grandfather's two men were pacing up and down, who looked as though they, too, had worn shoulder-cord and sword-belt when they were ten. Grandfather was to move into an Old Soldiers' Home. They spoke in turn, talked of the first-rate mess, the dapper old superintendent who could at times be the life and soul of the party, of the comrades whom they called the salt of the earth, and of the proud pleasure of war reminiscences, and then they said, always in unison, 'Truly, a fitting way for the life of a German front-line soldier to draw to a close!' They wanted grandfather out of the house because his one-room flat was required by the block-warden as a store-room for helmets, sandbags, water butts and fire beaters.

Grandfather had assumed his most imbecilic expression. His half-closed eyes gazed stupidly into empty space; he kept chewing at his snow-white moustache, slobbering over it. During the short pause which followed the mutual recital of the motto about the life of a front-line soldier, he would mutter incoherent and irrelevant rubbish which the men could not understand. 'Headaches he got, the old corporal,

Pierd em up den Dez pinkelt hadd.» Schließlich zogen sie ab, nachdem sie ihm ins Ohr gebrüllt hatten, daß sie am Tag drauf mit Möbelwagen und Taxe wiederkommen würden, um ihn im Heim abzuliefern.

Wir lauschten, bis das Poltern der Stiefel auf der Treppe verstummte. Großvater strich den feuchten Schnurrbart glatt und öffnete die Augen wieder.

«Ich nehme dich mit zu uns!» sagte ich.

«Sülwst is de Mann!» knurrte er und deutete zur Tür. Ich legte den Riegel vor, holte das Tuch aus dem Bett, schwang mich auf die Nähmaschine und ließ meine fünfundneunzig Pfennige auf die Fensterbank rollen. Großvater zählte tastend. Dann wurde Robinson herausgeholt, der Stift angefeuchtet. Ich schrieb, Großvater rechnete im Kopf. Dann lehnte er sich in den Korbstuhl zurück. Seine Lippen zitterten kein bißchen, als er sagte: «Morgen früh führen wi, Jung!»

5

Der Morgen hatte die schwülwarme Nacht mit einem kaum merklichen Hauch von Kühle beendet. Als ich auf die Straße trat, stand die Sonne erst fingerbreit über dem Krankenhausdach, aber schon spürte man die Hitze des fernen Mittags. Trotz des Tornisters, der hart auf meinen Rücken schlug, lief ich ein Stück neben einem Sprengwagen her, bis meine Beine pitschnaß waren und das Wasser in meinen Schuhen schmatzte. Erst dann erinnerte ich mich meiner Mutter, die aus dem Fenster lehnte, um ihrem Jungen einen Abschied zuzuwinken. Sicher war neben der Angst auch ein wenig Stolz in ihren Augen. Die Freude am frühen Sommerferientag, die der Sprengwagen gebracht hatte, verging, für einen Moment war Trennungsschmerz da und die Ahnung künftigen Heimwehs, aber dann siegte der Haß wieder, der die erste große Lüge meines Lebens rechtfertigte. Um ihre Ruhe zu haben, schickte

when the horse had peed on his nut . . .' At last they went away, after shouting in his ear that they would be back the next day with a furniture van and a taxi to convey him to the Home.

We listened until the din of their boots on the stairs died away. Grandfather smoothed out his damp moustache and opened his eyes again.

'I'll take you back to our house!' I said.

'Every man his own master!' he growled and pointed to the door. I bolted it, fetched the cloth from the bed, swung up on to the sewing machine and let my ninety-five pence roll on to the window-ledge. Grandfather felt the coins as he counted them. Then Robinson Crusoe was brought out, the pencil moistened. I wrote, grandfather added up in his head. Then he leant back in his wicker chair. His lips did not tremble a bit as he said: 'We're off, tomorrow morning, lad!'

5

The coolness of a scarcely perceptible morning breeze had put an end to the heavy warmth of the night. As I went out into the street only a sliver of sun was peeping above the roof of the hospital, but already the distant midday heat could be felt. Despite the rucksack which bumped heavily up and down on my back, I ran for a while alongside a watering-cart until my legs were soaking wet and the water squelched in my shoes. Only then did I remember my mother who was leaning out of the window to wave goodbye to her boy. As well as anxiety there was doubtless a little pride in her eyes. The joy at its being an early morning in the summer holidays, which the watering-cart had brought, ebbed away and for a moment there was the pain of separation and the presentiment of future home-sickness, but then my hate – the hate which justified the first big lie of my life – was again triumphant. For the sake of

sie mich ins Lager, sie sollte für immer ihre Ruhe vor mir haben.

Ich sah alles wie zum letzten Mal: die vertraute Fassade der Mietshäuser mit der winkenden Mutter darin, die Osram-Reklame auf der Brandmauer, die Lastwagen, die zum Güterbahnhof hinauffuhren, die zahme Elster des Zeitungsverkäufers unter der Brücke und die dumm lächelnden Puppen im Schaufenster von Kajot,[4] Uniformen für alle Gliederungen der Partei. Ich sah es genauer als sonst, aber ohne jeden Schmerz. Vielleicht hätte ich ihn empfunden, wenn ich die nach Leder und Imprägnierung riechende Uniform nicht hätte tragen müssen, die mich zu einer dieser Schaufensterpuppen machte. Mutter hatte viel Geld ausgegeben, um ihren Sohn vorschriftsmäßig ins Zeltlager zu schicken. Ich hatte die vergebens vertanen Scheine und Münzen ohne Bedauern in der Kasse des Kaufmanns verschwinden sehen; Geld interessierte mich nicht mehr, seitdem der notwendige Fahrpreis in der Blechbüchse lag.

Selbst der Abschied von Großvaters Wohnung brachte keinen Schmerz, eher ein Gefühl der Erlösung; es war unsere Stube nicht mehr, seitdem die Nähmaschine nicht mehr vor dem Fenster stand. Kitty, das Mädchen von nebenan, hatte sie zur Aufbewahrung bekommen; nur ich hatte das Recht, sie einmal zurückzufordern. Ich sagte: «Ja, Großvater!», aber ich dachte: Was soll ich an unseren Teichen mit einer Nähmaschine? Felljacken kann man damit doch nicht nähen.

Der Friedhofswärter, der gähnend das Tor an der Bergmannstraße öffnete, sah uns verwundert an, als wir früher als sonst mit Tornister und Hutschachtel an Blumenladen und Gefallenendenkmal vorbei hinter Nummer 231 in den Seitenpfad einbogen. Aber er fragte nichts, sagte nur etwas über die Hitze und ging in sein Häuschen zurück, um den Morgenkaffee zu kochen. An Großmutters Grab war es wie immer, nur erzählten wir ihr diesmal etwas geraffter als üblich, was

peace and quiet she was packing me off to camp; well, never again would I disturb her peace and quiet.

I saw everything as though for the last time; the familiar facade of the tenements where my mother was still waving to me, the Osram advert on the fire wall, the lorries which were driving up to the goods station, the tame magpie of the newspaper seller under the bridge and the stupid smiles of the dummies in the window at Kajot's, uniforms for all party ranks. I saw it all more clearly than usual, but felt no pain. Perhaps I should have felt some, had I not had to wear the uniform with its smell of leather and waterproofing, which turned me into one of those tailor's dummies. My mother had spent a lot of money in order to send her son to camp kitted out as prescribed. I had watched the uselessly wasted coins and notes disappear into the shopkeeper's till without regret; I had no interest in money now that there was enough in the tin box to pay for our fares.

Even taking leave of grandfather's flat caused no pain, in fact it brought a feeling of release; it had ceased to be our room since the sewing machine no longer stood in front of the window. Kitty, the girl from next door, had been entrusted with it; I alone had the right to ask for it back one day. I said 'Yes, grandfather', but I thought to myself: What am I supposed to do with a sewing machine at our pools? You couldn't sew fur jackets with it in any case.

The cemetery attendant who was yawning as he opened the gate on Bergmann St, looked at us in amazement, as, earlier than usual and carrying rucksack and hat-box, we walked past the flower stall and the war memorial and turned into the side-path behind grave No. 231. But he asked no questions, mumbled something about the heat and went back into his cabin to make his morning coffee. At grandmother's grave it was the same as ever, except that this time our report of the events since our last visit was rather more terse than usual. On

seit unserem letzten Besuch passiert war. Auf dem Weg zur
Gneisenaustraße, wo wir auf die 2 warten mußten, war nur
von alltäglichen Dingen die Rede. Ich war enttäuscht, daß
außer Gepäck und Uniform nichts anders war als sonst, daß die
Freude nur matt in mir glimmte. Sie wurde ganz gelöscht, als
ich Großvaters ständig wachsende Furcht bemerkte.

6

Am Bahnhof packte ihn vollends die Angst vor Verfolgern.
Er glaubte, daß man hinter ihm her wäre, um ihn in das Heim
zu sperren. Als ein Förster mit grünem Hut und Lodenmantel
zu uns ins Abteil stieg, begann Großvater zu zittern. Je länger
ich den Mann anstarrte, desto sicherer erkannte auch ich hinter
dem falschen Schnurrbart das Gesicht eines der Männer vom
Vortag. Von den Landschaften, die wir durchfuhren, sah ich
kaum etwas. Wir sprachen kein Wort. Der Förster schlief, als
wir ausstiegen, und wir hatten das Gefühl, ihn überlistet zu
haben.

Bei der hohen Pappel müsse von dem zum Dorf führenden
Fahrweg ein Pfad abzweigen, meinte Großvater, als wir auf
dem sandigen Bahnsteig standen und mißtrauisch die Leute,
die mit uns ausgestiegen waren, an uns vorbeiließen. Aber es
gab keine Pappel weit und breit, dafür aber viele Fahrwege,
die sich von einer Rampe aus in alle Richtungen verzweigten.
Lastwagen zogen Staubwolken hinter sich her. Der Himmel
war wolkenlos, aber die Hitze breitete Schleier vor die große,
nahe Sonne. Hinter dem Dorf, von dem man nur ein paar
flimmernde Dächer und den gedrungenen Kirchturm sah,
stand der Wald wie eine niedrige, schwarze Mauer.

In einem der tiefausgefahrenen Wagengeleise umgingen wir
das Dorf. Obwohl wir sehr schwitzten und das Atmen in der
gnadenlosen Hitze immer schwerer wurde, spürte ich jetzt
wieder einen Hauch der erwarteten Freude. Großvaters Auf-

the way to Gneisenau St, where we had to wait for a No. 2, we spoke only about everyday matters. I was disappointed that apart from our luggage and my uniform nothing was different, and that I felt only a faint glimmering of joy. It was totally extinguished when I noticed grandfather's constantly growing fear.

6

At the station, fear of pursuers took complete possession of him. He believed they were after him, to lock him up in the Home. When a forester with a green hat and a woollen overcoat came and sat in our compartment, grandfather began to tremble. The longer I stared at the man the more certain I became that I, too, could recognize behind the false moustache the face of one of the men from the day before. I hardly saw anything of the countryside through which we travelled. We did not say a word. When we got out the forester was asleep, and we felt as though we had outwitted him.

Near the tall poplar tree a path should branch off from the road to the village, grandfather said, as we stood on the sandy platform, suspiciously allowing the people who had got out at the same stop to pass by. But far and wide there was no poplar to be seen; instead there were many roads branching out in all directions from a raised mound of earth. Lorries dragged clouds of dust along behind them. There were no clouds in the sky, but the heat cast veils of haze between us and the sun which loomed large and low. Beyond the village, of which nothing could be seen except a few shimmering roof-tops and the squat tower of the church, the forest rose up like a low, dark wall.

Following one of the ruts cut deep by the lorries, we skirted round the village. Even though we were sweating profusely and were finding it increasingly difficult to breathe in the

forderungen, mich nach etwaigen Verfolgern umzusehen, wurden seltener. Ich beschrieb ihm die erkennbaren Häuser des Dorfes, aber er reagierte nicht darauf. Als einzelne Stämme und Wipfel sich aus der dichten Wand des Waldes zu lösen begannen, blieb Großvater stehen, hob die Nase und lächelte. Er roch den Wald.

Der Weg stieg kaum merklich an, er wurde sandiger, das silbergraue Korn daneben kleiner und spärlicher. Vor dem Wald bogen die Fahrspuren nach links ab. Ich ließ Großvater los und rannte über eine von Katzenpfötchen übersäte Brache auf den Wald zu. «Fodozoon!» schrie ich triumphierend, als ich den Tornister in das knisternde Moos fallen ließ. Keuchend und kichernd trippelte Großvater mir nach.

Wir rasteten nicht so lange, wie wir uns vorgenommen hatten. Das Wandern auf festem Waldboden lockte, die Erwartung, unsere Teiche zu sehen und ihre kühle Luft zu atmen, vertrieb jede Müdigkeit. An den steiler werdenden Höhenzügen, die wir überquerten, konnte Großvater sich orientieren. Ich sang ihm alle Lieder vor, die ich kannte. Gegen Mittag erreichten wir einen lichten Hang, von dem aus die Wellentäler der unendlichen Wälder zu übersehen waren. Großvater behauptete, daß man von dieser Stelle aus bei klarer Luft die hellere Färbung der Laubbäume im Tal der Prinzessin erkennen könnte. Es war aber mit der Mittagshitze auch der Dunst stärker geworden, der alle Farbunterschiede weißlich flimmernd ineinander verschmolz. Die schwache Staubwolke, die einige Minuten über den Wald zog und dann verging, war so unwirklich, daß ich sie Großvater verschwieg und auch selbst bald vergaß.

Sie kam mir erst wieder in den Sinn, als wir unversehens einen durch den Wald geschlagenen Weg mit frischen Autospuren kreuzten, über dem sich an Masten befestigte Drähte hinzogen. Großvater erschrak, als er den Abdruck der Profilreifen unter den Füßen spürte, dann aber begann er zu kichern.

merciless heat, I now felt again a trace of the joy I had hoped for. Grandfather's demands that I should look out for possible pursuers became less frequent. I described to him those houses in the village which could be made out, but there was no re-action. As individual trunks and tree tops became visible against the thick wall of the forest, grandfather stopped, sniffed and smiled. He could smell the forest.

Almost imperceptibly, the path began to slope upwards, it became sandier, the silver-grey corn at its edge smaller and more sparse. In front of the forest, the lorry tracks turned off to the left. I released grandfather's hand and ran towards the forest across a fallow field, dotted with cudweed. 'Fodozoon', I shouted triumphantly, dropping my rucksack in the rustling moss. Panting and giggling, grandfather pattered after me.

Our rest was shorter than planned. The idea of walking on the firm forest floor spurred us on, the prospect of seeing our pools and breathing in their cool air banished all tiredness. Grandfather was able to get his bearings from the ever steeper ridges which we crossed. I sang for him every song that I knew. Towards midday we reached an open slope from which the rolling hills and valleys of the endless forest could be sur-veyed. Grandfather claimed that on a clear day the lighter foliage of the deciduous trees in the valley of the princess could be distinguished from this spot. But with the heat of midday, the haze had also become denser and all the different colours were melted into a whitish shimmer. The faint cloud of dust which passed for a few minutes above the forest before fading away seemed so unreal that I did not bother grand-father about it, and soon forgot it myself.

It only sprang to mind again when our path happened to cross a roadway that had been driven through the forest; on it were fresh car tracks, and above, attached to poles, wires ran. Grandfather was startled to feel underfoot the impression left by the heavy tread of the tyres, but then he began to giggle.

Die Vorstellung, daß Menschen hier vorbeifuhren, ohne von unserem Paradies hinter dem übernächsten Waldhügel zu wissen, machte ihm Spaß. Ich bemühte mich vergeblich, die Freude festzuhalten und die aufsteigende Angst zu bekämpfen.

Der Wald blieb, wie er war, trocken, nichts als Kiefern und Sand, braune Nadeln am Boden, knackende Äste, unbewegte, heiße, nach Harz duftende Luft. Die Erinnerung an den Weg und die Autos, die Masten und Drähte verging, war aber spürbar als schwache, ungewisse Furcht, die dann plötzlich in der nächsten Senke riesenhaft anschwoll, Kopf und Glieder lähmte, als wir vor dem Zaun standen.

Betonpfähle, höher als Großvater, hielten weitmaschigen Draht; darauf gesetzt waren nach außen geneigte Eisenstangen, zwischen denen sich in fünf gleichlaufenden Linien Stacheldraht spannte. Innen lief ein kaum sichtbarer Trampelpfad entlang, nicht breiter als ein Wildwechsel, sonst war der Wald unberührt, soweit wir sehen konnten.

Wir lehnten am Zaun, die Hände in die Maschen gekrallt, zitternd, plötzlich müde und zu Tode erschöpft, hungrige Häftlinge, die teuflisch genarrt waren. Hatte ich das nicht schon einmal geträumt, das Gitter vor der Freiheit, oder gedacht, wenn ich «Fedezeen» nicht ausgesprochen hatte?

Großvater keuchte und stöhnte, als bliebe der Atem ihm weg; er hing an dem Zaun, wie vom Starkstrom festgehalten, dann stieß er sich zurück, fiel wieder nach vorn und riß an dem Draht. Und dann lief er los, an den Betonpfählen entlang. Ich hob Großmutters Hutschachtel auf und rannte ihm nach.

Der Zaun zog sich in grausamer Gleichförmigkeit dahin, bergauf, bergab durch unseren Wald; alle paar hundert Meter bog er stumpfwinklig nach innen ab. Die Sonne, die vorher rechts vor uns gestanden hatte, wanderte nach links hinüber. Der Wald veränderte sich; Grasbüschel, Farnkraut und Blaubeerstauden bedeckten den Boden, krüpplige Eichen wuchsen zwischen den Kiefernstämmen. Ein Kahlschlag öffnete sich.

He was amused by the idea that people drove along here without knowing about our paradise which lay just beyond the next wooded hill but one. I struggled in vain to retain my high spirits and combat the fear that rose within me.

The forest remained, as ever, dry, nothing but pines and sand, brown needles on the ground, cracking branches and hot, still air, filled with the smell of resin. The memory of the track, of the cars, the poles and the wires dimmed, but left a faint, uncertain fear, which in the next hollow suddenly swelled up immensely, paralysing both brain and body, as we stood in front of the fence.

Concrete pillars, taller than grandfather, supported a fence of broad-meshed wire; on top there were iron bars pointing outwards between which five parallel strands of barbed wire were stretched. On the inside, just visible, there ran a beaten track, no wider than an animal run, otherwise the forest was untouched for as far as we could see.

We leaned against the fence, fingers gripping the mesh, trembling, suddenly tired and completely spent, hungry prisoners who had been bitterly deceived. Had I not seen all this in my dreams, the bars in front of freedom, or thought it when I had not uttered 'Fedezeen'?

Grandfather panted and groaned as though he could not breathe; he hung on the fence as though in the grip of an electric current, he pushed himself away, fell forward again and tore at the wire. Then he darted off, following the line of concrete posts. I picked up grandmother's hat-box and hurried after him.

With cruel monotony the fence ran on, uphill, downhill, through our forest; every few hundred metres it turned inwards at an obtuse angle. The sun which earlier on had been on our right, moved slowly over to our left. The forest was changing; clumps of grass, ferns and bilberry bushes covered the ground; stunted oak trees grew among the pine trunks.

Einer der fallenden Bäume hatte den Zaun halb umgerissen. Wir kletterten hinüber, Großvater blutete an der Hand, ich am Knie. Hutschachtel und Tornister ließ ich fallen. Wir liefen einen Hang hinauf. Dahinter mußten unsere Teiche liegen. Oben brachen wir durch dichtes Gebüsch und sahen hinunter.

Einige der mächtigen Eichen, Erlen und Ulmen standen noch. Ihre weitausladenden Äste überragten einen Bunker, auf dessen flaches Dach Büsche und junge Bäume gepflanzt waren. Auf der anderen Seite des einstigen Tales waren gelbe Sandberge aufgeschüttet. Großvater brach, ohne einen Laut von sich zu geben, zusammen. Ich kniete mich neben ihn und schob trockenes Laub unter seinen Kopf. Wortlos bewegten sich seine Lippen.

Ich erschrak kaum, als ich die Schaftstiefel eines Soldaten neben mir sah. Was wir hier suchten, wollte er wissen.

«Unsere Teiche», sagte ich.

«Die Sumpflöcher sind zugeschüttet», sagte der Soldat. «Und ihr müßt verschwinden!»

Da hob Großvater mühsam den Kopf und sagte: «Tauschürt? Jih hebben sie tauschürt, die schöne Prinzeß!» Er ließ den Kopf wieder fallen. Das Laub raschelte ein wenig. Er schloß die Augen und öffnete sie auch nicht, als die Soldaten ihn wegtrugen. Auch beim Verhör in der Baracke sagte er nichts. Die Soldaten lachten, als ich Großvaters Namen sagte. Ich sah nur ihre Koppelschlösser, die mich kalt anstarrten, aber ich bin sicher, daß sie auch grinsten, als ich von der Fidizinstraße sprach.

Großvater sagte nur noch einmal etwas, bevor dieses furchtbare Zucken in sein Gesicht kam. Er sagte: «Ik komm all!» Er sagte es leise; Großmutter in ihrem weißen Papierhemd hörte es wohl auch so.

A clearing opened out in front of us. In falling, one of the trees had half torn down the fence. We clambered over; grandfather's hand was bleeding, so was my knee. I dropped the hat-box and the rucksack. We ran up a slope. Our pools must lie behind it. At the top we burst through the thick undergrowth and looked down.

Some of the mighty oaks, alders and elms were still standing. The broad sweep of their branches hung over a pill-box on the flat roof of which bushes and young trees had been planted. On the other side of what had once been the valley, yellow mounds of sand had been piled up. Grandfather collapsed without making a sound. I knelt beside him and pushed dry leaves under his head. His lips moved, but no sound came from them.

I hardly started when I saw the jack boots of a soldier at my side. He wanted to know what business we had to be there.

'Our pools,' I said.

'Those bogs have been filled in,' the soldier replied, 'and you had better make yourselves scarce.'

With great effort grandfather raised his head and said, 'Filled in? Yer've filled in the beautiful princess!' His head fell back again. The leaves rustled slightly. He shut his eyes and did not even open them as the soldiers carried him away. During the interrogation at the barracks he said nothing, either. The soldiers laughed when I told them grandfather's name. I could only see their buckles which stared coldly at me, but I am sure that they grinned, too, when I spoke of Fidizin St.

Grandfather spoke but once more before that terrible twitching passed across his face. He said, 'I'm coming!' He said it softly, yet grandmother in her white paper shroud would still have heard it.

THE RENUNCIATION

SIEGFRIED LENZ

Translated by Stewart Spencer

DER VERZICHT

MITTEN in jenem Winter kam er mit Fahrrad und Auftrag hierher, in einer hartgefrorenen Schlittenspur, die ihm nicht erlaubte, den Kopf zu heben und nach vorn zu blicken, sondern ihn unablässig zwang, die Spur, der er sich anvertraut hatte, zu beobachten, denn sobald er aufsah, schrammte die Felge jedesmal an den vereisten Schneewänden entlang, die Lenkstange schlug zur Seite, und wenn er sie herumriß, setzte sich das Vorderrad quer, festgestemmt in der engen Spur, so daß er – in dem langen Uniform-Mantel, den alten Karabiner quer überm Rücken – Mühe hatte, rechtzeitig abzuspringen. Mühsam kam er den Dorfweg herauf, der an der Schule vorbeiführt, allein und keineswegs eine überzeugende Drohung, vielmehr machte er in der grauen Februar-Dämmerung, vor den rauchfarbenen Hütten unseres Dorfes, den Eindruck eines verzweifelten und verdrossenen Mannes, dem die Spur, in der er zu fahren gezwungen war, bereits mehr abverlangt hatte, als er an Aufmerksamkeit, an Kraft und Geschicklichkeit aufbringen konnte.

Durch die Fenster der Schulklasse sahen wir ihn näherkommen, glaubten sein Stöhnen zu hören, seine Flüche und die Verwünschungen, mit denen er die kufenbreite Spur bedachte und mehr noch sein Los, in ihr entlangfahren zu müssen. Es war Heinrich Bielek. Wir erkannten ihn sofort, mit dem schnellen und untrüglichen Instinkt, mit dem man einen Mann aus seinem Dorf erkennt, selbst in schneegrauer Dämmerung, selbst wenn dieser Mann jetzt eine Uniform trug und einen alten Karabiner quer über dem Rücken: Heinrich Bielek, krank und mit weißem Stoppelhaar – wenn auch nicht so

THE RENUNCIATION

IT was in the middle of that winter when his bicycle and his orders brought him here along the solidly frozen tracks of a sleigh, which did not allow him to raise his eyes and look ahead but forced him to keep a constant watch on the tracks he had entrusted himself to, because every time he did look up, the rim of the wheel would immediately scrape against the frozen walls of snow, the handlebars would turn sideways, and when he twisted them back, the front wheel would go crooked, wedged firmly in the narrow tracks, so that – with the long coat of his uniform and the old carbine slung across his back – he had trouble dismounting in time. He toiled up the road into the village which runs past the school, alone and in no way convincing us that he was a threat but rather giving the impression – in the grey February gloom and set against the smoke-coloured cottages of our village – of a despairing and disgruntled man of whom the tracks which he was forced to follow had already demanded more attention, strength and skill than were his to give.

We saw him approaching through the classroom windows and imagined we could hear his groaning, his oaths and the curses he conferred both on the width of the sleigh-runners' track and, above all, on the fate which forced him to cycle along it. It was Heinrich Bielek. We recognized him at once, with that swift and unerring instinct with which people recognize a man from their own village, even in the snow-grey gloom, even when that man was now dressed in uniform, with an old carbine slung across his back – Heinrich Bielek, in poor health and with bristly white hair, though not in such poor

krank, daß sie in jener Zeit auf ihn hätten verzichten wollen. Sie konnten ihn zwar nicht beliebig verwenden oder – ihrem Lieblingswort gemäß – einsetzen, aber er trug ihre Uniform, vermehrte ihre Zahl und gab ihnen die Sicherheit einer Reserve.

Wir beobachteten, wie er sich am Schulhof vorbeiquälte, und glaubten ihn längst am Dorfausgang und unterwegs nach Schalussen oder wohin immer ihn die hartgefrorene Schlittenspur und sein Auftrag führen sollten, als ihn zwei Männer über den Korridor brachten, ihn ins Lehrerzimmer trugen und dort auf ein Sofa niederdrückten. Wie ich später erfuhr, legten sie seinen Karabiner quer über einen verkratzten Ledersessel, öffneten seinen Mantel und sahen eine Weile zu, wie er sich krümmte, nach mehreren Versuchen auf die Seite warf und beide Hände flach auf seinen Leib preßte, ohne einen einzigen Laut, und bevor sie ihm noch anboten, den Arzt aus Drugallen holen zu lassen, richtete er sich wieder auf und beschwichtigte die Männer durch einen Wink: es waren nur die überfälligen Magenkrämpfe, die er schon in der Nacht erwartet hatte und deren Verlauf er so gut kannte, daß er mit dem Schmerz allein fertig zu werden hoffte.

So war es wahrscheinlich auch weniger der Schmerz als der Gedanke an die bläuliche, hartgefrorene Schlittenspur, der ihn später auf dem Sofa im Lehrerzimmer festhielt, neben einer rissigen Wand, unter der Photographie eines uniformierten ·Mannes mit Kneifer, der sachlich auf ihn herabsah. Obwohl es ihm besser zu gehen schien, erhob er sich nicht, sondern verteilte liegend Zigaretten, ohne selbst zu rauchen, und erwiderte den erschreckend sachlichen Blick jenes Mannes auf der Photographie, den er für einen Lehrer gehalten hätte, wenn er ihm unbekannt gewesen wäre; doch Heinrich Bielek kannte ihn so gut, daß er selbst die Furcht verstand, die dieser Mann hervorrief oder hervorrufen sollte.

Nachdem er endgültig beschlossen hatte, daß die Magen-

health that at that period they might have wished to do without him. They could not of course employ or – to use their favourite word – engage him as they liked, but at least he was now dressed in their uniform, swelling their numbers and giving them the guarantee of a reserve.

We watched him labouring past the playground and imagined he must have left the village long before and already be on his way to Schalussen or wherever the solidly frozen tracks of the sleigh and his orders were to take him, when two men brought him across the corridor, carried him into the staffroom and forced him to lie down there on a sofa. As I later found out, they slung his carbine across a badly scratched leather armchair, undid his coat and for a while watched him writhing about, taking several attempts to roll over on to one side and then pressing both hands flat against his body, without a single sound. Even before they offered to have the doctor called from Drugallen he had sat up and beckoned to the men reassuringly: it was only the overdue stomach cramp he had expected the previous night and whose course he knew so well that he hoped to master the pain on his own.

So it was presumably not so much the pain as the thought of the bluish, solidly frozen tracks of the sleigh which subsequently kept him firmly on the staffroom sofa, beside a wall with cracks in it and beneath the photograph of a man in uniform wearing a pince-nez and looking down on him with a detached gaze. Although he appeared to be feeling better, he did not get up, but handed out cigarettes from his lying position, without taking one for himself, and countered the terrifyingly detached gaze of that man in the photograph, whom he would have taken to be a teacher had he been unacquainted with him; but Heinrich Bielek knew him so well that he even understood the fear that this man inspired or was supposed to inspire.

When he had finally decided that his stomach cramp would

krämpfe es ihm nicht mehr erlaubten, in der Schlittenspur weiterzufahren, zog er den schlechtsitzenden Uniform-Mantel aus, rollte ihn zusammen und schob ihn sich als Kopf-kissen unter und musterte aus seinen eichelförmigen Augen die beiden Männer. Er erkundigte sich nicht nach seinem Fahrrad, ein zusätzliches Zeichen dafür, daß er vorerst nicht weiterzufahren gedachte, vielmehr weihte er die Männer in seinen Auftrag ein, wodurch er erreichte, daß beide sich dem unerwünschten Zwang ausgesetzt fühlten, ihm, der ausge-streckt vor ihnen lag, zu helfen.

Das Vertrauen, in das er sie zog, ließ den Männern – einer von ihnen war Feustel, der pensionierte Rektor, ein nach Tabak und Zwiebeln riechender Junggeselle – keine andere Wahl, weshalb sie, noch bevor er sie darum bat, einen Jungen in das Lehrerzimmer riefen und neben das Sofa führten, auf dem Heinrich Bielek lag. Obwohl sie seinen Auftrag kannten, überließen sie es dem Liegenden, ihn an den Jungen weiter-zugeben, und als Bielek zu sprechen begann, lag auf ihren Gesichtern ein Ausdruck beflissenen und gespannten Interesses, so als hörten sie alles zum ersten Mal. Der Junge, Bernhard Gummer, mit wulstigem Nacken und schräg gelegtem Kopf – jeder bei uns kannte seinen sanften, freundlichen Schwachsinn – starrte auf den alten Karabiner, der quer auf dem Ledersessel lag, und verriet weder durch ein Nicken noch durch einen Blick, ob und wie er den Auftrag oder doch die Verlängerung des Auftrags verstanden hatte, was jetzt Feustel veranlaßte, dem Jungen eine Hand auf die Schulter zu legen und ihn auf-zufordern, das, was er gehört hatte, langsam zu wiederholen.

Der Junge enttäuschte sie nicht: ohne das Gesicht zu heben, wiederholte er, daß er nach Schalussen zu gehen habe, zu Wil-helm Heilmann, dem Alteisenhändler, und er sollte ihn hierher bringen, in die Schule, ins Lehrerzimmer, zu dem Mann in der Uniform, zu Heinrich Bielek. Wenn er nicht komme, werde man ihn noch heute holen, es sei dringend. Der ehemalige

no longer allow him to continue his journey along the tracks of the sleigh, he took off the ill-fitting coat of his uniform, rolled it up and shoved it under his head as a pillow and peered at the two men with his acorn-shaped eyes. He did not ask after his bicycle, an additional sign that he had no thoughts at present of continuing on his way, but instead initiated the men into the nature of his orders, with the result that both felt themselves the victims of an unwelcome compulsion to help this person who lay stretched out in front of them.

The confidence into which he drew them left these men – one of them was Feustel, the retired headmaster, a bachelor who stank of tobacco and onions – with no other choice and, even before he asked them to do so, they had summoned a youth into the staffroom and made him stand beside the sofa on which Heinrich Bielek was lying. Although they knew what his orders were, they left it to the recumbent man to communicate them to the youth, and when Bielek began to speak, their faces assumed an expression of studied and expectant interest, as though they were hearing it all for the first time. The youth, Bernhard Gummer, with that swollen neck of his which set his head at an angle – we all knew his harmless and amiable half-wittedness – stared at the old carbine, which lay slung across the leather armchair and gave no indication either by way of a nod of the head or a glance whether he had understood the task, why it had been extended, or in what way it was to be carried out. Feustel felt obliged to place one hand on the youth's shoulder and demand that he slowly repeat all he had heard.

The youth did not disappoint them: without raising his eyes, he repeated that he was to go to Schalussen, to Wilhelm Heilmann, the scrap-metal dealer, and bring him back here, to the school, to the staffroom, to the man in uniform, to Heinrich Bielek. If he did not come, someone would go that same day to fetch him, because it was urgent. The former head-

Rektor richtete sich zufrieden auf, und Bernhard Gummer zog bedächtig seinen Mantel an, setzte die Ohrenschützer auf, lauschte einen Augenblick, als höre er, wie ein Funker, schwache Signale in den Hörmuscheln; dann streifte er die an einer Schnur befestigten Fausthandschuhe über und verließ mit schleppendem Gang die Schule.

Der Junge kannte den Weg, er selbst wohnte in Schalussen, und er kannte auch – wie wir alle – die Hütte von Wilhelm Heilmann und den Schuppen und den Lagerplatz hinter dem Schuppen, auf dem ein Hügel von rostigem Eisen lag: alte Fahrradrahmen, Bleche, braunrotes Drahtgewirr, leere Pumpgehäuse, abgestoßene Hufeisen und zerbeulte Kessel, durch deren Löcher im Sommer der Löwenzahn herauswuchs oder Taubnesseln. Dieser Hügel schien uns mehr ein Wahrzeichen der Heilmanns als ihr Kapital, von dem sie lebten; denn er wurde nie flacher und geringer, wurde nie in unserer Gegenwart auf Lastwagen geladen, wurde nicht einmal, wie Erbsen, nach guten und schlechten Teilen verlesen, sondern lag nur da durch Jahreszeiten und Generationen, ein Hügel der Nutzlosigkeiten. Und doch mußten sie davon leben und gelebt haben, geheimnisvoll und gewitzt; ganze Geschlechter von ihnen hatten altem Eisen vertraut, ernährten sich mit seiner Hilfe, wuchsen heran und ließen den rostroten Hügel wieder den nächsten Heilmanns als Erbe zufallen, die es anscheinend weder mehrten noch minderten, sondern nur darauf aus schienen, es zu erhalten. Unsere Großväter, unsere Väter und wir: Generationen unseres Dorfes stahlen hinten von dem Hügel, wenn sie Groschen brauchten, und gingen vorn zu den Heilmanns und verkauften ihnen, was diese schon dreimal besaßen, wonach unsere Leute nur noch Zeugen wurden, wie der Krempel wieder auf den Hügel flog, so daß dieser zwar nicht seine alte Form, aber doch sein altes Gewicht hatte, was ihm jene seltsame Dauer verlieh. Obwohl Wilhelm Heilmann allein lebte, zweifelten wir nicht daran, daß eines Tages irgend-

master threw back his shoulders with a satisfied air, and Bern-hard Gummer put on his coat with deliberation, put on his ear-muffs and listened for a moment as though he were a radio operator and could hear weak signals in his head-phones; then he pulled on his mittens, which were fastened by a piece of string, and went shuffling out of the building.

The youth knew the way, for he, too, lived in Schalussen and – like the rest of us – he knew the cottage of Wilhelm Heilmann, the shed and the tip behind the shed on which stood a mound of rusty iron – old cycle frames, sheets of metal, a tangle of brownish-red wire, empty pump-casings, cast-off horseshoes and dented kettles through whose holes dandelions grew in summer, or else dead-nettles. It was as a symbol of the Heilmann family that we viewed this mound rather than as the capital on which they lived; for it never grew flatter or smaller; we never saw it loaded on to lorries, and it was never sorted out into good and bad piles, like peas, but simply remained there from one season and one generation to the next, a mountain of uselessness. And yet they must have lived off it, now and in the past, in some shrewd and mys-terious way; whole generations of them had entrusted their lives to scrap iron, supported themselves with its help, grown up and left the rusting red mound as legacy to the next genera-tion of Heilmanns, who to all appearances neither added to it nor reduced it but seemed only intent on maintaining it as it was. Our grandfathers, our fathers and we, too: generations of villagers stole things from the far side of the mound when-ever they needed money, then went round to the Heilmanns' front door and sold them what had been theirs three times already; and finally our people could witness how the junk was thrown back on to the heap, so that the mound retained not of course its former shape but its former weight, and in that way kept its remarkable permanence. Although Wilhelm Heilmann lived by himself, we had no doubts that one day

woher ein neuer Heilmann auftauchen werde, um den Hügel
aus altem Eisen in seinen Besitz zu nehmen – zu übernehmen
und zu verwalten wie jenes Holzscheit, an dem das Leben
hing.

Soviel ich weiß, fand der Junge an jenem Morgen Heilmann lesend im Bett. Er wunderte sich nicht, daß der alte
Mann angezogen unter dem schweren Zudeck lag, ging zu
ihm, setzte sich auf die Bettkante, schob die Ohrenschützer
hoch und wiederholte seinen Auftrag, und nachdem er fertig
war und sah, daß der Alte weder Überraschung noch Abwehr
oder Furcht zeigte, riet er ihm, sich zu verstecken oder die
Hütte zu verschließen, und wenn nicht dies, so doch ein Gewehr zu kaufen, da auch der andere ein Gewehr bei sich hatte,
doch Wilhelm Heilmann, der Letzte mosaischen Glaubens in
unserer hoffnungslosen Ecke Masurens,[1] lächelte säuerlich, das
Lächeln einer ertragbaren und unwiderruflichen Gewißheit,
und er schlug das Zudeck zurück und stand auf. Er hatte mit
Stiefeln im Bett gelegen. Der Junge ging in die Küche, setzte
sich auf eine Fußbank und brach sich ein Stück von einem
grauen Hefefladen ab und begann zu essen; er brauchte nicht
zu warten, denn der Alte wechselte nur seine Brille, die Lese-
brille gegen die Arbeitsbrille, stand schon in der dunklen
Küche und forderte den Jungen auf, ihn zu führen. Der alte
Mann blickte weder auf die gekalkte Hütte, die er unverschlos-
sen zurückließ, noch auf den schneebedeckten Hügel, unter
dem das rostige Erbe der Heilmanns lag, sondern ging dem
Jungen voraus neben der Schlittenspur, und unter ihren Schritten krachte der gefrorene Schnee. Vor den Weiden, die mit
einer Eisglasur überzogen waren, holte der Junge ihn ein einziges Mal ein und zeigte auf die dunkle, undurchdringbar
erscheinende Flanke des Waldes, deutete nur stumm hinüber,
wobei seine Geste und seine Haltung nichts als eine heftige
Aufforderung ausdrückten: Wilhelm Heilmann lächelte säuerlich und schüttelte den Kopf. Vielleicht wußte er, daß er in

some new Heilmann would turn up from heaven knows where to assume ownership of the mound of scrap iron, to take it over and guard it like that block of wood on which life itself hung.

As far as I know, the youth found Heilmann reading in bed that morning. It did not surprise him that the old man was lying there fully dressed under the thick blanket; but he went up to him, sat down on the edge of the bed, pushed up his ear-muffs and repeated his instructions; and when he had finished and saw that the old man showed no sign of surprise or resistance or fear, advised him to go into hiding or lock up the cottage or, failing that, buy a rifle, because the other man had a rifle with him; but Wilhelm Heilmann, the last man in our dismal corner of Masuria to profess the Mosaic faith, smiled bitterly, the smile of a bearable and irrevocable certainty, threw back the covers and got up. He had gone to bed wearing his boots. The youth went into the kitchen, sat down on a footstool and tore off a piece of grey yeast cake and set to eating; he had no need to wait because the old man only changed his glasses, the ones he wore for work in place of his reading glasses, came straight into the gloomy kitchen and called on the youth to show him the way. The old man glanced neither at the white-washed cottage, which he left unlocked, nor at the snow-covered mound beneath which lay the Heilmanns' rusting inheritance, but walked along in front of the youth, beside the tracks left by the sleigh, and the frozen snow crunched beneath their feet. The only time the youth caught up with him was in front of some willows, which were coated in a frosting of ice; there he pointed to the gloomy and apparently impenetrable edge of the wood, mutely indicating the direction in such a way that the movement of his hand and his whole attitude were expressive of one impassioned demand: Wilhelm Heilmann laughed bitterly and shook his head. Perhaps he knew that he was the last one in our corner

unserer Ecke der Letzte war, den sie lediglich vergessen oder
geschont, wahrscheinlich aber vergessen hatten, was ihn dazu
bringen mußte, unversöhnt zu warten bis zu dem Augenblick,
da die Reihe an ihn käme. Jetzt, da der Junge ihn holte, war er
versöhnt, etwas war erloschen in ihm: seine Wißbegier, die
Zweifel, denen er sich ausgeliefert fand, als sie nacheinander
die andern holten – wobei sie oft genug durch Schalussen und
an seiner Hütte und seinem Eisenhügel vorbeikamen –, ohne
ihm selbst zu drohen oder ihm auch nur anzukündigen, was er
insgeheim immer mehr erwartete. Zwei Jahre dauerte es, bis
ihre genaue Grausamkeit sich seiner weniger entsann als ihn
vielmehr hervorholte wie etwas, das man nur zurückgestellt,
sich aufgespart hatte für eine andere Zeit. Wilhelm Heilmann
hatte damit gerechnet und sich nicht ein einziges Mal die
Schwäche der Hoffnung geleistet.

In seiner knielangen erdbraunen Joppe ging er dem Jungen
voran, durch das Spalier der rauchfarbenen Hütten zur Schule,
die er einst selbst besucht hatte; ging den mit Asche und winzigen Schlackenbrocken gestreuten Weg hinauf, entdeckte das
Fahrrad, blieb neben ihm stehen, nickte lächelnd und schob
die Hände tief in die Taschen. Bernhard Gummer stellte sich
neben ihn, sein Gesicht veränderte und näherte sich dem alten
Mann, die aufgeworfenen Lippen bewegten sich, flüsterten
etwas dringend und unverständlich, dann wandte er sich um
und verschwand in der Schule, ohne zurückzublicken.

Der Alte wartete, bis er das Geräusch der genagelten Stiefel
auf dem Korridor hörte, stieß sich mit dem Rücken von der
Wand ab und trat dem uniformierten Mann entgegen, der in
einer Hand den Karabiner trug, sich mit der andern den
Mantel zuknöpfte. «Fertig, Wilhelm?» «Fertig, Heinrich.» Es
kam Wilhelm Heilmann nicht zu, mehr zu sagen, und es gab
nichts für ihn, das ihm wichtig genug erschienen wäre, als daß
er es hätte erfahren wollen: das Wissen, das er in sich trug wie
eine Konterbande, übertraf alles, was er von Heinrich Bielek

of the world, whom they had simply forgotten or spared, most likely just forgotten, so that he was bound to wait implacably until the moment when his turn came. Now that the youth had come to fetch him, he was reconciled, something in him had died – his curiosity, the doubts to which he found himself prey when they came to fetch all the rest of them, one after the other, when as often as not they would pass through Schalussen and by his cottage and his mound of iron without threatening him personally or even informing him of what he secretly came more and more to expect. It took two years for their painstaking cruelty not so much to recall his existence as to bring him out of storage, so to speak, treating him like something that had only been set on one side for use at a later date. Wilhelm Heilmann had taken that into account and never once allowed himself the weakness of hope.

He walked ahead of the youth, in his knee-length, earth-brown coat, passing through the line of smoke-coloured cottages leading to the school he himself had once attended; walked up the path strewn with cinders and tiny bits of slag, came across the bicycle, stopped beside it, nodded with a smile and shoved his hands deep into his pockets. Bernhard Gummer stood beside him, his face altered in expression and moved closer to the old man's, his protruding lips stirred and whispered some urgent and enigmatic message; then he turned and disappeared into the school without looking back.

The old man waited until he could hear the noise of his hobnailed boots in the corridor, then pushed himself away from the wall with his back and went to meet the man in uniform who was holding the carbine in one hand and buttoning up his coat with the other. 'Ready, Wilhelm?' 'Ready, Heinrich.' It was not for Wilhelm Heilmann to say anything else and there was nothing that struck him as sufficiently important that he might have wished to find out about it: the knowledge he bore within him as though it were contraband far exceeded

je hätte erfahren können, und so folgte er ihm einfach auf die Landstraße, wandte sich mit ihm um und winkte leicht zur Schule zurück, ging neben ihm durch unser Dorf mit der überzeugenden Selbstverständlichkeit eines Mannes, der den Weg und den Plan des andern kennt und teilt. Sie gingen an der Domäne² vorbei, über die alte Holzbrücke, an deren Geländer noch die Schrammen der Erntewagen vom letzten Herbst zu erkennen waren. Auf freiem Feld traf sie ein eisiger Wind, schnitt in ihre Gesichter. Wilhelm Heilmann spürte, wie sein Augenlid zu zucken begann. Ein verschneiter Wegweiser zeigte Korczymmen an, vierzehn Kilometer, Grenzgebiet. Flach über den Schnee lief ihnen der Wind entgegen, trieb eine schmerzhafte Kühle in ihre Lungen, und sie senkten ihre Gesichter und legten den Oberkörper nach vorn. «Es ist nicht der freundlichste Tag», sagte Heinrich Bielek. «Drüben in den Wäldern wird es angenehmer», sagte Wilhelm Heilmann. Ein Schlitten mit vermummten Leuten kam ihnen entgegen, sie traten zur Seite, Hände winkten ihnen zu, sie grüßten zurück, ohne zu erkennen, wem ihr Gruß galt. Das Gebimmel der Schlittenglocken verklang in einem Tal.

Als sie die Stelle erreichten, wo der Wald die Straße belagerte, hatte Heinrich Bielek ein Gefühl, als ob ein heißes Geschoß in seinen Magen eindrang; es traf ihn so überraschend, mit einer so vollkommenen Gewalt, daß er beide Hände erschrocken auf seinen Leib preßte, das Fahrrad fallenließ und auf den Knien in den Schnee sank. Seine Mütze fiel vom Kopf. Das Schweißband rutschte aus dem Kragen heraus. Der Riemen des Karabiners schnürte in seine Brust. Wilhelm Heilmann sah ausdruckslos auf ihn herab, und als ihn ein schneller, argwöhnischer Blick traf, hob er das Fahrrad auf und hielt es mit beiden Händen fest – wie eine Last, die er um keinen Preis loslassen wollte oder durfte, nur um damit schweigend zu bekunden, daß es ihm weder jetzt noch später darauf ankam, eine Gelegenheit auszunutzen. Es war weder

anything he could ever have found out from Heinrich Bielek, and so he simply followed him along the main road, turned round at the same time as he did and waved undemonstratively in the direction of the school and walked alongside him through our village with the convincing matter-of-factness of a man who knows and shares another's way and plan. They passed by the Crown land and over the old wooden bridge on whose handrails it was still possible to make out the scratches left by the harvest waggons the previous autumn. Once in the open fields, they were met by an icy wind which cut into their faces. Wilhelm Heilmann felt his eyelid beginning to twitch. A snowed-up signpost showed the way to Korczymmen, fourteen kilometres, border-district. The wind came rushing towards them, keeping low over the snow, driving a painful rawness into their lungs, and they lowered their heads and braced their bodies to meet it. 'Not a very nice day, is it?' Heinrich Bielek said. 'It'll be pleasanter over there in the woods,' Wilhelm Heilmann said. A sleigh with its occupants all muffled up came towards them, they stepped aside, hands waved at them and they returned the greeting without recognizing the people they were waving to. The tinkling of the sleigh-bells died away in a valley.

When they reached the place where the wood crowded up to the road, Heinrich Bielek suddenly felt as though a hot bullet had penetrated his stomach; it struck him so unexpectedly and with such utter force that he squeezed both hands against his body in panic, allowed the bicycle to fall over and sank down on his knees in the snow. His cap fell off his head. The sweatband slipped from inside his collar. The sling of his carbine cut into his chest. Wilhelm Heilmann looked down at him blankly and when a swift, suspicious glance caught him, he righted the bicycle and held it firmly with both hands – like a weight which he neither would nor could let go of at any price – bearing silent witness to the fact that he had no

Niedergeschlagenheit noch Schwäche, was er in diesem Augenblick bekundete, sondern das Eingeständnis, auf jede Handlung zu verzichten, die das, was er in seinem Lauschen und in seinen Träumen so oft erwartet, erlebt und durchstanden hatte, ändern könnte. Er hielt das Fahrrad fest und wagte nicht, über sein zuckendes Augenlid zu streifen, stand nur und blickte auf den uniformierten Mann im Schnee, der sich jetzt angestrengt auf alle viere erhob, lange zögerte, als ob er nach der entscheidenden Kraft suchte, die ihn auf die Beine bringen sollte, dann die Hände nah zusammenführte, sich hochstemmte mit einem Ruck, und eine Sekunde bang und ungläubig dastand, ehe er sich mit einer knappen Aufforderung an Wilhelm Heilmann wandte. «Also weiter, Wilhelm», sagte er.

Sie gingen in der Mitte einer frischen Schlittenspur durch unseren alten Wald, geschützt vor dem eisigen Wind, der hoch durch die Kiefern strich und überall Schneelasten von den Ästen riß, die stäubend zwischen den Stämmen niedergingen. In weitem Abstand neben dem Weg lagen Haufen geschnittener Stämme; die Schnittflächen leuchteten gelblich, zeigten ihnen an, wo die Spur verlief. Wilhelm Heilmann schob das Fahrrad, und der andere nahm den Karabiner ab und trug ihn in der Hand. Sie gingen nebeneinander, bemüht, auf gleicher Höhe zu bleiben, auch wenn der Weg es erschwerte, auch wenn er sie dazu zwang, schräg aus den Augenwinkeln auf den andern zu achten, nicht so sehr aus Furcht oder aus Mißtrauen, sondern aus dem Verlangen, gemeinsam vorwärtszukommen, sich ziehen zu lassen vom Schritt des andern. Ein fernes Donnern wie von einem Wintergewitter rollte über sie hin; Heinrich Bielek hob den Kopf, lauschte, ohne stehenzubleiben, und sagte leise: «Schwere Artillerie», worauf Wilhelm Heilmann ausdruckslos hochblickte – mit der gleichen Ausdruckslosigkeit, mit der er den alten Eisenkrempel auf seinen Hügel geschleudert hatte.

intention either now or later of exploiting any such opportunity. It was neither despondency nor weakness which he showed at that moment but an avowal to renounce every action that might affect the course of what he had so often anticipated, suffered and survived in his listening and his dreaming. He held the bicycle firmly, not daring to rub his twitching eyelid, but just stood and stared at the man in uniform lying there in the snow, struggling to raise himself on all fours, hesitating for a long time as if in search of the crucial strength that would bring him to his feet, then placing his hands close together, forcing himself up with a jerk and standing for a second afraid and disbelieving, before turning to Wilhelm Heilmann with a brief word of command. 'On we go then, Wilhelm,' he said.

They went along a newly formed sleigh track through our old wood, protected from the icy wind which swept through the tops of the pines, tearing down from their branches their burdens of snow and turning it to powder as it passed between the trunks. At distances along the road there lay piles of hewn tree-trunks; the cut surfaces gave off a yellowish light, showed them which way their trail went. Wilhelm Heilmann pushed the bicycle and the other unslung the carbine and carried it in his hand. They walked alongside each other, at pains to remain level, even when the road made it difficult to do so, even when it forced them to squint at each other from the corner of their eyes, not so much out of fear or distrust but out of a desire to keep together, to allow themselves to be drawn each by the other's step. A distant clap of thunder, as if from a wintry storm, growled overhead; Heinrich Bielek raised his eyes, listened, without stopping, and said quietly, 'Heavy artillery', whereupon Wilhelm Heilmann glanced blankly upwards – that same blank expression with which he had hurled scrap metal on to his mound.

The wood began to thin out, they passed the frozen marshes

Der Wald wurde freier, sie gingen an den gefrorenen Sümpfen vorbei und den Berg hinauf und wieder in den Wald, der sie mit derselben Bereitwilligkeit aufnahm, wie er sich hinter ihnen schloß, und als sie den verrotteten hölzernen Aussichtsturm erreichten, fiel Schnee. Die Straße teilte sich, ein zweiter Wegweiser zeigte Korczymmen an, elf Kilometer. Sie folgten dem Wegweiser wortlos, als hätten sie sich längst auf ein Ziel geeinigt.

Wilhelm Heilmann dachte an den Mann, der ihn führte oder vielmehr überführte, entsann sich dessen einäugigen Vaters, der Kate, in der die Bieleks wohnten, fleißige und geschickte Besenbinder, deren sichtbarster Reichtum dreckige Kinder waren, die im Frühjahr durch die Birkenwälder schwärmten, um elastische Reiser zu schneiden. Er dachte an den Knaben Heinrich Bielek, der auf den Bäumen gesessen hatte, um Lindenblüten für den Tee zu pflücken, der bis spät in den Oktober barfuß gegangen und bei einer Hochzeit unter die Kutsche gekommen war, in der die Braut gesessen hatte. Er entsann sich sogar jener Begabung Heinrichs, die sie damals immer wieder verblüfft hatte, die Begabung nämlich, ein Schnitzmesser mit der Spitze auf seinen Schenkel fallenzulassen, und zwar, so daß er sich nicht die geringste Wunde beibrachte. Wilhelm Heilmann wurde auf einmal gewahr, daß er zu schnell ging oder daß der Mann neben ihm langsamer wurde. Er blieb nicht stehen, versuchte nur, sich auf den Schritt des andern einzustellen, was ihm jedoch nicht gelang, so daß er schließlich, als er wieder einen Vorsprung hatte, doch stehenblieb, sich umwandte und Heinrich Bielek nicht mehr hinter sich in der Schlittenspur fand, sondern ihn durch den hohen Schnee seitwärts in den Wald stapfen sah, den Kolben des Karabiners als Stütze benutzend. Sofort hob er das Fahrrad an, kehrte zurück, noch bevor ihn der Befehl erreichte, zurückzukehren, und folgte den Fußstapfen, die zu einer Hütte aus Fichtenstämmen führten, wie sie sich unsere Wald-

and up the hillside and back into the wood, which welcomed them with the same willingness as it closed in after them, and by the time they reached the decaying wooden look-out tower, snow was falling. The road divided, a second signpost pointed towards Korczymmen, eleven kilometres. They followed the signpost without speaking, as though they had long ago agreed on a goal.

Wilhelm Heilmann was thinking of the man who was leading him – or rather handing him over – remembering his one-eyed father, and the shack in which the Bielek family lived, hard-working and skilled broom-makers whose most obvious wealth consisted of dirty children, who wandered through the birchwoods in spring cutting whip-like twigs. He was thinking about Heinrich Bielek as a boy, sitting in trees and gathering lime blossoms to make tea with, going barefoot until late into October and, on the occasion of a wedding, falling under the wheels of a coach in which the bride had been sitting. He even remembered that innate gift of Heinrich's, which at that time had never failed to amaze them, his gift for being able to drop a carving knife point downwards on to his leg in such a way that he never caused himself the slightest injury. Wilhelm Heilmann suddenly noticed that he was walking too quickly or that the man at his side was going more slowly. He did not stop, but simply tried to get into step with the other, something which he none the less could not manage to do, so that he finally did stop when he again found himself out in front, turned round and discovered that Heinrich Bielek was no longer following him in the tracks of the sleigh, but saw him trudging off into the wood through the deep snow, using the butt of his carbine as a support. He immediately shouldered the bicycle and set off back, even before the order reached him to return, and followed the footsteps which led to a cabin made of spruce logs like those our woodsmen build themselves for the summer. The door was

arbeiter für den Sommer bauen. Die Tür war nur mit Draht gesichert, sie bogen ihn auseinander und traten in die Hütte, in der auf dem nackten Fußboden vier Strohsäcke lagen. Kein Fenster, kein Ofen, nur ein Bord, auf dem angelaufene Aluminiumbecher standen; in den Pfosten neben der Tür waren Kerben geschnitten, in einer Ecke lag Schnee.

Heinrich Bielek ließ sich auf den ersten Strohsack hinab, streckte sich stöhnend aus und deutete stumm auf den Strohsack neben ihm, auf den sich, nachdem er das Fahrrad in die Hütte gestellt hatte, Wilhelm Heilmann setzte, dann seine Brille abnahm und sie sorgfältig am Ärmel der Joppe putzte. Danach stand er auf und ging zur Tür, um sie zu schließen: ein schwacher Befehl rief ihn zurück, und er sah, wie Heinrich Bielek vom Strohsack aus den Lauf des Karabiners auf ihn gerichtet hielt, den Lauf mühsam schwenkte und mitdrehte, während er langsam durch den Raum zu seinem Strohsack zurückkehrte. Die Tür blieb offen. Plötzliche kleine Böen schleuderten Schnee herein. Kalte Zugluft strömte über sie hin.

Der Schmerz hielt Heinrich Bielek fest wie in einem Griff, preßte ihn an den Strohsack, und er schlug mit den Beinen und warf den Kopf hin und her, ohne jedoch den Mann zu vergessen, der neben ihm saß und ruhig auf ihn herabblickte. Er vergaß ihn so wenig, daß er sich jetzt herumwarf und ihn fortwährend aus aufgerissenen Augen anstarrte, erschrocken, abwehrend, denn er erschien ihm durch den Schmerz hindurch riesenhaft vergrößert und in all seiner körperlichen Überlegenheit so sehr auf Flucht aus zu sein, daß er ihn bereits fliehen sah: die erdbraune Joppe hierhin und dorthin zwischen den Stämmen, hinter den Tannen, unerreichbar selbst für die Kugel, und Heinrich Bielek dachte: «Nicht, Wilhelm, tu das nicht.»

Dann spürte er, wie sein Koppelschloß ausgehakt, sein Mantel geöffnet wurde, das heißt, er spürte weit mehr die jähe

secured only by wire; they bent it apart and stepped into the cabin, where four straw mattresses lay on the bare earth. No window, no stove, only a shelf on which there stood some tarnished aluminium mugs. Notches had been cut into the post beside the door; snow lay in one corner.

Heinrich Bielek sank down on the nearest straw mattress, stretched himself out with a groan and mutely indicated the mattress beside him, where Wilhelm Heilmann, having first brought the bicycle into the cabin, sat down, took off his glasses and carefully cleaned them on his coat sleeve. Then he got up and went to the door intending to close it; a weak word of command called him back and he saw that, from his position on the straw mattress, Heinrich Bielek was holding the barrel of the carbine trained on him, brandishing and aiming the barrel with difficulty, until he had slowly returned the length of the room to his straw mattress. The door remained open. Sudden small gusts of wind hurled snow inside. A cold draught blew in over them.

Pain gripped Heinrich Bielek as though in a hold of iron, forced him down against the straw mattress and he kicked his legs and tossed his head to and fro, while never forgetting the man who was sitting beside him, quietly looking down at him. So little did he forget him that he now rolled over on to his other side and stared at him without respite, with gaping eyes, terrified, defensively, because he seemed to have grown, as a result of the pain, to gigantic proportions and, taking advantage of his physical superiority, to be so intent on flight that he could already see him fleeing, the earth-brown coat flashing between the tree-trunks, beyond the fir-trees, out of reach even of a bullet, and Heinrich Bielek thought, 'No, Wilhelm, don't do it.'

Then he felt the buckle of his belt being unfastened and his coat being undone, that is to say, what he felt was the sudden relief from pain rather than the individual events which led up

Erleichterung als die einzelnen Vorgänge, die dazu führten. Er ließ den Karabiner los, legte die Hände flach auf seinen Leib und fühlte nach einer Weile, wie der Krampf ihn freigab und der Griff sich lockerte, so fühlbar nachgab, daß er sich hinsetzte, den Rücken gegen die behauenen Stämme der Wand gelehnt. In einem Augenblick, da Wilhelm Heilmann die Hände vor das Gesicht zog, nahm er den Karabiner wieder an sich, legte ihn quer über seine Schenkel.

Sie saßen sich schweigend gegenüber, und beide hatten, nicht länger als einen Atemzug, den Eindruck einer Sinnestäuschung: keiner suchte den Blick des andern, keiner sagte ein Wort; vielmehr schienen sie einander wahrzunehmen durch ihre lauschenden, reglosen Körper, schienen auch im Einverständnis dieser Körper zu handeln, und als sich der eine erhob, erhob sich der andere fast gleichzeitig, stand in der gleichen Unschlüssigkeit da, setzte sich mit dem gleichen Zögern in Bewegung. Gemeinsam traten sie aus der Hütte, später, als es aufgehört hatte zu schneien, traten hinaus ohne Angst und ohne Hoffnung. Wilhelm Heilmann führte das Fahrrad, er dachte nicht an die verlorene Chance, zwang seine Erinnerung nicht zurück zu jenen Minuten, in denen er unbemerkt und risikolos die Hütte hätte verlassen oder tun können, was die absolute Wehrlosigkeit des andern nahelegte. Er ließ Heinrich Bielek vorangehen. Sie gingen weiter durch die Wälder, den Weg nach Korczymmen.

Vor dem Grenzdorf, das Wilhelm Heilmann kannte, aber seit Jahren nicht betreten hatte, bogen sie vom Hauptweg ab und folgten einer ausgetretenen Spur im Schnee, bis sie die klumpigen, gefrorenen Wälle des Grabens erreichten, der mitten durch den Wald lief. Sie hörten das Geräusch von Spitzhacken und Schaufeln und das Krachen von Erdklumpen, die gegen die Stämme geschleudert wurden.

Sie sahen Frauen in Kopftüchern und alte Männer auf dem Grund des Grabens arbeiten und sahen Kinder, die Steine,

to it. He let go of the carbine, flattened his hands against his body and soon felt the cramp releasing him and the iron hold loosening and slackening so perceptibly that he sat up and rested his back against the hewn logs of the cabin wall. As soon as Wilhelm Heilmann passed his hands over his face, he seized hold of the carbine once more and laid it at an angle across his knees.

They sat facing each other in silence and then, for the moment it takes to draw breath, both had the impression that they were seeing things: neither of them sought the other's gaze, neither spoke a word; they seemed instead to be aware of each other's presence through the agency of their listening, motionless bodies, seemed also to act with the agreement of those bodies, and when one of them got up, the other got up at almost the same time and stood there in the same indecision, began to stir with the same hesitating movements. Later, when it had stopped snowing, they left the cabin together, left it fearlessly and hopelessly. Wilhelm Heilmann pushed the bicycle, not thinking of the lost opportunity, not forcing his memory back to those minutes when he could have left the cabin unnoticed and without any risk to himself, when he could have done everything that the other's total helplessness might have prompted him to do. He let Heinrich Bielek walk in front. They walked on through the woods, along the road to Korczymmen.

Before entering the border village, which Wilhelm Heilmann already knew, although it was years since he had set foot in the place, they turned off from the main road and followed a trail that had been stamped down in the snow, until they reached the clod-covered, frozen embankments of the trench which ran through the middle of the wood. They heard the noise of picks and shovels and of earth breaking as it was hurled in clods against the trunks of trees.

They saw women in head-scarves and old men working at

Wurzeln und harte Brocken von Erde an den Wänden hoch-
stemmten. Wilhelm Heilmann nickte ihnen im Vorübergehen
zu. Weit vor ihnen schoß ein Maschinengewehr, und danach
hörten sie einzelne Revolverschüsse. Hinter den Wällen standen Posten. Auf einen Wink lehnte Wilhelm Heilmann das
Fahrrad gegen einen Baum und ging sofort weiter in die Richtung, aus der sie die Schüsse gehört hatten. Ein junger, breit-
gesichtiger Mann kam ihnen entgegen, sein Gewehr schräg
vor der Brust. Er trat zwischen sie. Er befahl Heinrich Bielek
zurückzugehen. Als er sich umdrehte, bemerkte er, daß der
Mann in der erdbraunen Joppe, den er weiterzuführen hatte,
ihm bereits mehrere Schritte stillschweigend vorausgegangen
war.

the bottom of the trench and saw children heaving stones, roots and solid lumps of earth up the walls. Wilhelm Heilmann nodded to them as he passed. From the distance in front of them came the sound of machine-gun fire, after which they heard isolated revolver shots. Sentries were standing behind the embankments. At a given sign Wilhelm Heilmann leant the bicycle against a tree and continued, without pausing, in the direction from which they had heard the shots. A broad-faced young man came to meet them, his rifle held across his chest. He strode between them. He ordered Heinrich Bielek to go back. When he turned round, he saw that the man in the earth-brown coat, the one he had to take on with him, had already gone on ahead several paces without saying a word.

THE DOGS

INGEBORG BACHMANN

Translated by Francis Kyle

DAS GEBELL

DIE alte Frau Jordan, die schon drei Jahrzehnte «die alte Frau Jordan» genannt wurde, weil es danach eine junge Frau Jordan gab und jetzt wieder eine junge Frau Jordan, wohnte zwar in Hietzing,[1] aber in einer verlotterten Villa, in einer Einzimmerwohnung mit einer winzigen Küche und einem Bad, in dem es nur eine Sitzbadewanne gab. Von ihrem berühmten Sohn Leo, dem Professor, bekam sie 1000 Schilling im Monat, und sie brachte es fertig, damit zu leben, obwohl diese 1000 Schilling in den letzten zwanzig Jahren so an Wert verloren hatten, daß sie nur mit Mühe eine ältere Frau zahlen konnte, eine gewisse Frau Agnes, die zweimal in der Woche zu ihr «hereinsah» und ein wenig aufräumte, «das Gröbste», und sie sparte davon auch noch für die Geburtstagsgeschenke und für Weihnachtsgeschenke für ihren Sohn und für ihren Enkel aus der ersten Ehe des Professors, der pünktlich zu Weihnachten von der ersten jungen Frau geschickt wurde, um sein Geschenk entgegenzunehmen, und Leo wiederum hatte zuviel zu tun, um darauf zu achten, und seit er berühmt war und sein Lokalruhm in einen internationalen Ruhm überging, hatte er noch mehr zu tun. Eine Änderung trat erst ein, als die neueste junge Frau Jordan, so oft sie konnte, zu der alten Frau kam, ein wirklich nettes sympathisches Mädchen, wie die alte Frau sich bald eingestand, und sie sagte nur jedesmal: Aber Franziska, das ist nicht richtig, Sie sollten nicht so oft kommen, und was für eine Verschwendung. Ihr werdet selber genug Auslagen haben, aber der Leo ist halt ein so guter Sohn!

Franziska brachte jedesmal etwas mit, Delikatessen und Sherry, etwas Gebäck, denn sie erriet, daß die alte Frau gerne

THE DOGS

OLD Mrs Jordan – who had been known for thirty years as 'old Mrs Jordan', because after her there had been a 'young Mrs Jordan', and now there was another 'young Mrs Jordan' – lived in the fashionable district of Hietzing, but in a villa that had seen better times. All she had, in fact, was a bedsitting room, plus a tiny kitchen and a bathroom with a hip-bath. Her son Leo, the well-known professor, gave her an allowance of £30 a month, and she managed to get by on this, even though this sum of money had lost so much of its value over the last twenty years that she could only just afford a cleaning lady, Agnes by name, who looked in once or twice a week and did a bit of basic housework for her. Even then, she still put a little money aside with which to buy birthday and Christmas presents both for her son and also for her grandson from the Professor's first marriage. Every year at Christmas the boy was sent by his mother to collect his present. As for Leo, he was too busy to concern himself with her problems, all the more so now that his local reputation was developing into an international one. Things changed, however, when the latest Mrs Jordan started calling on the old lady as often as she could manage. She was a really kind-hearted girl, as the old lady soon realized, and every time she came Mrs Jordan would say to her, 'Franziska dear, it really isn't right for you to come and see me so often, and look what it's costing you. You are bound to have enough expenses as it is. But, then, Leo is such a good son!'

Whenever she came, Franziska would bring something with her, delicacies of one sort or another, some pastry perhaps, or a bottle of sherry, for she guessed that the old lady

einen Schluck trank, und etwas mehr noch, daß sie großen Wert darauf legte, etwas zum «Aufwarten» zu haben, denn Leo konnte doch vorbeikommen, und er durfte nicht merken, daß sie nichts hatte und den ganzen Tag darüber nachgrübelte, wie das Geld einzuteilen sei und was für die Geschenke übrigbleiben mußte. Ihre Wohnung war peinlich sauber, aber es war ein leichter Geruch darin nach alter Frau, von dem sie nichts wußte und der Leo Jordan rasch in die Flucht trieb, ganz abgesehen davon, daß er keine Zeit zu verlieren hatte und absolut nicht wußte, worüber er mit seiner fünfundachtzigjährigen Mutter reden sollte. Belustigt war er nur manchmal gewesen – soviel wußte Franziska –, wenn er mit einer verheirateten Frau eine Beziehung hatte, denn dann schlief die alte Frau Jordan nicht und machte seltsame, umständliche Anspielungen, da sie für sein Leben zitterte und sich verheiratete Männer von Frauen, die mit Leo Jordan lebten, für gefährlich und eifersüchtig und blutrünstig hielt, und sie beruhigte sich erst wieder, als er Franziska geheiratet hatte, die keinen eifersüchtigen Mann im Gebüsch lauern hatte, sondern jung und fröhlich war, eine Waise, zwar nicht aus einer Akademikerfamilie, aber einen Bruder hatte sie, der Akademiker war. Akademikerfamilie und Akademiker waren für Frau Jordan von einer großen Wichtigkeit, obwohl sie nie unter Leute kam und nur von ihnen erzählen hörte. Aber ihr Sohn hätte ein Recht darauf gehabt, in eine Akademikerfamilie zu heiraten. Die alte Frau und Franziska sprachen fast nur von Leo, da er das einzige ergiebige Thema zwischen ihnen sein konnte, und Franziska mußte viele Male das Fotoalbum ansehen, Leo im Kinderwagen, Leo in einem Strandbad und Leo durch alle Jahre, auf Wanderungen, beim Briefmarkenkleben und so fort, bis zu seiner Militärzeit.

could not say no to a 'little drop' now and again. And she realized also that she set great store on having something 'to offer visitors'. After all, Leo might drop in, and he must not notice how little she had or how much trouble she had just to make ends meet and still have something left for presents. Her flat was meticulously clean, but there remained nevertheless a faint odour of old ladies, of which she herself was unaware. It was quite enough, however, to drive Leo Jordan away, especially as he had so little time to spare, and was absolutely unable to think of anything to talk about with his eighty-five year-old mother. The only occasions, in fact, when he had been cheerful on a visit to her – this much Franziska did know – was when he was having a relationship with a married woman. This used to give his mother insomnia, and she would make curious, indirect references to the situation. She imagined that the husbands he was deceiving must be dangerous, jealous and blood-thirsty individuals and she feared for his safety. She only calmed down again, in fact, after he had married Franziska, who was not shadowed by a jealous husband, but on the contrary was young and light-hearted. Franziska was an orphan, to be precise, and, though she did not come from an academic family, she did, at any rate, have a brother who was an academic. For, in the old lady's eyes, academics, and an academic family background, carried a great deal of weight, even though she had no social life of her own and only heard about such people from others. After all, it was her son's special right, she had felt, to marry into an academic family. The old lady and Franziska hardly ever spoke about anything else except Leo. He was the one subject of conversation they could always come back to. And so the photograph album was always being brought out, and Franziska had to look at the snaps of Leo in his pram, or Leo on the beach – in fact, Leo all through his childhood, on excursions, with his stamp collection, and so on, right up to the time of his National Service.

Es war ein ganz anderer Leo, den sie durch die alte Frau kennenlernte, als den, mit dem sie verheiratet war, und wenn dann beide Frauen ihren Sherry tranken, sagte die alte Frau: Er war ein kompliziertes Kind, ein merkwürdiger Bub, es war eigentlich alles vorauszusehen, was dann aus ihm geworden ist.

Franziska hörte eine Zeitlang diese Beteuerungen mit Freude an, auch daß Leo so gut zu seiner Mutter war und ihr immer aufs Erdenklichste geholfen hatte, bis sie merkte, daß etwas nicht stimmte, und sie fand bestürzt heraus, was nicht stimmte: Die alte Frau fürchtete sich vor ihrem Sohn. Es fing damit an, daß die alte Frau – denn sie hielt das für eine geschickte Taktik, die Franziska niemals durchschauen würde, da sie ihren Mann blind bewunderte – manchmal hastig und beiläufig sagte: Aber bitte kein Wort zu Leo, Sie wissen ja, was für ein besorgter Mensch er ist, es könnte ihn aufregen, sagen Sie ihm bloß nicht, daß mit meinem Knie etwas nicht in Ordnung ist, es ist ja eine solche Kleinigkeit, aber er könnte sich aufregen.

Franziska kam zwar zum Bewußtsein, daß Leo sich doch überhaupt nie aufregte, jedenfalls nicht seiner Mutter wegen, und ihren Berichten daher abwesend zuhörte, aber sie unterdrückte ihr erstes Begreifen. Das von dem Knie hatte sie ihm leider schon erzählt, schwor aber der alten Frau, kein Wort davon zu sagen, denn Leo hatte sowieso ärgerlich reagiert und dann, sie begütigend, gemeint, wegen einer solchen Lappalie könne er wirklich nicht nach Hietzing fahren. Sag ihr doch – er gebrauchte rasch ein paar medizinische Ausdrücke –, sie soll sich das und das kaufen und möglichst wenig tun und herumgehen. Franziska kaufte widerspruchslos die Medikamente und behauptete in Hietzing, sie habe heimlich, ohne einen Namen zu nennen, mit einem Assistenzarzt ihres Mannes gesprochen, der ihr diesen Rat gegeben habe, aber wie sie, ohne Pflegerin,

The Leo whom she came to know through the old lady was an altogether different person from the man to whom she was married. When the two women had their sherry together, the old lady would say, 'Oh yes, he was a complex child all right, quite a remarkable boy, in fact, even then you could have predicted what kind of person he would become.'

In the beginning Franziska was glad to hear this praise, how Leo was always so kind to his mother, always ready to help her in every conceivable way. But gradually she came to see that something did not quite fit, and then all of a sudden it dawned on her what it was: the old lady was afraid of her son. It started off when the old lady (who obviously considered this to be a subtle approach, and one which Franziska would never see through in her blind admiration for her husband) would sometimes throw in casually: 'but please don't mention this to Leo, you know how many worries he has already, it might make him anxious. Don't say anything about my knee to him, it is only a tiny thing, but it might worry him.'

Franziska came to see, though, that Leo never worried about anything – at any rate, not about his mother, and for that reason only half listened to her reports. At first she would not face up to this fact. Unfortunately, she had already told him about his mother's knee by then, but she had sworn to the old lady that she would not breathe a word about it. In fact, it had annoyed Leo, though he had added, to placate her, that he obviously could not go all the way down to Hietzing just for a little thing like that. 'Just tell her,' he said (and here he threw off a couple of medical terms) 'she should get herself this and that and move about and do as little as possible.' Franziska did not argue, but went and bought the medicine, maintaining when she got to Hietzing that she had found an opportunity to speak to an assistant of her husband's, without mentioning the old lady by name, and that this was the advice he had given her. How she would succeed in keeping the old lady in bed,

die alte Frau im Bett halten sollte, das wußte sie auch nicht.
Und sie hatte keine Courage mehr, deswegen Leo zu fragen,
denn eine Pflegerin kostete Geld, und nun fand sie sich zwischen zwei Fronten. Auf der einen Seite wollte Frau Jordan
nichts wissen davon, auf der andren wollte Leo Jordan, wenn
auch aus ganz andren Gründen, einfach nicht zuhören. In der
Zeit des entzündeten Knies log sie ihren Mann einige Male an,
sie fuhr schnell nach Hietzing, um angeblich zum Friseur zu
gehen, räumte die kleine Wohnung auf und brachte alles
mögliche mit, sie kaufte ein Radio, und danach wurde ihr
allerdings unbehaglich, denn Leo würde diese Ausgabe bemerken, und so buchte sie schnell noch einmal alles um und
griff ihr weniges Geld auf dem Sparbuch an, von dem abge-
macht worden war, daß es ihre eiserne Reserve sein solle für
irgendeinen Notfall, der hoffentlich nie eintreten würde und
auch nur kleiner Notfall hätte sein dürfen, denn sie hatte mit
ihrem Bruder das Wenige geteilt, was nach dem Tod ihrer
ganzen Familie geblieben war, außer einer Keusche in Süd-
kärnten, die langsam verfiel. Sie rief dann einen praktischen
Arzt aus der Nebenstraße und ließ ihn eine Weile die alte Frau
behandeln, bezahlte wieder aus ihrer eisernen Reserve und was
viel wichtiger war – sie durfte dem Arzt nicht zu erkennen
geben, wer sie war und wer die alte Frau war, denn es hätte
Leos Ruf nur geschadet, und Leos Ruf lag auch im Interesse
von Franziska, aber viel selbstloser dachte die alte Frau, denn
sie konnte von ihrem berühmten Sohn nicht noch verlangen,
daß er sich ihr Knie ansah. Einen Stock hatte sie schon früher
benutzt, aber nach der Kniegeschichte brauchte sie den Stock
wirklich, und darum fuhr Franziska sie manchmal in die Stadt.
Es was etwas mühsam, mit der alten Frau einkaufen zu gehen,
sie brauchte einmal nur einen Kamm, aber es gab keine
Kämme mehr wie «zu ihrer Zeit», und wenn die alte Frau auch

however, without the help of a nurse, she had no idea. And she did not have the courage to consult Leo, for a nurse would be expensive. She thus found herself caught between two stools. On the one hand the old lady would not let her do anything about it, and on the other – though for very different reasons – Leo Jordan simply would not take any notice. During this period, when the old lady was suffering from her inflamed knee, Franziska sometimes had to deceive her husband. Ostensibly on a visit to her hairdresser, she would hurry down to Hietzing and clean up the small flat. She would take with her anything she could, and she also bought a radio, though this caused her some worry for it was an expense Leo was quite likely to notice. So she quickly doctored her accounts and drew this money out of the small reserve that had been set aside for an emergency which hopefully would never occur. In any case, there was only sufficient for a minor emergency, since she had already shared with her brother the small inheritance that had come to them after the death of the rest of her family. All that was left, in fact, was a small cottage in South Kärnten and this was slowly going to ruin. Franziska put the old lady in the care of a doctor from the neighbourhood. She paid for this once again out of her reserve, and moreover had to be careful not to let the doctor know who she and the old lady were, for this could only have damaged Leo's reputation, which would not have been in her own interest. But the old lady's motivation was much less personal: it would not have been right, she thought, to have asked her famous son to look at her knee. In the past she had used a walking stick from time to time, but after she had her knee trouble she really needed it badly. For this reason Franziska would sometimes drive her into town. Shopping with the old lady was a rather tiresome business. On one occasion she wanted to buy a comb, but it was no longer possible to buy a comb like the combs people used to have 'in the old days'.

höflich war, würdevoll in dem Geschäft stand, so verärgerte sie doch die kleine Verkäuferin, indem sie mißtrauisch auf die Preise sah und sich nicht enthalten konnte, Franziska laut zuzuflüstern, daß das räuberische Preise seien, daß sie besser woanders hingingen. Die Verkäuferin sagte frech, da sie nicht wissen konnte, wie groß dieses Problem des Kammkaufens für die alte Frau war, zu andren Preisen gebe es nichts und nirgendwo. Franziska verhandelte verlegen mit der Mutter, sie nahm den Kamm, der gefallen hatte, der aber der alten Frau ein Vermögen zu kosten schien, und bezahlte ihn rasch, sie sagte: Er ist einfach schon ein Weihnachtsgeschenk von uns, ein Vorausgeschenk. Die Preise sind jetzt wirklich überall horrend gestiegen. Die alte Frau sagte kein Wort, sie fühlte ihre Niederlage, aber wenn es doch räuberische Preise waren und früher so ein Kamm zwei Schilling gekostet hatte, heute aber sechzig, dann gab es für sie nicht mehr viel zu verstehen in dieser Welt.

Nach der Zeit, in der das Thema «guter Sohn» erschöpft war, lenkte Franziska die Unterhaltung öfter auf die alte Frau selbst, denn sie wußte nur, daß Leos Vater früh gestorben war, an einem Infarkt oder Schlaganfall, ganz plötzlich, auf einer Treppe, und das mußte lange her sein, denn wenn man nachrechnete, dann war diese Frau schon fast seit fünfzig Jahren Witwe, zuerst noch Jahre beschäftigt, ihr einziges Kind großzuziehen, und dann eine alte Frau, um die sich niemand mehr kümmerte. Von ihrer Ehe sprach sie nie, sondern nur im Zusammenhang mit Leo, der eben ein ganz schweres Leben gehabt hatte, ohne Vater, und sie stellte, besessen von Leo, keinen Bezug her zu Franziska, die beide Eltern früh verloren hatte, denn schwer konnte es nur ihr Sohn gehabt haben, und heraus kam dann eigentlich, daß er es so schwer nicht gehabt hatte, weil ein entfernter Vetter ihm dann das Studium bezahlt

Standing there in the shop, courteous and dignified as she was, the old lady succeeded nevertheless in irritating the little shop assistant by looking askance at the prices, then whispering loudly to Franziska that such prices were nothing short of 'daylight robbery', and that they should go and look somewhere else. The shop assistant did not appreciate how big a problem this was for the old lady and replied impertinently that you could not get such a comb at a lower price anywhere else. Franziska was embarrassed by the old lady's behaviour. She took the comb which had caught her eye but seemed to the old lady to cost a fortune, and quickly paid for it, saying: 'it is a Christmas present from us – just a little present in advance. It is true that prices everywhere have just rocketed nowadays.' Conscious of her defeat, the old lady said nothing, but she thought to herself: when you consider that a comb used to cost just a few pence and now you have to pay five shillings for it, well, it's still daylight robbery. And she felt she really could not understand anything any more.

There came a time, too, when they ran out of things to say about her 'fine son'. Then Franziska would steer the conversation towards the old lady herself. All she knew about her was that Leo's father had died early on, as the result of a heart-attack or a stroke, quite suddenly, as he was coming upstairs. That must have been a long while ago, for the old lady had been a widow now for a good fifty years – first as a young woman preoccupied with bringing up her only child, and then later as an old lady whom no one cared about. She would never talk about her marriage, or at any rate only in so far as it related to Leo, who had had, in her view, a hard time without a father. In her obsession with Leo she failed to consider Franziska, who had in fact lost both parents at an early age, for to her mind it was only her son who could have had a hard time. It emerged, in fact, from all this, that he had not had such a difficult time after all, as a distant cousin had paid for his

hatte, dieser Johannes, von dem Franziska noch wenig gehört hatte, nur ein paar abfällige, kritische Sätze über diesen Verwandten, der im Geld schwimme und das Leben eines ewigen Müßiggängers führe, jetzt eines älteren, mit allen Lächerlichkeiten, der sich ein wenig mit Kunst beschäftige, chinesische Lackarbeiten sammle, einer dieser Schmarotzer eben, wie sie in jeder Familie vorkommen. Daß er homosexuell war, wußte Franziska auch, und war nur etwas scharf verwundert, daß jemand wie Leo, der schon durch seinen Beruf angehalten war, Homosexualität und noch ganz andere Phänomene neutral und wissenschaftlich zu sehen, sich über diesen Vetter ausließ, als hätte er sich schuldhaft Kunstgegenstände, Homosexualität und auch noch ererbtes Geld zugezogen, aber damals bewunderte Franziska ihren Mann noch so sehr, um mehr als irritiert und verletzt zu sein. Auch hörte sie erleichtert von der alten Frau, als auf diese schweren Zeiten die Rede kam, daß Leo nämlich von einer unermeßlichen Dankbarkeit war und diesem Johannes sehr geholfen hatte, der in vielen persönlichen Schwierigkeiten steckte, über die man besser nicht sprach. Die alte Frau zögerte und sagte ermutigt, weil sie immerhin der Frau eines Psychiaters gegenübersaß: Sie müssen nämlich wissen, der Johannes ist sexuell.

Franziska beherrschte sich und unterdrückte ein Lachen, es war sicher die größte Kühnheit, zu der sich die alte Frau aufgerafft hatte seit Jahren, aber mit Franziska wurde sie immer offener und sie erzählte, wie Johannes sicher oft einen Rat bekommen hätte von Leo und selbstverständlich, ohne zahlen zu müssen, aber mit Johannes sei es eben hoffnungslos, und wenn jemand keinen guten Willen hatte, sich zu ändern, war das begreiflich, daß jemand wie Leo vor den Kopf gestoßen war, denn es solle ja alles weitergehen mit Johannes, wie eh und je. Franziska übersetzte sich vorsichtig diese naive Erzählung in die Wirklichkeit, verstand immer weniger, warum Leo so

schooling. This was Johannes, about whom Franziska had heard very little up to that point. All that she had registered were one or two derogatory comments, to the effect that he was rolling in money and led an idle life. He was ageing a bit now, and becoming all the more ridiculous, dabbling in art and collecting Chinese lacquerwork – one of those good-for-nothings that every family throws up from time to time. Franziska knew, too, that he was a homosexual, but it hurt her to see how Leo – who for professional reasons alone should have been obliged to view homosexuality and such phenomena in an unbiased, scientific light – would go to town in criticizing this cousin, as if he personally was to blame for his art collection, his homosexuality and even the money he had inherited. At that time, though, Franziska was too overawed by her husband to feel more than simply irritated or pained by such outbursts. And when the conversation turned to these difficult times, she was relieved to hear from the old lady of Leo's great capacity for gratitude, and the fact that he had given this cousin of his a great deal of help at a time when he had many personal problems which were better left unmentioned. The old lady would hesitate at this point, and then, remembering that after all, she was talking to the wife of a psychiatrist, she would pluck up courage and add: 'Well, I really ought to tell you that Johannes is sexual.'

Franziska had to control herself to avoid laughing, as this was certainly the boldest statement the old lady had come out with for many years. Indeed, she was becoming more open with Franziska all the time. She told her how she was sure Johannes had often consulted Leo (naturally, without paying). But Johannes was a hopeless case, and if a person did not have the will to change, well, it was understandable how he could have offended someone like Leo – for there was no changing Johannes, he would never mend his ways. Franziska cautiously translated this naïve account into real terms, but only suc-

abfällig und boshaft über den Vetter sprach, und sie kam damals nicht auf den naheliegenden Grund, daß Leo ungern erinnert sein wollte an eine Verpflichtung, wie er ungern an seine Mutter und seine früheren Frauen erinnert sein wollte, die eine einzige Konspiration von Gläubigern für ihn darstellten, denen er nur entkam, wenn er sie herabsetzte vor sich und anderen, denn so ähnlich gingen ja auch seine Reden über seine erste Frau, die ein Ausbund an Teufelei und Unverständnis und Niedertracht gewesen sein mußte, was sich bei der Scheidung erst ganz herausstellte, als ihr nobler Herr Vater ihr einen Anwalt genommen hatte und einen Teil des Gelds sicherstellen wollte für das Kind, Geld, das sie ihm gegeben hatte in den zweiten schwierigen Zeiten als junger Arzt. Es war eine für Franziska erschreckend hohe Summe, aber wie sie hörte, war von der «Baronin», wie Leo sie immer ironisch nannte, nichts anderes zu erwarten gewesen, denn diese Familie hatte ihn ja immerzu wie einen Emporkömmling behandelt, ohne die geringste Ahnung zu haben, wen sie vor sich hatte, und auch daß die «Baronin» danach nie mehr heiratete, sondern völlig zurückgezogen lebte, vermerkte er belustigt, denn außer ihm hätte sich kein Trottel gefunden, jung und dumm und arm wie er damals war, der dieses preziöse Fräulein geheiratet hätte. Von seiner Arbeit habe sie nichts, einfach nichts verstanden, und was die Abmachungen des Sohnes wegen betraf, so verhielt sie sich zwar fair, sie schickte ihn regelmäßig, und lehrte den Sohn, seinen Vater zu achten, aber natürlich nur, um aller Welt zu beweisen, wie nobel sie war, aus keinem anderen Grund.

Der dornenreiche, leidvolle Aufstieg eines genialen Arztes war schon Franziskas Religion zu der Zeit, und immer wieder

ceeded in understanding even less why it was that Leo spoke so badly of his cousin. On this occasion she did not get any closer to the real reason – that Leo did not like being reminded of an obligation – just as he did not like being reminded of his mother or the other women in his past life, whom he saw as a collective conspiracy of creditors, from whom he could only escape by denigrating them in his own eyes and in front of others. This was precisely the case whenever he referred to his first wife, who must have been a dreadful mixture of stupidity, mischief and deceit, though this did not fully emerge until they were divorced. Her aristocratic father had engaged a lawyer on her behalf in order to secure a portion of her money for her child – the same money that she had made over to him in the second difficult stage of his career when he was making his way as a young doctor. To Franziska it seemed an appallingly large amount of money, but Leo explained that you could not have expected any other kind of behaviour from someone like the 'baroness' (as he always referred to her sarcastically), for her family had always treated him like an upstart without having the faintest idea of the kind of person he was. He was pleased to observe, too, that, after this experience, the 'baroness' had never married again, but lived like a hermit without any social contacts, for, apart from himself – young and innocent and indigent as he had been at the time – there would have been nobody else stupid enough to have married this young lady with all her fine airs. She had totally failed to understand anything at all about his work. So far as the arrangements regarding their son were concerned, she had, it was true, be-haved quite correctly, regularly sending him to visit his father and teaching him to respect him. But evidently all this was only in order to impress upon the world what a fine person she was, and not for any better reason.

During this period Franziska had almost made a religion out of her husband's thorny, painful career and his emergence as a

hielt sie sich vor, wie er, unter unsäglichen Mühen und trotz
dem Hindernis dieser furchtbaren Ehe, seinen Weg nach oben
gemacht hatte. Auch die Last, die seine Mutter doch darstellte,
finanziell und moralisch, war für ihn keine leichte, und die
wenigstens konnte Franziska ihm abnehmen. Obwohl es ihr
sonst vielleicht nicht gerade in den Sinn gekommen wäre, ihre
freien Stunden mit einer alten Frau zu verbringen, wurden die,
im Gedanken an Leo, zu etwas besonderem, zu einer Handrei-
chung, einem Liebesbeweis für ihn, damit er seinen Kopf ganz
frei hatte für die Arbeit.

Leo war eben auch zu gut zu ihr, er sagte ihr, das sei übertrieben, wie sie sich um seine Mutter kümmere, ein Anruf hie
und da genüge auch. Seit ein paar Jahren hatte die alte Frau ein
Telefon, das sie aber mehr fürchtete als liebte, denn sie telefonierte nicht gerne und schrie immer zu sehr hinein und hörte
schlecht, was der andere sagte, außerdem kostete das Telefon
zuviel, aber das dürfe Franziska Leo ja nicht sagen. Die alte
Frau, von Franziska angeregt und vor einem zweiten Glas
Sherry, fing einmal doch an, von früheren Zeiten zu sprechen,
von den ganz frühen, und es stellte sich heraus, daß sie aus
keiner Akademikerfamilie war, ihr Vater war Handschuh- und
Sockenstricker in einer kleinen Fabrik in Niederösterreich
gewesen, und sie war das älteste von acht Kindern, aber dann
hatte sie trotzdem eine wunderbare Zeit gehabt, als sie in
Stellung ging, denn sie kam zu einer griechischen Familie, zu
immens reichen Leuten, die einen kleinen Buben hatten, das
schönste Kind, das sie je gesehen hatte, und sie wurde seine
Gouvernante, denn Gouvernante war eine sehr gute Stellung,
nichts Erniedrigendes, und die junge Frau des Griechen hatte
ja Dienstboten genug, oh ja, sie hatte schon ein besonderes
Glück gehabt, denn es war damals schwierig gewesen, eine so

brilliantly gifted doctor, and she was always reminding herself of how he had risen in his profession by dint of immeasurable exertions and in spite of the obstacles put in his path by this disastrous marriage. The responsibility for his mother, both financially and morally, weighed heavily on him, and Franziska felt that this burden at least was one of which she could relieve him. Although, under other circumstances, she would not exactly have chosen to spend her free hours with an old lady, she did so for Leo's sake, and these hours came to have a special meaning for her: they became a kind of gift, a proof of her love for him, which would enable him to concentrate entirely on his work.

In point of fact, Leo was almost too good to her, saying that she was really overdoing it to bother so much about his mother – a telephone call now and again ought surely to be enough. For a couple of years the old lady had had a telephone, but she was more afraid than fond of it. She did not like using it, as she always shouted too loudly into the speaker, and then could never make out what the other person was saying. Moreover, it was too expensive – though of course Franziska should not mention that to Leo. On one occasion, stimulated by the conversation with Franziska, and after her second glass of sherry, she began to speak about the past, going right back to her youth. Franziska learnt that she did not come from an academic family at all, but that her father had worked in a small factory making gloves and stockings in Lower Austria, and that she was the eldest of eight children. But she had been wonderfully happy when she took her first paid position. She had gone to live with a Greek family, immensely wealthy people, who had a small boy – the most beautiful child she had ever seen. She had become his governess, which was a very good position to have, nothing lowering about it at all. The young wife of the family had plenty of servants. Yes, indeed, she had certainly been very lucky, for at that time it had been

gute Stellung zu finden. Kiki hatte das Kind geheißen. Kiki wurde es jedenfalls damals von allen genannt. Wenn die alte Frau immer häufiger von Kiki zu sprechen anfing und jedes Detail ihr einfiel, was Kiki gesagt hatte, wie drollig und zärtlich er war, welche Spaziergänge sie miteinander gemacht hatten, kam ein Glanz in ihre Augen, der niemals darin war, wenn sie von ihrem eigenen Kind sprach. Kiki war einfach ein kleiner Engel gewesen ohne Unarten, betonte sie, ohne alle Unarten, und die Trennung mußte so furchtbar gewesen sein, Kiki hatte man verheimlicht, daß das Fräulein wegging, und sie hatte die ganze Nacht geweint, und Jahre später hatte sie noch einmal versucht, herauszufinden, was aus der Familie geworden war, einmal hieß es, sie seien auf Reisen, dann wieder in Griechenland, und nun wußte sie überhaupt nicht, was aus Kiki geworden war, der jetzt über sechzig Jahre alt sein mußte, ja, über sechzig, sagte sie gedankenvoll, und gehen hatte sie müssen, weil die Griechen damals eine erste lange Reise machen mußten und sie nicht mitnehmen konnten, und sie hatte zum Abschied ein wunderbares Geschenk bekommen von der jungen Frau. Die alte Frau stand auf und kramte in einer Kassette, sie zeigte ihr die Brosche von Kikis Mutter, eine echte, mit Brillanten, aber sie fragte sich noch heute, ob man sie nicht hatte gehen lassen, weil die junge Frau gemerkt hatte, daß Kiki mehr an ihr hing als an seiner Mutter, verstehen könnte sie es schon, aber es sei der schwerste Schlag gewesen, und sie sei nie ganz darüber hinweggekommen. Franziska schaute nachdenklich die Brosche an, die vielleicht wirklich sehr wertvoll war, sie hatte aber keine Ahnung von Schmuck, nur die erste Ahnung, daß dieser Kiki der alten Frau mehr bedeutet haben mußte als Leo. Denn sie zögerte oft, etwas von Leos Kinderzeit zu erzählen, oder sie fing an, brach erschreckt ab und sagte rasch: Es waren eben Kindereien, Buben sind eben so schwer aufzuziehen, und absichtlich hat er es nicht

difficult to find such a good position. The boy had been called Kiki. Or at any rate, Kiki was what everyone called him. The old lady would talk more and more about Kiki, recalling in every detail what he had said, how sweet and affectionate he had been, and the walks they had taken together. As she went back over those times her eyes would sparkle in a way that they never did when she spoke of her own child. Kiki had been, quite simply, a little angel, she insisted, without a trace of malice in him, and it must have been dreadful when they had to part. They had kept it a secret from Kiki that his governess was leaving, and she herself had wept the whole night through. Years later she had tried to find out what had become of the family. She had heard at first that they were travelling, later that they were back in Greece, then she had lost all track of what had happened to Kiki. By now he must be over sixty, she reflected. She had had to leave them at that time because they were about to set off on their first long journey and they could not take her with them. When she left she had been given a wonderful present by the young mother. The old lady stood up and rummaged around in a little box, taking out from it the brooch she had been given by Kiki's mother. It was a very fine one, inset with diamonds. Even today, though, she still wondered whether she had not been dismissed because the young woman had realized that Kiki had grown fonder of her than of his own mother. She could understand that, of course, but it had been a bitter blow and she had never quite got over it. Franziska looked thoughtfully at the brooch, which was perhaps a really valuable one, but then she did not know anything about jewellery. What she did begin to see, though, was that this Kiki must have meant more to the old lady than Leo. For she would often hesitate before saying something about Leo's childhood, or she would start off and then suddenly check herself, adding quickly, 'Well, anyhow, those were just children's tricks, boys are so hard to bring up, and he did not

getan, aber damals hatte er eben eine so schwierige Zeit und ich hatte schon meine liebe Not, aber man bekommt das ja alles tausendfach zurück, wenn ein Kind groß ist und dann seinen Weg macht und so berühmt wird, er war eigentlich mehr seinem Vater ähnlich als mir, wissen Sie.

Franziska gab behutsam die Brosche zurück, und die alte Frau erschrak wieder. Bitte, Franziska, aber sagen Sie nur ja kein Wort zu Leo, wegen der Brosche, er weiß nichts davon, und es könnte ihn verärgern, aber ich habe so meine Pläne, denn wenn ich krank werde, dann könnte ich sie verkaufen, damit ich ihm nicht noch mehr zur Last fallen muß. Franziska umarmte die alte Frau furchtsam und heftig. Das dürfen Sie niemals tun, versprechen Sie's mir, daß Sie diesen Schmuck nie verkaufen. Sie fallen uns doch nicht zur Last!

Auf der Heimfahrt machte sie Umwege kreuz und quer, denn es war eine solche Turbulenz in ihr, diese arme Frau wollte doch wohl nicht diese Brosche verkaufen, während sie und Leo ziemlich viel Geld ausgaben, reisten, Gäste hatten, und sie überlegte immerzu, was sie eigentlich Leo sagen müsse, aber etwas warnte sie, es war ein erster leiser Alarm in ihr, denn in irgend etwas, auch wenn sie schrullig war und übertrieb, mußte die alte Frau recht haben, und deswegen sagte sie dann doch kein Wort zuhause, nur fröhlich, daß es der Mutter ausgezeichnet gehe. Vor der Reise zu einem Kongreß nach London schloß sie aber heimlich mit einer Garage, die Autos vermietete und Taxis privat auf Bestellung schickte, einen Vertrag, den sie anzahlte, und zu der alten Frau sagte sie vor der Reise: Uns ist da so eine Idee gekommen, weil Sie nicht allein zu weit gehen sollten; Sie rufen jetzt jedesmal ein Taxi, es kostet so gut wie nichts, es ist einfach eine Gefälligkeit von einem alten Patienten, aber reden Sie nicht darüber und vor allem nicht mit Leo, Sie kennen ihn ja, er mag nicht, daß Sie sich bedanken und so, und Sie fahren in die Stadt, wenn Sie

do it intentionally, but he had such a hard time then, and I had my own problems too. But one reaps the rewards a thousand times over once a child has grown up, and has been successful and become famous. You see, he took more after his father than after me.'

Franziska gave her back the brooch gingerly, which made the old lady shudder once again. 'Please, Franziska,' she said, 'don't mention that brooch to Leo, he does not know anything about it, and it might annoy him. I have my own plans, you see. If I became ill, then I could sell it, so I would not be even more of a burden on him.' Franziska was quite startled, and gave the old lady a vigorous hug. 'You mustn't ever do that, please promise me that you won't ever sell this jewellery. You are not a burden for us at all!'

On her way back home she went wrong several times, for she was in quite a state. It was shameful for this poor old lady to consider selling her brooch, while she and Leo had plenty of money to spend, and could travel when they wanted, entertain guests, and so on. She tried to work out what she should say to Leo. Eccentric though the old lady was, and prone to exaggerate, Franziska had a kind of premonition – as if an alarm had been triggered off in her – that there was an element of truth in what she said. She therefore made no mention of it when she got home, only commenting cheerfully that the old lady was absolutely fine. But before setting off for a conference in London she made a secret arrangement on her own account with a garage which hired out cars and provided chauffeur-driven vehicles on request. She said to the old lady before the journey, 'We've had an idea, as we've been thinking that it's not a good thing for you to go around too much by yourself. Whenever you need one, you can call a taxi – it costs next to nothing – it's a favour in fact from a former patient of Leo's. But don't refer to it, especially not in front of Leo – you know how he is, he doesn't like you to be thanking

etwas brauchen und lassen den Wagen warten und lassen sich nur von Herrn Pineider fahren, dem jungen. Der weiß übrigens nicht, daß sein Vater ein Patient von Leo war, das fällt unter die ärztliche Schweigepflicht, wissen Sie, ich komme gerade von ihm, und Sie versprechen mir, Leo zuliebe, daß Sie den Wagen nehmen, es beruhigt uns einfach. In der ersten Zeit machte die alte Frau wenig Gebrauch von diesem Wagen, und Franziska schimpfte sie aus, als sie aus England zurückkam, denn mit dem Bein ging es wieder schlechter und die alte Frau hatte natürlich alle Einkäufe zu Fuß gemacht und war sogar einmal mit der Straßenbahn in die Innere Stadt gefahren, weil man in Hietzing fast nichts bekam, und Franziska sagte energisch wie zu einem widerspenstischen Kind, das dürfe einfach nicht mehr vorkommen.

Auch die Zeit der Gespräche über Kiki, das Leben einer jungen Gouvernante im Wien vor dem ersten Weltkrieg und vor der Heirat gingen vorüber, und manchmal erzählte auch nur Franziska, besonders wenn sie von einer Reise zurückgekommen war mit Leo, etwa was für einen großartigen Vortrag Leo gehalten hatte auf dem Kongreß, und daß er ihr jetzt diesen Sonderdruck für die Mutter mitgegeben habe. Die alte Frau las mühsam und angestrengt den Titel: «Die Bedeutung endogener und exogener Faktoren beim Zustandekommen von paranoiden und depressiv gefärbten Psychosen bei ehemaligen Konzentrationslagerhäftlingen und Flüchtlingen.» Franziska versicherte, es sei nur eine kleine Vorarbeit für eine viel größere, an der er arbeite, und sie dürfe jetzt auch schon mitarbeiten, es werde wahrscheinlich das bedeutendste und erste wichtige Buch auf diesem Gebiet sein. Von einer noch unabsehbaren Bedeutung.

Die alte Frau war merkwürdig stumm, sie verstand sicher nicht die Tragweite dieser Arbeiten, vielleicht überhaupt nicht,

him for things. Anyhow, go into town whenever you need something, and have the car wait for you. And only ask for Mr Pineider as your driver, the younger one, I mean. He doesn't know that his father was once a patient of Leo's. Professional discretion, you see. I have just been with him now, as it happens. Promise me now, for Leo's sake, that you will use the car – we shall feel so much better if you do.' To begin with, the old lady used the car very little. Franziska upbraided her over it when she returned from England, for her leg was getting worse again, and of course the old lady had been doing all her shopping on foot. She had even taken the tram into the centre on one occasion, because you could hardly get anything you wanted in Hietzing. Franziska had to address her quite sharply, like a naughty child, to make it clear that such a thing should not happen again under any circumstances.

In course of time she also stopped talking about Kiki and her life as a young governess in Vienna before the First World War and before she was married. Sometimes it was only Franziska who did the talking, especially on those occasions when she had just returned from a trip with Leo, and she would go on about the splendid paper Leo had read at the conference, a special copy of which he had given to her to give to his mother. The old lady read the title of it laboriously: 'The significance of endogenous and exogenous factors in the genesis of psychosis of the paranoid and depressive type in former inmates of concentration camps and refugees ...' Franziska assured her that this represented only the preliminary stage of a much more extensive work on which he was now engaged and in which she, too, was now allowed to share. It would probably prove to be the first definitive book on this subject – of an importance beyond anything she could imagine.

The old lady was unusually silent. Evidently, she did not understand the scope of his work. Perhaps she had no idea at

was ihr Sohn tat. Dann sagte sie überraschend: Wenn er sich nur nicht zu viele Feinde damit macht, hier in Wien, und dann ist da noch etwas ...

Franziska erregte sich: Aber das wäre sogar sehr gut, es ist auch eine Provokation, und Leo fürchtet niemand, denn für ihn ist das die einzig wichtige Aufgabe, die noch weit über ihre wissenschaftliche Bedeutung hinausgeht.

Ja, natürlich, sagte die alte Frau schnell, und er weiß sich zu verteidigen, und Feinde hat man überhaupt, wenn man berühmt ist. Ich habe nur an Johannes gedacht, es ist aber schon so lange her. Wissen Sie, daß er eineinhalb Jahre, vor dem Kriegsende, im KZ war? Franziska war überrascht, sie hatte es nicht gewußt, verstand dann aber den Zusammenhang nicht. Die alte Frau wollte nicht weiterreden und tat es dann doch. Für Leo war es schon eine gewisse Gefahr, damals, einen Verwandten zu haben, der, nun Sie verstehen schon. Ja, natürlich, sagte Franziska. Sie blieb aber etwas verstört, denn die alte Frau hatte manchmal eine so umständliche Art, Dinge zu sagen und doch nicht zu sagen, und sie fand sich dann nicht zurecht, obwohl sie auf einmal ganz von Stolz erfüllt war, daß jemand aus Leos Familie etwas so Furchtbares durchgemacht hatte, und daß Leo, in seiner taktvollen bescheidenen Weise, ihr nie etwas darüber gesagt hatte, auch nicht in welcher Gefahr er sich, als junger Arzt, befunden haben mußte. An diesem Nachmittag wollte die alte Frau nicht mehr weitersprechen, sondern sagte, zusammenhanglos: Hören Sie das auch?

Was?

Die Hunde, sagte die alte Frau. Früher hat es nie so viele Hunde gegeben in Hietzing, ich habe wieder welche bellen gehört, und nachts bellen sie auch. Die Frau Schönthal nebenan hat jetzt einen Pudel. Der bellt aber wenig, er ist ein sehr lieber Hund, ich treffe sie fast jeden Tag beim Einkaufen, aber wir grüßen einander nur, der Mann ist nicht Akademiker.

all what her son was doing. Then all of a sudden she came out with, 'If only it does not make him too many enemies, here in Vienna. And then there is another thing . . .'

Franziska became enthusiastic: 'But that would even be a good thing – it would be a kind of challenge – and Leo isn't afraid of anybody. His work is the only thing that matters, and it means far more to him than its specific contribution to science.' 'Of course, of course,' the old lady said quickly. 'And he knows how to look after himself. When you are famous you cannot help having a few enemies. I was only thinking of Johannes – but then that was all such a long time ago. Did you know that he spent eighteen months in a concentration camp before the end of the War?' This was a surprise for Franziska, but she did not see the connection. The old lady did not want to go on, but she did all the same. 'For Leo,' she said, 'there was an element of danger in having a relative who . . . well, you see what I mean.' 'Yes, of course,' Franziska said. It disturbed her, though, for the old lady sometimes had such a roundabout way of putting things – or of not putting them – and she was not quite sure how to see it all. She felt very proud that a member of Leo's family should have undergone such a terrible experience, and also that Leo, in his typically discreet and modest way, had never referred to it, nor to the danger in which he himself must have been at the time, when he was a young doctor. On that particular afternoon, the old lady would not speak about it any more, but suddenly observed to Franziska, 'Can you hear it, too?'

'Hear what?'

'Dogs,' said the old lady. 'There never used to be so many dogs in Hietzing. But just then I heard them barking again. They bark at night too. Mrs Schönthal next door has a poodle. He does not bark much though, he is a very well-behaved dog. I usually meet them when I go shopping. But we only exchange greetings – after all, her husband isn't an academic.'

Franziska mußte rasch heimfahren in die Stadt, und diesmal wollte sie Leo fragen, ob das etwas zu bedeuten habe, daß seine Mutter auf einmal von Hunden sprach, ob es ein bedenkliches Symptom war, es konnte mit dem Alter zusammenhängen. Aufgefallen war ihr auch, daß die alte Frau sich irgendwann einmal aufgeregt hatte, wegen zehn Schilling, die auf dem Tisch gelegen waren, dann nicht mehr da waren, als die Frau Agnes weggegangen war, und diese Erregung wegen der zehn Schilling, die fehlten, was sie sich aber gewiß nur einbildete, das waren doch Anzeichen von einem Prozeß, denn die Bedienerin konnte sie unmöglich genommen haben, sie war, was man, in manchen Kreisen, den besseren, eine kreuzbrave Frau nennt, die mehr aus Mitleid kam als des Geldes wegen, das sie überhaupt nicht brauchte, es war eine Gefälligkeit, weiter nichts. Auch die hilflosen Geschenke der alten Frau Jordan, eine abgeschabte uralte Handtasche oder sonst ein unnützer Gegenstand hätten diese Frau Agnes kaum veranlaßt, zu kommen, denn daß es weder von der Alten noch von ihrem Sohn etwas zu erwarten gab für sie, das hatte sie längst begriffen, und von Franziskas eifervollen Gedanken, die Lage zu verbessern, wußte sie nichts, und Franziska hatte deswegen der alten Frau gut zugeredet wie einem Kind, denn sie wollte nicht, daß die kostbare Hilfe verlorenging, wegen einer Altersstörrischkeit und einem Verdacht, der haltlos war.

Sie fand die alte Frau immer öfter am Fenster, wenn sie kam, und sie saßen nicht mehr beisammen, wenn Franziska kam, um den Sherry zu trinken und kleines Gebäck zu knabbern, und es ging also weiter mit diesen Hunden, während zugleich doch ihre Schwerhörigkeit zuzunehmen begann, und Franziska war ratlos, denn es mußte doch etwas geschehen, und Leo, dem sie zwar alles fernhielt, würde eines Tages auch nicht darum herumkommen, sich mit seiner Mutter beschäftigen zu müssen. Nur fing gerade damals etwas an, kompliziert zwischen Leo und ihr zu werden, und sie entdeckte, daß er sie

Franziska hurried home. She wanted to ask Leo if there was anything significant in the fact that his mother had suddenly started talking about dogs. Was it a serious symptom? Did it perhaps have something to do with old age? She had also noticed that the old lady had got in quite a state on one occasion describing an incident when, according to her, she had left a few shillings lying on the table, and these had suddenly vanished after her cleaning lady Agnes had left the house. She had obviously imagined the whole thing, but this fuss over the few shillings was presumably symptomatic of a certain condition. Agnes would never have taken the money. She was what in well-to-do circles would be called 'a treasure', and only came at all out of pity and kindness, certainly not for the money, which she did not need. 'Old' Mrs Jordan would give her pathetic little presents sometimes, such as an old, worn-out handbag or some other useless object, but these certainly would not have been sufficient to induce her to come. Indeed, she had long since realized that she would not get anything out of either the old lady or her son. She also knew nothing about Franziska's efforts to improve the situation. Franziska, therefore, spoke to the old lady soothingly, like a child, for she was anxious not to lose this valuable source of help simply because of her obstinacy and misplaced suspicions.

When Franziska came to see her now, she was very likely to find her seated at the window. They no longer had their sherry and pastries together. The old lady kept on talking about the dogs. Her hearing was steadily deteriorating and Franziska was at a loss to know what to do – something obviously had to be done. She kept this from Leo, but she knew the day would come when he would no longer be able to avoid involving himself with his mother's problems. Franziska's own relationship with Leo was becoming more difficult at this time. She had become so overawed by her husband, she now realized, that she was actually afraid of him. On one occasion,

schon dermaßen eingeschüchtert hatte, daß sie sich fürchtete
vor ihm, aber wenigstens einmal, in einem Anfall von ihrem
alten Mut, ihre unbegreifliche Furcht überwindend, schlug sie
beim Abendessen vor: Warum nehmen wir denn die Mutter
nicht zu uns, wir haben doch Platz, und dann wäre doch unsere Rosi immer bei ihr und du brauchtest dir nie Sorgen zu
machen, außerdem ist sie so still und ohne Bedürfnisse, sie
würde dich niemals stören und mich schon gar nicht, ich sage
es deinetwegen, weil ich weiß, welche Sorgen du dir machst.
Leo, der an diesem Abend bei guter Laune war und sich über
etwas heimlich freute, und sie erriet nur nicht worüber, aber
sie nutzte die Gelegenheit, antwortete lachend: Was für eine
Idee, du hast überhaupt kein Gefühl für die Situation, mein
Schatz, alte Leute darf man nicht mehr verpflanzen, es würde
sie nur bedrücken, und sie braucht ihre Freiheit, sie ist eine
starke Frau, die Jahrzehnte allein gelebt hat, und wie ich sie
kenne, kennst du sie wohl kaum, sie würde ja vor Angst um-
kommen hier, schon der Leute wegen, die zu uns kommen,
und dann womöglich stundenlang Skrupel haben, auch nur
ins Bad zu gehen, vor Ängstlichkeit, daß einer von uns auch
ins Bad wollen könnte. Aber, Franziskalein, bitte, nicht so ein
Gesicht, ich finde deine Anwandlung rührend und lobenswert,
aber du würdest sie glatt damit umbringen, mit deiner wunder-
baren Idee. Nur, glaub mir, über diese Dinge weiß ich eben
doch besser Bescheid.

Aber diese Sache mit den Hunden ... ? Franziska fing zu
stottern an, denn sie hatte davon gar nicht sprechen wollen und
hätte gern sofort jedes Wort zurückgenommen. Sie war nicht
mehr fähig, ihre Besorgnis richtig auszudrücken.

Was, fragte ihr Mann, völlig verändert, will sie noch immer
einen Köter? Ich verstehe nicht, antwortete Franziska. Wieso
sollte sie – du meinst doch nicht, daß sie einen Hund haben
will?

however, she recovered enough of her old self to overcome this irrational fear, and in the course of dinner suggested to him: 'Why don't we ask your mother to come and live with us? We have got enough room for her, and Rosie would always be near her, so you would not have any worries. Anyway, she is so quiet, and has so few needs, she would never bother you. She certainly would not bother me at all. I'm only suggesting it for your sake, as I know she's on your mind.' On this particular evening Leo was in a good mood and was secretly very pleased about something – what it was she could not guess, but it gave her an opportunity to make her point. He laughed, and replied: 'What an idea! My dear, you just don't appreciate the situation at all. You cannot move old people around like that, it has an upsetting effect on them. My mother needs her freedom. She is a strong character and she has lived on her own for so many years. I know her far better than you can, and I know she would positively die of anxiety if we brought her here – if only because of all the people who come and see us. She would probably agonize for hours over whether or not to use the bathroom, imagining that one of us might want to use it at the same time. My dear Franziska, please don't make a face like that, I'm very touched by this impulse of yours, I think it's very praiseworthy of you. But it's quite simple – this extraordinary idea of yours would just be the end of her. Do believe me. I really do know more about this sort of thing.'

'But what about this business with the dogs?' Franziska stammered. She wished she had not raised the subject at all and could take it all back. She had gone beyond the point of being able to put her anxiety into words. 'What was that you said?' her husband asked in a completely different tone of voice.

'Does she really still want a wretched dog?'

'I don't understand you,' Franziska answered. 'Why shouldn't she . . . Do you mean that she wants to have a dog?'

Aber natürlich, und ich bin nur froh, daß dieses kindische Zwischenspiel rasch vorübergegangen ist, denn sie würde doch nicht, in ihrem Alter, noch mit einem Hund zurechtkommen, sie soll auf sich selber aufpassen, das ist mir wichtiger, ein Hund ist eine derartige Plage, von der sie sich, bei dieser fortschreitenden Senilität, doch keine Vorstellung macht. Sie hat nie etwas gesagt, erwiderte Franziska schüchtern, ich glaube nicht, daß sie einen Hund will. Ich wollte etwas ganz anderes sagen, aber es ist ohne Bedeutung, verzeih. Nimmst du einen Cognac, arbeitest du noch, soll ich dir etwas abtippen?

Bei ihrem nächsten Besuch wußte Franziska nicht, wie sie es anstellen sollte, aus der alten Frau, die auf der Hut war, etwas herauszufragen, was sie wissen mußte. Sie fing es auf einem Umweg an und sagte beiläufig: Ich habe übrigens heute den Pudel von der Frau Schönthal gesehen, wirklich ein hübscher Hund, ich mag Pudel sehr, überhaupt alle Tiere, weil ich doch auf dem Land aufgewachsen bin, wir hatten immer Hunde, ich meine, meine Großeltern und alle Leute im Dorf, und Katzen natürlich auch. Wäre es für Sie nicht gut, einen Hund zu haben, oder eine Katze, jetzt wo Sie sich mit dem Lesen schwer tun, so was geht zwar vorüber, aber ich zum Beispiel würde schrecklich gern einen Hund haben, nur, wissen Sie, in der Stadt, das ist eine Mühe und für einen Hund nichts Rechtes, aber in Hietzing, wo er im Garten herumtollen kann und man spazieren gehen kann . . .

Die alte Frau sagte erregt: Einen Hund, nein, nein, ich will keinen Hund! Franziska merkte, daß sie etwas falsch gemacht hatte, aber sie fühlte zugleich, daß sie die alte Frau nicht gekränkt hatte, als hätte sie ihr vorgeschlagen, sich einen Papagei zu halten oder Kanarienvögel, es mußte etwas ganz anderes sein, was sie so erregt hatte. Nach einer Weile sagte die alte Frau sehr ruhig: Nuri war ja ein sehr schöner Hund, und ich bin gut mit ihm ausgekommen, das war, lassen Sie mich nachdenken, das muß schon fünf Jahre her sein, aber ich habe ihn

'Obviously. And it is just as well that this childish episode is over now, as she could not possibly look after a dog at her age. She ought to look after herself rather. A dog is such a nuisance, and that is something she cannot appreciate in her senile condition, which isn't getting any better.'

'But she hasn't said anything about a dog,' Franziska replied timidly. 'I don't think she wants one. I did not mean that at all. Anyway, it is not important, forgive me. Would you like a brandy now? Are you going to work, do you want anything typed?'

The next time she went to see her Franziska was uncertain as to how she should set about finding out from the old lady what she wanted to know, as she was very much on her guard. She broached the subject indirectly, beginning casually, 'I saw Mrs Schönthal's poodle today. What a fine dog he is. I'm very fond of poodles – in fact I like all animals – that's because I was brought up in the country and we always had dogs – I mean my grandparents did, and all the people in the village. Cats as well, of course. Wouldn't it be a good thing for you, perhaps, to have a dog, or a cat? Now that reading is becoming difficult for you? That will get better, of course. But I mean, in my case, I should love to have a dog myself, only it would be a lot of trouble in town, and would not be fair on the animal. But out here in Hietzing, where he could run around in the garden, and one could go for walks . . .' The old lady replied vehemently: 'A dog! Good gracious, no! I don't want a dog!' Franziska realized that she had said the wrong thing, but at the same time she was aware that she had not offended the old lady, as if she had suggested getting a parrot or a canary. There had to be some other reason why she had got so excited. After a while the old lady said very quietly: 'Nuri was such a beautiful dog, and we got on so well with each other. Let me think now, that must have been at least five years ago. But then I gave him away, to a home, or wherever it is they find new

dann weggegeben, in so ein Asyl oder wo sie die weiterver-
kaufen. Leo mag Hunde nicht. Nein, was sage ich da, es war
ganz anders, in diesem Hund war etwas, was ich mir nicht
erklären kann, er konnte Leo nicht leiden, er ist ihn jedesmal
angeflogen und hat gebellt wie verrückt, wenn Leo auch nur
auf die Tür zugegangen ist, und dann hätte er ihn beinahe
gebissen, und Leo hat sich so empört, das ist ja natürlich, ein
Hund, der so scharf ist, aber das war er sonst nie, mit keinem
Fremden, und dann habe ich ihn selbstverständlich weggegeben. Ich konnte doch Leo nicht von Nuri anbellen und beißen
lassen, nein, das war zuviel, denn Leo soll es doch gemütlich
haben, wenn er zu mir kommt und sich nicht ärgern müssen
über einen unerzogenen Hund.

Franziska dachte, daß Leo, obwohl kein Hund mehr da war,
der ihn anflog und nicht leiden konnte, doch reichlich selten
kam und immer weniger, seit Franziska ihm das abnahm.
Wann war er denn überhaupt hier gewesen? Einmal hatten sie
zu dritt eine kleine Spazierfahrt gemacht über die Weinstraße
und ins Helenental und in einem Gasthaus gegessen mit der
Mutter, aber sonst kam doch nur Franziska.

Sagen Sie Leo nur ja nichts, das mit Nuri hat ihn sehr getroffen, er ist sehr verletzlich, wissen Sie, und ich kann es mir
heute noch nicht verzeihen, daß ich so egoistisch war, Nuri
haben zu wollen, aber alte Leute sind eben sehr egoistisch,
liebe Franziska, das verstehen Sie noch gar nicht, Sie sind noch
so jung und gut, aber wenn man sehr alt ist, dann kommen
diese egoistischen Wünsche, und man darf sich da nicht nach-
geben. Wenn Leo nicht für mich sorgte, was wäre dann aus
mir geworden, sein Vater ist ja so plötzlich gestorben und hat
an nichts mehr denken können, und Geld war auch keines da,
mein Mann war ein bißchen leichtsinnig, nein, nicht ein Ver-
schwender, aber er hat es schwergehabt und keine glückliche
Hand mit dem Geld, da ist ihm Leo nicht nachgeraten, nur
habe ich damals noch arbeiten können, denn es war ja für den

owners for them. Leo does not like dogs. No, no, what am I saying, it was not like that at all. There was something about this dog which I could not understand. He could not stand Leo. He used to fly at him whenever he came and bark like a mad thing, even when he was only on the doorstep. He would nearly bite him, which made Leo so furious – well, it's only natural, if a dog gets as fierce as that. Nuri wasn't like it with anyone else, not even strangers. So of course I had to give him away. I couldn't have Leo being barked at and bitten by Nuri, that would have been too much. I wanted Leo to enjoy coming to see me, and not to have to bother about a badly behaved dog.'

Franziska thought to herself, 'Even though there's no dog to pester him now, he still makes precious few visits.' Even fewer since she herself had taken on this duty. When had he last been there? On one occasion the three of them had gone for a short drive along the Weinstrasse and up into the Helenental valley and then had a meal in an inn. Usually Franziska came by herself.

'Don't mention that to Leo, will you,' the old lady said. 'That business with Nuri really got him down. You see, he is a very vulnerable person, and even today I cannot forgive myself for being so selfish and wanting to keep Nuri. But old people are very egotistic, Franziska dear, you won't understand that yet, you are so young and good. But when you are very old you get these selfish desires and you shouldn't give in to them. If Leo had not looked after me, what would have become of me? His father died so unexpectedly, and he did not have time to think of anything. There wasn't any money, anyway. My husband was a bit irresponsible; not exactly a spendthrift, but he had his problems and he wasn't good with money – luckily Leo did not inherit that. Of course, at that time I could still go out to work – well, I had to for the sake of the boy, and I was still young then. But what can I do about

Buben, und ich war noch jung, aber was sollte ich heute denn tun? Meine einzige Angst war immer, in ein Altersheim zu müssen, und das würde Leo nie zulassen, und hätte ich nicht diese Wohnung, müßte ich in ein Heim, und das ist wohl ein Hund nicht wert. Franziska hörte ihr verkrampft zu, und sie sagte in sich hinein: Das also ist es, das ist es, und sie hat ihren Hund für ihn weggegeben. Was sind wir für Menschen, sagte sie sich – denn sie war unfähig zu denken, was ist mein Mann für ein Mensch! – wie gemein sind wir doch, und sie hält sich für eine Egoistin, während wir alles haben! Um nicht ihre Tränen zu zeigen, packte sie rasch ein kleines Paket von Meinl[2] aus, mit Kleinigkeiten, und tat, als hätte sie nichts verstanden. Ach, übrigens, wo hab ich bloß meine Gedanken, ich habe Ihnen nur den Tee und den Kaffee gebracht und ein bißchen Lachs und russischen Salat, ganz zusammen paßt es wohl nicht, aber ich war heute ziemlich verdreht beim Einkaufen, weil Leo abreist und ein Manuskript noch nicht fertig ist, er wird Sie aber heute abend anrufen, und er kommt ja schon in einer Woche zurück.

Er sollte ausspannen, sagte die alte Frau, sorgen Sie doch dafür, ihr habt doch noch keine Ferien gehabt in diesem Jahr. Franziska sagte lebhaft: Das ist ein guter Gedanke, ich bekomme ihn schon irgendwie herum, man muß das ein bißchen listig machen, aber das ist ein guter Rat, den Sie mir da geben, denn er überarbeitet sich ja ständig, und ich muß ihn einmal bremsen.

Was Franziska nicht wußte, war, daß es ihr letzter Besuch bei der alten Frau war, und sie keine kleine List mehr nötig hatte, weil andere Geschehnisse kamen und von einer so orkanartigen Stärke, daß sie beinahe die alte Frau vergaß und vieles andre mehr.

Die alte Frau, in ihrer Furcht, fragte ihren Sohn am Telefon nicht, warum Franziska nicht mehr kam. Sie beunruhigte sich, aber ihr Sohn klang vergnügt und unbesorgt, und einmal kam

that today? My only fear had always been that I should have to go into an old people's home, which Leo would never permit. If I did not have this apartment now, that is certainly what I should have to do – and it's not worth it for no sake of a dog.' As Franziska listened to her she found herself clenching her fists. 'So that's what's behind it!' she murmured, 'that's what it is, she had to give her dog away for his sake! What monsters we all are!' she said to herself (for she was incapable of thinking 'what a monster my husband is'.) 'What a miserable way to behave! And the old lady considers herself an egotist, when we are the ones with everything!' To hide her tears, she busied herself unpacking a small parcel of things she had bought at Meinl's, and carried on as if she hadn't understood at all. 'Anyway,' she said, ' I must have been in another world today. I bought you tea and coffee and some salmon with some Russian salad, which doesn't make much of a meal. I was rather distracted whilst I was shopping. Leo is just about to go off on a trip, and his manuscript isn't finished yet. He'll ring you this evening, and he will be back in a week's time.'

'He ought to take a rest,' the old lady said. 'Why don't you arrange it? After all, you haven't had a holiday yet this year.' 'What an excellent idea,' Franziska replied warmly, 'I'll talk him round to it somehow – you have to be a bit crafty with him. That's a very good suggestion of yours. He really does overwork himself all the time, and for once I should get him to slow down.'

Franziska could not have known that this was to be the last time she would visit the old lady. The time was past for her to resort to craftiness. Other events now occurred, of such a cataclysmic nature, that she practically forgot the old lady altogether, and much else besides. The old lady was too afraid to ask her son on the telephone why Franziska did not come to see her any more. She was worried, but her son sounded quite happy and relaxed. He even visited her himself on one occa-

er sogar und blieb zwanzig Minuten. Das Gebäck rührte er nicht an, den Sherry trank er nicht aus, von Franziska sprach er nicht, aber eine ganze Menge von sich, und das machte sie überglücklich, denn er hatte schon lange nicht mehr von sich selber gesprochen. Er verreiste jetzt also, ausspannen müsse er, nur bei dem Wort «Mexiko» bekam die alte Frau einen gelinden Schrecken, denn gab es dort nicht Skorpione und Revolutionen, und Wilde und Erdbeben, aber er lachte sie aus, küßte sie und versprach zu schreiben, er schickte auch ein paar Ansichtskarten, die sie andächtig las. Franziskas Grüße fehlten darauf. Von Franziska bekam sie einmal einen Anruf aus Kärnten. Ach, was diese jungen Leute da an Geld hinauswarfen! denn Franziska erkundigte sich nur, ob alles gut ginge. Sie sprachen dann von Leo, nur die alte Frau schrie immer im unpassendsten Moment: Es wird aber zu teuer, Kind, aber Franziska redete weiter, ja, es sei ihr gelungen, er spanne jetzt endlich aus, und sie habe zu ihrem Bruder fahren müssen, etwas sei zu regeln hier, deswegen habe sie Leo nicht begleiten können. Familienangelegenheiten in Kärnten. Wegen des Hauses. Dann bekam die alte Frau noch ein merkwürdiges Kuvert, mit ein paar Zeilen von Franziska, außer Herzlichkeiten stand nichts weiter darin, als daß sie ihr gerne eine Fotografie lassen möchte, die sie selber gemacht habe, das Foto zeigte Leo, vermutlich auf dem Semmering,[3] lachend, in einer Schneelandschaft, vor einem großen Hotel. Die alte Frau beschloß, Leo nichts zu sagen, und fragen würde er ohnehin nicht. Sie versteckte das Bild unter der Brosche in der Kassette.

Bücher konnte sie jetzt überhaupt nicht mehr lesen und das Radio langweilte sie, nur nach Zeitungen verlangte sie, die

sion and stayed for as long as twenty minutes. He didn't touch the cakes she offered him, or finish his sherry, nor did he mention Franziska, but he talked a great deal about himself, however, which delighted her, as he had not done that for a long time. It seemed he was off on a journey to get some rest. It was only when he mentioned Mexico that the old lady had a bit of a shock. Wasn't that the place where there were scorpions, and revolutions? Where you were likely to encounter savages, not to mention earthquakes? But Leo just laughed at her fears. He hugged her and promised he would write. He actually did send a couple of postcards, which she read with appropriate reverence. There was no message on them from Franziska. On one occasion Franziska telephoned her from Kärnten. 'How careless these young people are with their money,' the old lady thought, for Franziska had only called to find out whether everything was all right with her. They talked a little about Leo, but the old lady kept butting in at the most unsuitable moments with, 'but this is costing you too much, child!' Franziska carried on, however. She had had her way, she said, now Leo really was taking a rest. She herself had gone to stay with her brother, as there was something that had to be seen to, and that was why she hadn't been able to go with Leo. Family problems down in Kärnten. Something to do with the house they had there. Then the old lady received a strange letter from Franziska containing just a few lines. Apart from some friendly words, it said nothing of consequence – only that Franziska wanted to give her a photograph she had taken herself. The photograph – presumably taken at a winter resort – showed Leo standing and laughing against a background of snow, in front of a large hotel. The old lady resolved not to mention this to Leo. In any case, he was not likely to ask her. She tucked the picture under the brooch in the little box.

By now she was no longer able to read books, and she found the radio boring. All she wanted was newspapers, which

Frau Agnes ihr brachte. In den Zeitungen, für die sie Stunden brauchte, las sie die Todesanzeigen, es war immer eine gewisse Befriedigung in ihr, wenn jemand gestorben war, der jünger war als sie. So, also auch der Professor Haderer, er konnte höchstens siebzig Jahre alt sein. Die Mutter von Frau Schönthal war auch gestorben, an Krebs, noch nicht einmal fünfundsechzig. Sie kondolierte steif in der Milchhandlung und schaute den Pudel nicht an, und dann ging sie wieder nach Hause und stellte sich an das Fenster. Sie schlief nicht so wenig, wie man oft von alten Leuten behauptet, aber oft wachte sie auf, und schon hörte sie die Hunde. Wenn die Bedienerin kam, erschrak sie, denn es störte sie schon jedes Kommen von jemand, seit Franziska nicht mehr kam, und ihr selber war, als veränderte sie sich. Denn jetzt ängstigte sie es wirklich, daß sie plötzlich auf der Straße umfallen könne oder sich nicht mehr in der Kontrolle hatte, wenn sie etwas in der Stadt brauchte, und sie rief darum gehorsam immer nach dem jungen Herr Pineider, der sie herumfuhr. Und sie gewöhnte sich an diese kleinen Bequemlichkeiten aus Sicherheitsgründen. Den Zeitsinn verlor sie ganz, und als Leo einmal, braungebrannt, zu ihr kam, auf einen Sprung, wußte sie nicht mehr, ob er jetzt aus Mexiko zurück war oder wann er überhaupt dort gewesen war, aber sie war zu klug, um sich zu erkundigen, und dann entnahm sie einem Satz, daß er geradewegs aus Ischia kam, von einer Italienreise. Sie sagte zerstreut: Gut, gut. Das hat dir gut getan. Und während er ihr etwas erzählte, fingen die Hunde zu bellen an, mehrere gleichzeitig, in großer Nähe, und sie war so eingekreist von dem Gebell und einem sehr sanften, sanften Schrecken, daß sie sich vor ihrem Sohn nicht mehr fürchtete. Die Furcht eines ganzens Lebens wich auf einmal aus ihr.

Agnes would bring her. She spent hours reading these, particularly the obituary columns, and she derived a certain kind of satisfaction from reading of the deaths of people younger than herself. 'Now it's Professor Haderer's turn – and he cannot have been more than seventy.' Mrs Schönthal's mother had also died, from cancer, and she couldn't have been sixty-five. She offered her condolences rather stiffly the next time she went to the dairy, and did not look at the poodle. Then she went home again and sat at the window. She did not sleep quite as little as it is sometimes claimed old people do, but she would often wake up in the night, and then she would hear the dogs again. She would be startled by the arrival of her cleaning lady. Now that Franziska no longer came to see her, the arrival of anyone at all would be sufficient to startle her. Inwardly, too, she felt as if she were undergoing some kind of change. She began to have fears about falling over in the street, or that somehow she would lose control. Whenever she wanted to go into town, therefore, she would always call for young Mr Pineider, as she had been told to do, who would drive her from one place to another. She became accustomed to this little luxury, which she permitted herself on the grounds of safety. She lost her sense of time completely, and once when Leo dropped in with a good sun-tan, she could not remember any more whether he had just got back from Mexico, or when it was that he had been there. But she was too clever to ask him directly, and then he let fall something which made it clear that he had just returned from Ischia, after a trip to Italy. 'Good,' she said absent-mindedly, 'that's good. It must have been nice for you.' Just as he was in the middle of telling her something, the dogs started to bark, several of them at the same time, quite near by. Surrounded by this noise, she experienced a gentle sensation of fear, and she made the discovery that she was no longer afraid of her son. The fear of an entire lifetime suddenly left her.

Als er ihr sagte, im Gehen: Das nächste Mal bringe ich dir Elfi mit, du mußt sie endlich kennenlernen!, wußte sie überhaupt nicht, wovon er sprach. War er nicht mehr verheiratet mit Franziska, und seit wann eigentlich nicht mehr, und die wievielte Frau war das nun eigentlich, sie erinnerte sich nicht mehr, wie lange er mit Franziska gelebt hatte und wann, und sie sagte: Bring sie nur. Gut. Wenn es nur gut für dich ist. Einen Augenblick lang hatte sie die Gewißheit, Nuri sei wieder bei ihr und würde ihn anfliegen, anbellen, so nahe war jetzt das Gebell. Er sollte doch endlich gehen, sie wollte allein sein. Aus Gewohnheit bedankte sie sich, vorsichtshalber, und er fragte verwundert: Aber wofür denn? Jetzt habe ich doch tatsächlich vergessen, dir mein Buch mitzubringen. Ein phänomenaler Erfolg. Ich lasse es dir schicken.

Also vielen Dank, mein Bub. Schick es nur, aber deine dumme Mutter kann ja leider kaum mehr lesen und versteht so wenig.

Sie ließ sich von ihm umarmen und fand sich schon wieder allein, diesem Bellen ausgesetzt. Es kam aus allen Gärten und Wohnungen von Hietzing, eine Invasion der Bestien hatte angefangen, die Hunde näherten sich ihr, bellten ihr zu, und sie stand aufrecht, wie immer, da und träumte nicht mehr von der Zeit mit Kiki und den Griechen, sie dachte nicht mehr an den Tag, an dem der letzte Zehnschillingschein verschwunden war und Leo sie angelogen hatte, sondern versuchte nur noch angestrengt, die Dinge besser zu verstecken, sie wollte sie auch wegwerfen, besonders die Brosche und die Fotografie, damit von Leo nichts gefunden würde nach ihrem Tod, aber es fiel ihr kein gutes Versteck ein, nur der Kübel mit den Abfällen, aber der Frau Agnes traute sie auch immer weniger, denn ihr hätte sie den Mistkübel geben müssen, und sie hatte den Verdacht, daß diese Person ihn durchstöberte und dann die Brosche finden würde. Etwas zu unfreundlich sagte sie einmal:

As Leo left, he said to her: 'Next time I'll bring Elfi, it's about time you met her!' The old lady had no idea what he was talking about. Wasn't he married to Franziska any more? If not, how long had this been so? How many wives had Leo now had? She could no longer remember precisely how long he had lived with Franziska, or when that had been, and all she could say was, 'Yes, do bring her. That would be nice. Just as long as it is good for you.' The barking seemed so close now, that for a brief moment she was convinced Nuri was right there beside her again and that he would bark at Leo and go for him. 'If only he would go now, and leave me alone,' she thought. Out of habit she cautiously thanked him, but he replied, with some surprise: 'What are you thanking me for? This time I really did forget to bring you my book. It has had an amazing success. I shall put it in the post to you.'

'Thank you very much, my son,' she said. 'Do send it, but remember that your poor simple old mother can hardly read any more, and understands very little now.'

They hugged each other, and then the old lady found herself alone again with the barking. It seemed to reverberate around her from all the gardens and apartments of Hietzing; a full-scale invasion was under way, and now the dogs were getting closer, and howling at her. She stood there, erect as ever, and her thoughts were no longer of the days with Kiki and the Greek family, or of the day when her very last ten shilling note had vanished and Leo had lied to her. Her only concern now was how to conceal things. She wanted to throw them away, especially the brooch and the photograph, so that Leo shouldn't find any of these things after she was dead. But she could not think of a suitable hiding-place, apart from the rubbish bin. She was thinking of Agnes, whom she trusted less and less, and whose job it was to empty the rubbish. She suspected that she would rummage around in the bin and find the brooch. On one occasion she said to her in a rather un-

Geben Sie doch wenigstens die Knochen und die Reste den Hunden.

Die Bedienerin schaute sie erstaunt an und fragte: Welchen Hunden? Den Hunden natürlich, beharrte die alte Frau herrisch, ich möchte, daß es die Hunde bekommen!

Eine verdächtige Person, eine Diebin, die würde sich die Knochen wahrscheinlich nach Hause tragen.

Den Hunden, sage ich. Verstehen Sie mich denn nicht, sind Sie schwerhörig? Kein Wunder, in Ihrem Alter.

Dann bellten die Hunde leiser, und sie dachte, jemand habe die Hunde entfernt oder einige Hunde weggegeben, denn es war nicht mehr das starke und häufige und feste Bellen von früher. Je leiser sie bellten, desto unbeugsamer wurde sie, sie wartete nur auf die Wiederkehr des stärkeren Bellens, man mußte warten können, und sie konnte warten. Es war auf einmal endlich nicht mehr ein Bellen, obwohl es unzweifelhaft von den Hunden kam aus der Nachbarschaft, auch nicht ein Knurren, nur hin und wieder das große, wilde, triumphierende Aufjohlen eines einzigen Hundes, ein Gewimmer danach und im Hintergrund das sich entfernende Gebell aller anderen.

Eines Tages erhielt Herr Dr. Martin Ranner, fast zwei Jahre nach dem Tod seiner Schwester Franziska, eine Rechnung von einer Firma Pineider, über Taxifahrten, die genau datiert waren, auch von Frau Franziska Jordan angezahlt und in Auftrag gegeben worden waren, aber da nur wenige Fahrten zu ihren Lebzeiten gemacht worden waren, die meisten nach ihrem Tod, rief er die Firma an, um eine Erklärung für diese mysteriöse Rechnung zu bekommen. Die Erklärung erklärte ihm zwar nur wenig, aber da er nicht wünschte, seinen ehemaligen Schwager anzurufen oder ihn noch einmal im Leben wiederzusehen, bezahlte er, ratenweise, diese Fahrten einer Frau, die er nicht gekannt hatte und die ihn überhaupt

friendly tone: 'Do at least give the bones and whatever else there is left to those dogs.' The cleaning lady looked at her in astonishment and asked, 'What dogs are you talking about?'

'Those dogs there, of course,' the old lady insisted dictatorially. 'I want the dogs to have the scraps.' A suspicious creature, a thief like her would probably take the bones home with her, she thought to herself.

'The dogs. Can't you understand me? Are you hard of hearing? No wonder, at your age.'

Then the dogs began to bark more quietly, and she thought: 'Someone must have taken them further off, or perhaps given some of them away' – for she could no longer make out the loud, insistent and vigorous barking she had heard earlier. As the dogs grew quieter, the old lady became more inflexible. All she was waiting for now was the return of the earlier louder barking. Waiting was the only thing to do, and she was quite capable of that. Then at last it was no longer a barking, though undoubtedly it still came from the dogs not far away; nor was it even a growling, only now and again a savage and triumphant upsurge of howling from a solitary dog, followed by whimpering, and then in the background, gradually dying away, the sound of all the other dogs barking together.

One day, almost two years after the death of his sister, Franziska, Dr Martin Ranner received an invoice from a firm by the name of Pineider in respect of certain taxi rides, and bearing the exact dates on which these had been taken. Some of these had been ordered and a deposit paid for them by Mrs Franziska Jordan, but, since the bulk of them had been after her death, Dr Ranner telephoned the firm for an explanation of this mysterious invoice. The explanation did not really satisfy him, but, as he had no desire to ring his former brother-in-law, or for that matter, ever to set eyes on him again, he decided he would pay in instalments for these taxi rides taken by a lady he had never known and who meant nothing to him.

nichts anging. Er kam zu dem Schluß, daß die alte Frau Jordan, die dieser Pineider gefahren hatte, vor einiger Zeit gestorben sein mußte, denn die Firma hatte mehrere Monate seit der letzten Fahrt, aus Pietät vielleicht, verstreichen lassen, ehe sie ihre Forderungen geltend machte.

He came to the conclusion that old Mrs Jordan, whom Pineider had been driving around, must have died a little while
back, for the firm, possibly out of respect for the dead, had
allowed several months to elapse after the last ride before sub-
mitting their invoice.

LOBELLEN GROVE

JOHANNES BOBROWSKI

Translated by Ray Ockenden

LOBELLERWÄLDCHEN

ALSO Lobellen.

 Nein, Lobellen gar nicht.

 Aber na ja doch.

 Aber na nein.

 Da muß man erklären, daß Lobellen ein Dorf ist, ziemlich lang hingestreckt, an einer vielbefahrenen Chaussee, und Lobellerwäldchen eine Gastwirtschaft, ein Gartenlokal, ein Etablissement und ganz gehörig abgelegen von Lobellen. Wer Pferde hat, in Lobellen, fährt nach Lobellerwäldchen mit Fuhrwerk. Und nimmt die andern nicht mit, die andern Lobeller, die kein Pferd haben. Höchstens den Herrn Tesche, den Zollbichs,[1] Zoller, Zöllner, Zolloberwachtmeister oder wie sich das nennt. Es ist so üblich hier. Man kauft ihm auch Bier und der Lene, das ist Tesches Frau, Limonade, in Lobellerwäldchen.

 Das reicht dann ja, und es ist schön hier am Sonntag. Gastwirt Ambrassat deckt draußen Tischtücher auf und muß sechsmal hintereinander Marie schreien, ehe seine Frau dazukommt und die Gartenstühle zurechtrückt.

 Es sind ja schon Leute da, Klempner Borbe mit seiner Frau, der Hebamme, und Kakschies von der Fähre und Bauer Bussat mit seinem Bruder, genannt Herr Bussat, und nicht ohne die Bussatsche, wie meistens.

 Hier ist man so schön im Wald. Ambrassat holt das Grammophon heraus und zieht es auf und steckt die Kurbel wieder in die Tasche. Jetzt geht die Musik los, Lützows wilde, verwegene Jagd,[2] vom Berliner Lehrergesangverein auf beunruhigende Weise vorgetragen. Die tiefen Stimmen, die da

LOBELLEN GROVE

WELL now, Lobellen.

No, not Lobellen at all.

But yes, why not?

But no, not that.

It should be explained that Lobellen is a village, stretching quite far along a busy high road, and the Lobellen Grove is an inn, a rustic pub, an establishment a fair distance from Lobellen. Anyone in Lobellen who has a horse goes out to the Lobellen Grove with horse and cart. Without taking the others along, the other inhabitants of Lobellen who don't have a horse. Except maybe Herr Tesche, the fellow from the customs, the excise man, the tax-gatherer or Chief Preventive Officer or whatever he's called. That's a regular thing here. People buy him beer, too, and lemonade for Lene, that's Tesche's wife, in the Lobellen Grove.

That's enough in the way of people, and it's beautiful out here on Sundays. Ambrassat, the innkeeper, lays table-cloths out of doors and has to shout for Marie and go on shouting half a dozen times before his wife comes out and puts the garden chairs straight.

Some people have already arrived, plumber Borbe with Frau Borbe, the midwife, and Kakschies from the ferry and farmer Bussat with his brother, known as Herr Bussat, not forgetting, as is generally the case, Bussat's wife.

It's beautiful out here in the woods. Ambrassat brings out the gramophone and winds it up and puts the winding-handle back in his pocket. Now the music starts up, *Lützow's wild and daring Hunt*, performed in a disturbing manner by

ganz unten herumgurgeln und auf einmal samtweich werden, weil es höher hinaufgeht, mit denen kommt man ja mit, aber diese Tenöre, wie machen die das, da so ganz oben, na ich weiß ja nicht.

Und überhaupt dieses Grammophon.

Ambrassats Schwiegervater, der verstorbene Lehrer Fett, hat es im Jahre 93 von der Chicagoer Weltausstellung mitgebracht. Er war da nämlich hingefahren, über den Atlantik, und tatsächlich zurückgekommen. Da hatte er die restlichen dreißig Jahre zu erzählen gehabt.

Ambrassat hält es gut unter Öl, jeder außer ihm bedreckt sich, wenn er es anfaßt, Ambrassat bedient es auch ganz allein. Hat er dem Schwiegervater, als der sein Testament aufsetzte, in die Hand versprochen. Aber es lohnt ja auch, nicht wahr.

Noch besser wäre es, wenn die Platten länger spielten, doch der Apparat ist nicht so besonders groß, er schaffte es vielleicht nicht. Immerhin, ein stabiler Kasten aus Holz, in die Seitenwände sind Glasscheiben eingelassen, da sieht man den Klappmatismus, wie Ambrassat sagt. Er geht ganz gleichmäßig langsam, die Geschwindigkeit kommt durch die Übersetzung, sagt Ambrassat. Auf einer der Platten singt der bekannte Caruso Afrikanisches[3] von Meyerbeer. Und der Ton kommt aus dem grünen Blechtrichter, der sich großartig über dem Kasten erhebt. Stundenlang könnte man zusehen, wie alles funktioniert.

Und wenn man schon ein Stück die Waldlichtung hinuntergegangen ist und den Fluß sehen kann, die Szeszupe,[4] die sich bekanntlich erst hinter Lenkeningken und bei Lobellen noch längst nicht mit der Memel vereinigt, hat man die Musik sehr angenehm im Rücken, den Lindenbaum[5] oder O Täler weit, o Höhen.[6]

the Berlin Teachers' Choir. The bass voices, gurgling away in the depths and suddenly becoming soft and velvety as they go higher up the scale, they're easy enough to follow, but those tenors, how they manage it, right up at the top, well, I just don't know. And that gramophone, come to think of it.

Ambrassat's father-in-law, the late schoolmaster Fett, brought it back from the Chicago World Exposition in 93. He went over there, you see, across the Atlantic, and actually came back again. That gave him enough tales to tell for his remaining thirty years.

Ambrassat keeps it well-oiled, anyone who touches it apart from him gets covered in the stuff, and in fact Ambrassat is the only one who works it. That's what he solemnly pledged when his father-in-law was drawing up his will. But it's better that way, you'll agree.

It would be even better if the records played a bit longer, but the contraption isn't all that big, it probably couldn't manage it. At any rate, it's a solid wooden box, with glass panels let into the sides so that you can see 'the mechanicalities', as Ambrassat calls them. It goes round at the same slow pace, the speed is controlled by the transmission, so Ambrassat says. On one of his records the famous Caruso sings something African by Meyerbeer. And the sound comes out of the green metal horn which rears up over the box in imposing fashion. You could spend hours watching it all work.

And even when you go a little way down through the clearing, so that you can see the river, the Szeszupe, which, as everyone knows, doesn't join the Memel till it gets to the other side of Lenkeningken, a long way beyond Lobellen, you can still hear the music sounding pleasantly from behind you, the song about the linden tree or the one that goes 'Broad valleys, and ye hillsides'.

Da denkt man, daß es hier ein Land ist wie Musik. Die Lichtung öffnet sich immer breiter, der Wald endet mit einem jungen Birkenbestand, ein paar Büsche noch, dann fangen die Wiesen an und senken sich langsam, katzenhaft weich auf das Sandufer hinab. Auch ohne die Musik, die man jetzt nicht mehr recht hört, die wohl auch schon aufgehört hat.

Nicht einmal das Geschrei reicht bis hierher, mit dem Krauledats Kinder die Schaukel in Bewegung bringen, die große, mit Stangen an zwei Kiefern aufgehängte Kiste, in der immer gleich vier Personen Platz nehmen. Oder sechs Kinder.

Zu erzählen gibt es genug, und wenig zu reden, hier unten am Wasser. Die Barsche springen ein bißchen nach den Fliegen und den grünen Mücken, auch die andern Fische steigen herauf aus der Dämmerung unten, aber bewegen sich kaum, stehen und lassen sich die dunklen Rücken bescheinen.

Sonntag heißt Sonntag, weil da die Sonne scheint. Es ist so gut hier, daß einem nichts Vernünftigeres einfällt.

Da kann man auch wieder gehn. Sich zu den Pferden stellen, ihnen die schwarzen Fliegen von den Augen und die metallharten, rasselnden Bremsen von den Flanken wegfangen. Eine Beschäftigung, die ihren Lohn im Himmel hat, hier auf Erden ist sie nutzlos, es gibt zuviel von dem Zeug.

Musik und die Schaukel und große Kaffeekannen, weiß emailliert, und Blechfladen, und es geht nach und nach auf Sonntagabend zu. Und Tesches sind heute nicht da, bei Tesches ist Taufe.

Und Ambrassats wußten das nicht. Was Sie nicht sagen, Herr Bussat!

Der Heinrich, der eigentlich Franz Kirschnick heißt, steht bei den Pferden. Willst wieder koppschellern,[7] fragt Bauer Bussat hinüber.

Der Heinrich handelt mit Vieh, er ist dumm und hat Geld, da kann er zusetzen, da lebt er ganz gut, als Junggeselle.

It makes you think that the country here is just like music. The clearing opens out more and more, the wood comes to an end in a new plantation of young birches, there are just a few bushes after that and then the meadows begin, descending gradually and soft as cat's fur to the sandy river bank. Even without the music, which you can no longer hear very clearly, indeed it's probably stopped anyway.

Down here, not even the shouts of Kraudelat's children reach you as they set the swing going, the big crate hung on poles from two pine trees, with room for four people in it. Or six children.

There is plenty to tell, and little to discuss, down here by the water. The perch leap now and again for flies and green midges, other fish come up from the twilight down below as well, but they scarcely move, they simply float and let the sun fall on their dark backs.

Sunday is called Sunday because the sun shines. It is so pleasant here, that no more sensible explanation occurs to you.

And then you can set off again. Walk over to your horses and brush the black flies off their eyes and the metal-hard, rustling horse-flies from their flanks. An occupation that has its reward in Heaven, here on earth it's useless, there are too many of the things.

Music and the swing and large coffee-pots, white-enamelled, and thin griddle-cakes, and little by little Sunday evening draws on. The Tesches are not here today, there's a christening at the Tesches'.

And the Ambrassats knew nothing about it. Well, you do surprise us, Herr Bussat.

Heinrich, whose real name is Franz Kirschnick, is standing by the horses. 'Thinking of a bit of horse-trading, then?' shouts farmer Bussat to him.

Heinrich deals in livestock, he's stupid and has money, he's got plenty to spend, he can live quite well, as a bachelor.

Ach was, eure Kobbeln, sagt Heinrich, die könnt ihr behalten.

Das ist etwas anderes bei diesem Heinrich, er denkt nicht gleich immer an Kaufen. Wo Vieh ist, stellt er sich·eben dazu, wie alle Kirschnicks, das weiß man ja, das haben sie von ihrem Großvater Heinrich, deshalb werden sie ja auch alle nach ihm benannt.

Also du willst nicht?

Kann man ja drüber reden, sagt Heinrich.

Und jetzt fahren auch die ersten los, Bussats und Borbes. Der alte Kakschies bleibt noch. Die Zahnärztin Willmann will nach Hause, aber ihr Gatte nicht, nein, der nicht. Herr Bussat redet noch mit Förster Krauledat, der Frau und Kinder schon in sein Auto gepackt hat. Also der Herr Bussat bleibt noch, und der Krauledat fährt ab.

Und der Tesche kommt, jetzt, abends und per Rad, dienstlich, heute am Sonntag. Da ist womöglich die Taufe schon vorbei? Nein, das nicht, sondern: Dienst ist Dienst.

Das sagt man so. Aber man sagt auch, gleich hinterher: Und Schnaps ist Schnaps. Und das ist wahr. Das letzte Wort ist dann: Wo er recht hat, hat er recht.

Schnaps also. Eine besondere Sorte Korn, genannt Kornus, mancher sagt, aber unterschiedslos auf allen Schnaps, Branntwein, wir sagen besser Kartoffelsprit. Man kauft gewöhnlich ein Quartierchen am Wochentag, was ein Viertel bedeutet, und füllt mit Wasser auf. Aber hier wird ausgeschenkt. Und das Besondere besteht darin, daß der Schnaps in sieben Farben schillert. Da hat man zu zählen, und verzählt sich leicht, und hat sich die Augen zu schärfen, und feuchtet sie also an, von innen. Und wer erst genug gezählt hat und die Farben jetzt hersagt, der hat dann auch das Mundwerk flott, da wird der

'What, your nags?' says Heinrich. 'No, you can keep them.'

Heinrich is different, buying isn't always the first thing he thinks of. Wherever there are animals, he just goes and stands beside them, like all the Kirschnicks, everyone knows that, they get it from their grandfather Heinrich, that's why they're all called by the same name.

'Not interested in buying, then?'

'We could always talk about it,' says Heinrich.

And now the first ones are beginning to leave, the Bussats and the Borbes. Old Kakschies stays on. Frau Willmann the dentist's wife wants to go home, but not her husband, no, he doesn't want to go. Herr Bussat is still talking to Krauledat the forester, who has already packed his wife and children into his car. So, Herr Bussat stays on, and Krauledat drives off.

And then Tesche arrives, at this time, in the evening, on his bicycle, on duty, and today being Sunday, too. So presumably the christening is over already? No, it's not that; but duty is duty.

As they say. And someone will add at once: 'And booze is booze.' Which is true. And finally someone else says: 'If he's right, he's right, you know.'

So booze, then. A special kind of corn-whisky, known as kornus, some people call it brandy (but then they call all spirits that), let us rather say potato-brandy. On a weekday you usually buy a 'quarter' – that's just a small tot – and fill up with water. But out here you get full measure. And the special thing about this brandy is that it is shot with seven colours. You have to try and count them, and it's easy to lose count, and so you have to focus your eyes and moisten them for the effort, from inside of course. And when someone has counted long enough and reels off all the colours, you know his tongue's well and truly oiled, you're in for a long evening

Abend lang, da sollte die Ambrassatsche schon längst schlafen-
gegangen sein.

Hau bloß ab, sagt Kakschies, und zu Ambrassat: Deine Alte
schneidet ganz gemein. Er schiebt das Glas hinüber, und
Ambrassat gießt bis zum Eichstrich nach.

Und Zahnklempner Willmann ist abgefahren, unter Ge-
sang. Da singt seine Frau lieber mit, damit es nicht so besoffen
klingt.

Und Heinrich muß immer hinters Haus. Schwache Blase.

Der Kaiser, sagt Bussat, der brauchte überhaupt nicht. Der
saß und saß, hat der Herr Landrat gesagt. Da hatten sich die
Herren bei den Gardeulanen unter dem Tisch solche Töpfe
angebracht. Aufstehen ging ja nicht, wenn der Kaiser da saß
und saß, und immer von diesem.

Bussat gießt sein Glas hinunter und winkelt dabei elegant
den Arm.

Landläufige Geschichten.

Tesche steht auf und geht hinters Haus.

Wart mal, sagt er zu Heinrich, den er an der Hausecke trifft,
und Heinrich bleibt stehn und knöpft sich umständlich zu und
wartet. Da geht das Mondlicht über den Wald, ganz gelb.

Und Tesche kommt an der Wand entlang und sagt, hinter
Heinrichs Rücken: Du wirst mir bezahlen.

Heinrich sagt: Dann kommt es ja aber raus.

Nichts kommt raus, sagt Tesche, du zahlst alles auf einmal.
Wieviel?

Achthundert.

Bist du verrückt? Und woher?

Du kommst von Wallenthal, du hast eingenommen.

Und weil Heinrich schweigt: Na los, dann die Hälfte. Fürs
erste.

Komm jetzt rein, sagt Heinrich.

Wir reden noch, sagt Tesche.

and Frau Ambrassat should have gone to bed a long time
ago.

'Get away with you,' says Kakschies, and then, turning to
Ambrassat: 'Your old woman pours a mean drink.' He
pushes the glass across and Ambrassat fills it up as far as the
gauge-line.

And Willmann the dentist or tooth-plumber has gone off,
singing loudly. His wife prefers to join in his singing, so that
it doesn't sound so sozzled.

And Heinrich has to keep slipping round the corner of the
house. Weak bladder.

'The Emperor never needed to at all,' says Bussat. 'He just
sat and sat, that's what the District President told me. So
the lancers of the Imperial Guard had these pots fixed under
the table for them. Getting up wasn't allowed, not so long
as the Emperor sat there and sat there and kept doing this.'

Bussat downs his glass, sticking his elbow out at an elegant
angle.

Familiar stories.

Tesche gets up and goes behind the house.

'Just a moment,' he says to Heinrich, when they meet at
the corner of the house, and Heinrich stands still and takes
his time buttoning himself up and waits. The moonlight,
quite yellow, strides over the wood.

And Tesche comes along the wall and says, behind Heinrich's back: 'You'll have to pay me.'

Heinrich says: 'But then it'll all come out.'

'Nothing's going to come out,' says Tesche, 'you'll pay me
the lot at one go.'

'How much?'

'Eight hundred.

'Are you crazy? Where can I get that from?'

'You've just come from Wallenthal, you must be loaded.'

Da sitzen sie eine Weile in der Gaststube. Dann sagt Kakschies: Werden wir nehmen und gehn.

Da gehn sie also.

Da gehn sechs Männer durch den Wald.

Und vier gehn nach Hause. Drei nach Lobellen ins Dorf. Der Kakschies zum Fährhäuschen hinunter. Vor Lobellen biegt der Weg nach der Szeszupe ab. Und zwei bleiben im Wald. Der Tesche hat ein Quartierchen mitbekommen.

Das wird zugeführt, nämlich dem Gemüt. Und nicht im Stehen.

Und unter allerlei Reden, einem langwierigen Hinundher um Geld, achthundert und in zwei Hälften, und: Los, mach schon, du hast doch.

Ja sicher, er hat. Geld hat der Heinrich, und das Kind bei Tesches ist auch von ihm.

Müde bin ich,[8] sagt Tesche.

Geh zur Ruh, sagt Heinrich.

Läßt sich aufs Kreuz sinken und schläft auch schon.

Und Tesche sitzt noch eine Weile. Der Mond ist abgezogen.

Jetzt ist die Flasche leer und fliegt in die Büsche.

Na schön.

Kurze Nächte, im Sommer.

Heinrich wacht auf. Etwas Feuchtes fährt ihm in kurzen Abständen übers Gesicht. Wie kommt das? Die Gedanken finden sich nicht zusammen, in all dem Schnaps, schwimmen da herum. Und Angst hat er auch nicht, nicht einmal einen Schreck kriegt er, ganz tief im Schnaps wie in einer Decke, im siebenfarbigen Schnaps.

Da leckt mich doch einer, denk ich.

Nun hat er die Augen offen.

Da steht also ein Hirsch über ihm, breitbeinig, und läßt seine rauhe Zunge immer noch einmal dem Heinrich übers Gesicht gehn.

Das ist gar nicht so unangenehm, bloß es kitzelt, und da

And when Heinrich says nothing: 'Come on then, give me half of it. For a start.'

'Let's go inside,' says Heinrich.

'We'll discuss it later,' says Tesche.

So they all sit for a while in the bar parlour. Then Kakschies says: 'One for the road, and then we'll go.'

And so off they go.

Six men walking through the wood.

Four of them are going home. Three to the village, to Lobellen. Kakschies is going down to his ferryman's hut. The path down to the Szeszupe turns off before Lobellen. And two stay in the wood. Tesche has got his 'quarter' with him.

And applies it, to his emotions that is. As he walks.

And talking all the time, a tedious wrangling about the money, 'eight hundred and in two instalments,' and: 'Come on, out with it, I know you've got it.'

Yes, of course he has. Money is one thing Heinrich has, and the child at Tesche's house is his, too.

'Tired am I,' says Tesche.

''Tis time for bed,' says Heinrich.

And he collapses on to his back and is asleep.

And Tesche sits for a while. The moon has withdrawn.

Now the bottle is empty and flies into the bushes. Well, then. Short nights, in summer.

Heinrich wakes up. Something damp keeps passing over his face, at short intervals. How can that be? His thoughts cannot link up, in all that brandy, they just swim around in it. And he isn't afraid, he doesn't even have a sense of alarm, enfolded as in a blanket in his brandy, the brandy with the seven hues.

'Someone's licking me, I think.'

Now his eyes are open.

There, standing over him, is a stag, foursquare, running his rough tongue once again over Heinrich's face.

It's not all that unpleasant, but it tickles, and so Heinrich

muß Heinrich lachen, und da erschrickt aber der Hirsch und macht sich, nicht sehr eilig, fort ins Gebüsch.

Im Dämmerlicht erkennt Heinrich, während er sich aufrichtet, daß es ein weißer Hirsch ist.

Neben ihm liegt der Tesche und grunzt, als Heinrich ihn anstößt.

Na gewiß doch, sagt Tesche, so einer findet sich immer.

Heinrich erzählt ihm nämlich, daß ihn einer geleckt hat.

Aber du weißt ja gar nicht wer, sagt Heinrich, und nun ist er beinahe aufgeregt.

Ach geh mir doch vom Acker. Weißer Hirsch.

Dabei weiß es Tesche doch auch: Diese weißen Hirsche gibt es, drüben im Trappöner Forst, sie sind grau, etwas dunkler als Isländisch Moos.

Das bringt, wer weiß, Glück? Heinrich kann sich gar nicht beruhigen. Er steht auf und reckt sich und fängt an zu pfeifen, aber das sticht ein bißchen im Kopf, da hört er gleich wieder auf.

Und Tesche hat ein Wort verstanden, das heißt Glück.

Also wie ist mit vierhundert, sagt er.

Na gut, sagt Heinrich und setzt sich zu ihm. Aber Quittung.

Natürlich, unter uns Männern, sagt Tesche.

Heinrich zählt vier Scheine ab und tut die übrigen in die Brieftasche zurück.

Mindestens noch zehn Lappen, geht es Tesche durch den Kopf. Auch solch ein Gedanke allein schmerzt schon, bei dem vielen Schnaps, da braucht man gar nicht erst zu pfeifen.

Und ich hab doch mein Rad stehenlassen, in Lobellerwäldchen, sagt Tesche.

Das kommt nicht weg, sagt Heinrich.

Und jetzt kann man einfach zu Ende erzählen.

can't help laughing, but that startles the stag and it takes itself off, not too hurriedly, into the bushes.

In the gloaming Heinrich can make out, as he lifts himself up, that it is a white stag.

Beside him lies Tesche, who grunts when Heinrich nudges him.

'Well, yes, of course,' says Tesche, 'someone like that is always turning up.'

Heinrich has told him, you see, that someone was licking him.

'But you don't even know who it was,' says Heinrich, and begins almost to get worked up.

'Ah, tell me another one. White stag, indeed.'

But in fact Tesche knows very well that such white stags exist, over there in Trappön forest, they're grey, a little darker than Iceland moss.

'That should bring me, who knows, good fortune?' Heinrich can't calm down. He stands up and stretches and begins to whistle, but that gives him rather a sharp pain in the head, so he stops again straight away.

And Tesche has caught one of his words: fortune.

'Well, shall we say four hundred, then?' he says.

'All right then,' says Heinrich, and sits down beside him. 'For a receipt.'

'Of course, between the two of us,' says Tesche.

Heinrich counts out four notes and puts the rest back in his wallet.

'At least another ten like that,' the thought passes through Tesche's mind. But even the thought hurts, after all that brandy, without having to start whistling.

'And I left my bicycle back at the Lobellen Grove,' says Tesche.

'No one will take it,' says Heinrich.

And now the rest of the story can be simply told.

Tesches Kind wächst auf als Tesches Kind, von Heinrich keine Rede. Es heißt Martha und hat, als Kind, blonde Haare, später werden sie dunkel.

Heinrich bleibt verschwunden. Wir waren ja da zusammen, sagt Bussat, in Lobellerwäldchen. Er wollte noch nach Kloken rüber, sagt Tesche. Da ist er wohl versoffen, sagt Kakschies. Na wer weiß, sagt Ambrassat, wo sich so allerhand Gesindel herumtreibt, hier an der Grenze.

Wie letzte Gedanken aussehen, kann man nicht sagen. Doch wohl von Fall zu Fall ganz verschieden.

Letzte Worte – da ist es anders, die werden manchmal weitergetragen, da erfährt man etwas, die gehn, manchmal, noch lange um.

Diese nicht.

Was wird er auch schon gesagt haben?

Weißt du: ganz komisch, da steht er über einem, und solch eine Zunge, sag ich dir, ein weißer Hirsch, rein zum Lachen.

Na gewiß doch, sagt Tesche.

Und Heinrich will sich aufrichten: Tesche, laß sein, hör auf, Tesche.

Da ist nun schon alles erzählt. Man fährt nach Lobellerwäldchen, redet dies und das. Ambrassats Grammophon. Ambrassats Schaukel. Ambrassats siebenfarbiger Kornus. Hier ist man so schön im Wald. Ihr sauft auch wie die Löcher, sagt die Bussatsche. Der Kaiser, sag ich euch, sagt Herr Bussat, der saß und saß.

Tesche's child grows up as Tesche's child, no mention of Heinrich at all. She's called Martha and has fair hair as a child, as she grows older it turns dark.

And Heinrich never turns up.

'But we were all there together,' says Bussat, 'in the Lobellen Grove.'

'He was on his way over to Kloken,' says Tesche.

'He must have got drowned,' says Kakschies.

'You can't be so sure,' says Ambrassat, 'with all the riff-raff that roams about in these parts, so close to the frontier.'

What last thoughts are like it is impossible to tell. Presumably different in each case.

Last words – that's another matter, sometimes they are handed down, they may tell us something, they circulate, sometimes, for quite a while.

Not these.

What might he have said, anyway?

'You know, it's odd really, him standing over me, and a tongue like that, I can tell you, a white stag, simply makes you laugh.'

'Well, yes, of course,' says Tesche.

And Heinrich tries to get up: 'Tesche, lay off, stop it, Tesche.'

So the whole story is told now. They go out to the Lobellen Grove, discuss this and that. Ambrassat's gramophone, Ambrassat's swing. Ambrassat's seven-hued kornus. It's beautiful out here in the woods. 'You drink like fishes,' says the Bussat woman. 'The Emperor, I tell you,' says Herr Bussat, 'he just sat and sat.'

ANITA G.

ALEXANDER KLUGE

Translated by Simon Caulkin

ANITA G.

Haben Sie nicht eine erfreulichere Geschichte?

I

DAS Mädchen Anita G. sah, unter dem Treppenaufbau hockend, die Stiefel, als ihre Großeltern abgeholt wurden. Nach der Kapitulation kamen die Eltern aus Theresienstadt[1] zurück, was keiner geglaubt hätte, und gründeten Fabriken in der Nähe von Leipzig. Das Mädchen besuchte die Schule, glaubte an eine ruhige Weiterentwicklung. Plötzlich bekam sie Angst und floh in die Westzonen. Natürlich beging sie Diebstähle auf ihrer langen Reise. Der Richter, der sich ernstlich Sorgen um sie machte, gab ihr vier Monate, von denen sie aber nur die Hälfte abzusitzen brauchte. Für die andere Hälfte bekam sie Bewährungsauflagen und eine Bewährungshelferin, die aber die Betreuung übertrieb, also floh das Mädchen weiter nach WIESBADEN. Von WIESBADEN, wo sie Ruhe fand, nach KARLSRUHE, wo sie verfolgt wurde, nach FULDA, wo sie verfolgt wurde, nach KASSEL, wo sie nicht verfolgt wurde, von dort nach FRANKFURT. Sie wurde aufgegriffen und (da ein Fahndungsersuchen wegen Bruchs der Bewährungsauflagen vorlag) nach HANNOVER auf Transport gebracht, sie aber floh nach MAINZ. Warum begeht sie auf Reisen immer wieder Eigentumsdelikte? Sie wird unter verschiedenen Namen im Fahndungsblatt gesucht. Weshalb ordnet dieser intelligente Mensch nicht seine Angelegenheiten befriedigend? Häufig wechselt sie ihr Zimmer, sie hat meist gar keines, weil sie sich mit den Wirtinnen überwirft. Man kann nicht wie ein Zigeuner in der Gegend herumziehen. Warum verhält sie sich nicht dementsprechend?

ANITA G.

Don't you have a more cheerful story?

I

SQUATTING under the stairs, Anita G. saw the boots as her grandparents were taken away. After the capitulation, her parents returned from Theresienstadt – a thing no one would have believed possible – and set up factories near Leipzig. The girl went to school and expected a quiet life thenceforth. Suddenly she took fright and fled to the western zones. The journey was long and inevitably she began stealing. The magistrate took her case to heart and gave her four months, of which however she only had to serve half. For the other half she got probation and a female probation officer who overdid the aftercare, so she moved on again to WIESBADEN. From WIESBADEN, where she found a little peace, on to KARLSRUHE, where she was pursued, to FULDA, where she was again pursued, to KASSEL, where she was not pursued, and from there to FRANKFURT. She was picked up and, being wanted for breach of probation, transported to HANOVER; but she escaped to MAINZ. Why over and over again these petty thefts on her travels? She was wanted in the police register under various names. How come that an intelligent human being should make such a mess of her affairs? She switched lodgings frequently; indeed, mostly had none at all because of a tendency to fall out with her landladies. It doesn't do to go wandering the countryside like a gypsy: why not adjust and act accordingly? Why didn't she throw in her lot

Warum schließt sie sich dem Mann nicht an, der sich um sie bemüht? Warum stellt sie sich nicht auf den Boden der Tatsachen? Will sie nicht?

2

Den Mann, den sie gestern kennengelernt hatte, nahm sie mit in das Zimmer, das ihr schon nicht mehr gehörte. Komm, hier, sagte sie leise, als sie hörte, wie er sich in dieser Dunkelheit vorsichtig hinter ihr hertastete. Er konnte sich nicht ganz lautlos bewegen. Er war überhaupt nicht geschickt. Sie bewegte sich in dieser Dunkelheit auf ihn zu und führte ihn, an der Hand gefaßt, vorbei an den Räumen ihrer früheren Wirtin bis zu ihrem Zimmer. Sie schloß ab und machte Licht.

Der Mann mißbilligte dieses Theater, aber er wußte auch nicht, weshalb es veranstaltet wurde. Vermutlich nahm er an, daß sie auf Verwandte Rücksicht nahm, bei denen sie wohnte. Er hätte es vorgezogen, seinen Besuch bei diesen Verwandten zu machen und so die neue Verbindung mit dem schönen Mädchen zu legalisieren. Geheimnistuerei war ihm fremd. Er sagte das auch. Sie wollte ihm aber jetzt nicht erklären, inwiefern ihr dieses Zimmer nicht mehr gehörte. Der Grund, weshalb die Schepp sie hinausgeworfen hatte oder weshalb das Mädchen seinerseits das Mietsverhältnis beendet hatte, woraufhin sie von der Schepp hinausgeworfen worden war, war nicht mit ein paar Worten faßbar. Die Schepp: großer, ungewöhnlicher Hut, große, funkelnde Augen, voller Eitelkeiten. Ihr Mann, sagen wenigstens einige Leute, soll sich vom Balkon des 3. Stocks auf die Straße gestürzt haben, während sie im Nebenzimmer hantierte. Vielleicht rechnete die Schepp damit, daß das Mädchen heimlich zurückkäme? Das Mädchen bewegte sich ohne jeden Laut im Zimmer, was ihr leichter fiel, als Lärm zu machen, sie gehörte zu den Leuten, deren

with the man who was taking real trouble over her? Why this refusal to base herself on reality? No wish to, perhaps?

2

She had met him the day before and now took him back to her room (it wasn't in fact hers any longer). 'Come on, over here,' she said softly, hearing him feel his way gingerly behind her in the darkness. He was incapable of absolutely silent movement; not at all adroit. She moved over to him in the dark and led him by the hand, past her ex-landlady's quarters, up to her room. She closed the door and switched on the light.

The man wasn't keen on this performance, but then he had no idea why it had been put on. Doubtless he assumed that she was bothered about relatives with whom she shared the house. He would have preferred to call on them and legitimize his new relationship with this most attractive girl. Furtiveness was something alien to his nature. Indeed, he told her so. But at that moment she had no desire to explain how and why the room was no longer hers. The reason Frau Schepp had thrown her out, or why the girl for her part had given notice and had thereupon been thrown out, was hard to sum up in a couple of words. Frau Schepp had a large and peculiar hat, large sparkling eyes, and was shallow and vain. Her husband was supposed to have thrown himself off a third-floor balcony into the street below whilst she was busy in the next room – that's what some people said at least. Maybe she reckoned the girl might slip back in on the quiet? The girl moved soundlessly about the room – something that came more easily to her than making a noise. She was one of those people whose imaginations don't stretch to being noisy. The man bumped

Phantasie zum Lärmmachen nicht reicht. Der Mann stieß an das Eisenbett. Sie zitterte, da sie mit der Schepp rechnete.

An die Wärme und Sicherheit, die von dem neben ihr liegenden Körper ausging, glaubte A. nicht. Die bleiche, großporige Haut, die engen Brustwarzen, von einzelstehenden langen Härchen umgeben, schienen selbst schutzbedürftig. Sie hatte keinen Schutz zu vergeben. Wenn es nicht in wichtigen Punkten sie selbst beträte, fände sie diesen Mann vielleicht sogar lächerlich mit seinen Besorgnissen, der Furcht, sich auf etwas Unerlaubtes einzulassen. Sie hatte nicht die Fähigkeit, sich Menschen lange auszusuchen. Ungeduldig nahm sie den auf, der bereit war, sich mit ihr abzugeben. Es war eine Chance, ihr Leben wieder in den Zustand von Sicherheit und Ordnung zu bringen. Insofern wollte sie ihren Vorteil wahren.

Sie fror in dem ungeheizten Raum und spürte die kommende Erkältung wie etwas, auf das sie sich freute und das sie doch gleichzeitig mißbilligte, weil es hinderlich sein würde, alles so ähnlich wie ein Kind bekommen – sie suchte die Wärme in dem neben ihr liegenden Körper, an den sie sich erst wieder gewöhnen mußte. Sie genierte sich nicht mehr vor ihm. Sie lieferte ihm jeden Teil ihres Körpers aus, den er haben wollte. Sie gab sich mit einer Einfachheit, die es auch bei einfachen Leuten nicht gibt, und sorgte dafür, daß die Erzählungen, die ihre Vergangenheit betrafen, natürlich blieben. Sie richtete ihre Vergangenheit so zu, daß sie ihn nicht stören konnte. Pläne machte sie nicht, sondern wartete auf seine Vorschläge für den nächsten Tag. Sie vergewisserte sich des neben ihr schlafenden Körpers durch die dünne Decke. Sie schlief, wenn er da war, außerhalb der Decke, am Bettrand, auf der Seite liegend und etwas angelehnt an den Berg unter der Decke; sie hätte sonst befürchtet, ihn zu stören, wenn sie sich bewegte, was sie nachts nicht in der Kontrolle hatte.

into the iron bedstead. She thought of Frau Schepp and shivered.

A. had little faith in the warmth and security emanating from the body by her side. The pallid, coarse-grained skin, the pinched nipples surrounded by long, solitary hairs seemed rather to demand protection. She had no protection to give. If it hadn't touched upon her own self so significantly she might even have found him ridiculous, with his worries and his fear of letting himself in for anything illicit. She was not good at searching people out; she soon gave up and seized impatiently on anyone prepared to be interested in her. It was an opportunity to bring her life back to a safe and ordered pattern; and as such it was an advantage she would not let go.

She was freezing in the unheated room and felt a cold coming on as something to be welcomed and yet resented for its potential inconvenience; a bit like having a baby. She sought warmth in the body next to her, first having to accustom herself to it again. She was no longer embarrassed with him. Whatever part of her body he wanted, she gave him. She gave herself with a simplicity which simple people don't in fact have, and took care to keep her stories about the past natural. She arranged her past in such a way that it couldn't disturb him. She made no plans, content instead to await his suggestions for the next day. Through the thin cover she made sure of the body sleeping next to her. With him there, she slept outside the blanket, on the edge of the bed, lying on her side and leaning slightly against the mound under the clothes; fearing that otherwise she would disturb him with movements which at night she couldn't control.

Gegen Morgen erwachte der Mann und wandte sich ihr noch einmal zu. Sie hätte ihn gern geschont, weil sie auf keinen Fall wollte, daß er mehr tat, als er selbst wollte. Sie wollte nicht, daß er diese Nacht, die vielleicht die letzte war, in fader Erinnerung hätte. Aber sie konnte sich andererseits nicht gut gegen ihn wehren, wenn sie einfach und natürlich sein wollte. Sie gab sich Mühe, beteiligt zu erscheinen, was ihr nicht gut gelang. Sie war gespannt auf das, was er sagen würde, und verpaßte so, was er zu ihr sagte. Sie deckte den Erschöpften zu und machte sich Vorwürfe, ihm nicht nützlich gewesen zu sein. Sie schmiegte sich an die Decke, die ihn umgab, und wartete, bis er eingeschlafen war. Sie wollte ihn auf keinen Fall ausnützen. Insbesondere wollte sie ihn nicht auf diese Art ausnützen, die ihr nichts half.

Sie konnte sich bewegen, ohne irgendein Geräusch zu machen, und öffnete auch jedes Schloß ohne Geräusch. Der Mann stolperte, als sie ihn hinausbrachte, aber das ging im Morgenlärm des Hauses unter. Es zerschnitt ihr das Herz, als er sich in der Kälte des Zimmers ankleidete, aber sie konnte an dem Zustand nichts ändern, da sie eigentlich ja nicht einmal dieses Zimmer benutzen durfte. Sie entließ ihn schnell, damit sich diese Momente nicht in seiner Erinnerung einprägten. Sie selbst verließ, sobald er sich entfernt hatte, diese Wohnung.

3

Sie wollte ihn noch einmal sehen, bevor sie abreiste. Seit mehreren Wochen verlängerte sie sich von Tag zu Tag diese Beziehung, obwohl ihre Lage in der Stadt immer gefährlicher wurde. Sie suchte nach ihm und sah ihn später im Café am Dom. Er sah noch immer müde aus, schlaffer Mund und etwas hohle, eingefallene, «kandierte» Lippen. Eine ziemlich läppische Unterhaltung. Zu einem Nebenmann: Er hätte Nachtschicht gehabt . . ., wenn man mit einer temperament-

Towards morning the man woke and turned over to her again. She would willingly have spared him this; she was particularly anxious that he shouldn't do more than he himself felt inclined to. This might be their last night: she didn't want him to remember it with distaste. On the other hand, she couldn't very well fob him off if she was trying to be simple and natural. She tried, not very successfully, to seem interested. She waited tensely to hear what he would say, and thus missed what he finally did say to her. He was spent and she covered him up and berated herself for not having been any use to him. She snuggled up to his covering blanket and waited till he went to sleep. On no account must she exploit him; especially not in this way, which profited her not at all.

She could move quite soundlessly, and soundlessly she unlocked the doors. The man stumbled as she led him out, but the sound was lost in the morning noise of the house. Seeing him dress in the cold of that room cut her to the quick, but since she wasn't in fact even supposed to use the room herself she could do nothing to change the situation.

She packed him off quickly before these moments had a chance to fix themselves in his memory. As soon as he had gone, she left the house herself.

3

She wanted to see him once more before she left. For several weeks she had been spinning out the relationship day by day, even though her position in the town was becoming ever more dangerous. She went to look for him and later on found him in the café near the cathedral. He still looked tired, his mouth slack, with sunken, sagging, 'glacéed' lips. The conversation was hardly inspiring. To a man sitting next to him he remarked that he had been working nights . . . going with

vollen Frau zusammen sei . . . Er spürte nicht, daß sie in seiner Nähe war.

Sie erschrak. Dies war alles, was die Liebe bewirkt. Sie hätte gewünscht, daß sie schon gestern abgereist wäre. Was sie von ihrer Kraft in diesen Mann investierte, er blieb platt. Sie gab die Hoffnung auf, ihn für sich einzuspannen. Sie begleitete den Mann aus einiger Entfernung zum Amtsgebäude, in dem er wie jeden Tag verschwand. Später beruhigte sie sich. Sie beschloß, mit ihm noch einen weiteren Versuch zu machen.

4

Die Vorgeschichte ist mit wenigen Worten wiedergegeben:

Sie hätte mit diesem Mann nie ein Wort gesprochen, wenn der Unfall nicht als Vermittler dagewesen wäre. A. wollte an dem betreffenden Tag Mai 1956 die Stadt MAINZ verlassen, weil sie in mehreren Pensionen in der Bahnhofsgegend Schulden gemacht hatte und sich auch aus anderen Gründen in der Stadt nicht mehr sicher fühlte. Bevor sie die Stadt verließ, besuchte sie die auf einer Anhöhe gelegene Universität. Sie überbrückte den Tag in den Aufenthaltsräumen der Universität und in Vorlesungen. Sie wollte nach WIESBADEN hinüberfahren und dort vielleicht arbeiten, aber an der Torausfahrt der Universität wurde sie, als sie die Straße überquerte, von einem Auto erfaßt (es kann auch sein, daß sie in das Fahrzeug hineinlief). Sie erhob sich vom Sturz und prüfte die Schrammen an ihrem Körper. Der Autobesitzer kam auf sie zu und ohrfeigte sie. Sie wußte keine Reaktion darauf. Später lernte sie diesen Mann näher kennen. Wenn der Unfall nicht gewesen wäre, hätte sie nie ein Wort mit ihm gesprochen. Der Mann hielt sie an, in MAINZ zu bleiben, sich ein Quartier und Arbeit zu suchen. Er wünschte, daß sie richtig mit Geld versorgt wäre und eine Arbeit hätte.

someone who was all woman . . . He had no inkling that she was there.

She was appalled. This was all that love could do? She wished she had gone the day before. He was shallow and trivial, and remained so however much of her own energy she put into him. She gave up hope of harnessing him to her own aims. She followed him at a distance to the office building into which he daily disappeared. Later she calmed down and resolved to give him one more try.

4

There is little to tell by way of introduction.

She would never have said a word to him without the accident as intermediary. A. was going to leave MAINZ on that particular day in May 1956: both because of the debts she had run up in several lodging-houses near the station and for other reasons she no longer felt safe in the town. Before leaving she went up the hill to the university. She got through the day in university common rooms and lectures. She was intending to move on to WIESBADEN and perhaps find work; but coming out of the university gateway she was knocked down by a car as she crossed the street (it could have been her, of course, who ran into the car). She picked herself up and examined the cuts and scratches on her body, whereupon the owner of the vehicle came over and slapped her. She did not know how to react. Later she got to know the man better. But for the accident she would never even have spoken to him. He urged her to stay in MAINZ, find a room and get work. He wanted to be sure she was properly provided for, with money and a job. He was worried that he might otherwise be saddled with obligations arising out of her enforced idleness.

Er hätte sonst befürchtet, daß aus ihrer Untätigkeit Belastungen resultierten. Obwohl er Belastungen jeder Art ausdrücklich ablehnte, gebrauchte er selbst im weiteren Verlauf dieser Beziehung nicht die nötige Vorsicht. Sie erkannte die Folgen seiner Unvorsichtigkeit, behielt aber diese Tatsache für sich, wahrscheinlich, weil sie sich vor seiner Reaktion darauf fürchtete und er auch nicht danach fragte.

5   Auf der Suche nach einem Anwalt

Das Mädchen war auf einen Zeitungsartikel aufmerksam geworden, der von der Tätigkeit des Frankfurter Anwalts Dr. Sch. berichtete. Sie reiste nach FRANKFURT und versuchte mit diesem Verteidiger in Verbindung zu kommen. Den Vormittag über war er jedoch in seinem Büro nicht zu erreichen. Nachmittags sah sie ihn von weitem im Justizgebäude, der Bürovorsteher des Anwalts hatte ihr geraten, ihn dort zu suchen. Sie wagte nicht, ihn anzusprechen, als er, umgeben von einem Pulk Fragender, den Sitzungssaal verließ und die mächtige Freitreppe hinabstieg. Am späteren Nachmittag war er wieder unerreichbar, so oft sie auch in seinem Büro anrief. Sich für einen der nächsten Tage anmelden wollte sie nicht, sie hatte bereits die Hoffnung aufgegeben, an den berühmten Mann heranzukommen und ihn für ihren Fall zu interessieren. Mit einem der Assessoren, die im Anwaltsbüro zur Verfügung standen, wollte sie nicht sprechen, weil sie nur zum Anwalt selbst Vertrauen hatte und außerdem glaubte, daß nur bei dem Verteidiger selbst eine Beratung ohne Geld möglich sei. Ihr Fehler war, daß sie zu Anfang ihrer Versuche, genaugenommen bei ihrem ersten Anruf, zu zaghaft gefragt hatte. Sie erhielt daher eine ablehnende Antwort des Büropersonals.

Tageslauf des Verteidigers: Der berühmte Mann trieb sich den

Even though he expressly rejected obligations of any kind, he did in fact himself fail to take the necessary precautions as their relationship progressed. She was aware of the consequences of his lack of foresight but kept the knowledge to herself, probably for fear of his reaction; also because he didn't ask.

5   *Looking for a lawyer*

The girl noticed a newspaper article dealing with the activities of Dr Sch., the Frankfurt lawyer. She went to FRANKFURT and tried to get in touch with him. All morning, however, he was unobtainable at his office. During the afternoon she caught a distant glimpse of him at the law-courts, where she had been advised by his office manager to look for him. He left the courtroom and came down the imposing flight of steps surrounded by people asking him questions; she did not dare to speak to him. Later that afternoon, however many times she rang his office, he was still unavailable. She wouldn't make an appointment to see him another day, for she had already given up hope of getting through to this famous person and arousing his interest in her case. Nor would she speak to any of the legal advisers available in the office; the barrister and defence counsel himself was the only one she had any confidence in, and the only one furthermore who she thought would advise her free of charge. Her mistake was to have been too hesitant at the start – in fact when she telephoned first of all. It ensured her a negative response from the office staff.

A day in the life of the defence counsel: The famous person spent

Vormittag über im Bademantel in seiner Wohnung herum. Er war nicht neugierig auf den neuen Tag. Er telefonierte mit Wiesbaden und mit Zürich und saß dann an seinem Tisch.

Seine Hand lag auf dem Tisch, gestützt auf den zweiten und fünften Finger, der Daumen ruhig daneben, der dritte und vierte Finger knieten. Wenn er den vierten Finger langsam hochzog und nach vorn zog, schnappten an einem bestimmten Punkt die beiden knieenden Finger gemeinsam nach vorn und die Hand fiel flach auf den Tisch. Er antwortete nicht, wartete, bis die Sekretärin das Klopfen aufgab und von der Tür verschwand. Dicke Adern auf dem schmalen und etwas behaarten Handrücken, die beiden knieenden Finger nach vorn geschleudert und die Hand lag flach, gewissermaßen atemlos, auf dem Tisch. Er sah sie da, war nicht neugierig auf den Tag.

Später brauchten Mitarbeiter seine Zustimmung zu einer eiligen Entscheidung. An der Beratung eines Gnadenaktes in der Staatskanzlei nahm er fernmündlich teil. Die Telefonate belebten ihn etwas. Wenn er lange genug Interesse an diesen Gesprächen heuchelte, bekam er Interesse. Einer nach dem anderen riefen seine Mitarbeiter über das Haustelefon an und baten um Weisungen. Er hatte keine Lust. Ein vitaler Mensch kann nicht aufgeklärt sein. Wie viel Schwäche ist nötig, damit einer aufgeklärt ist?

Der Mittelteil des Tages rollte nach einem Zeitplan ab, auf den er nur insofern Einfluß hatte, als er jeweils den Aufbruch von einer Veranstaltung oder Verabredung zur anderen hinauszögern konnte, was aber sein ausgezeichneter Chauffeur, der ihn durch den Nachmittagsverkehr brachte, zum Teil wieder ausglich. Seine beiden Assessoren erwarteten ihn vor dem Portal des Justizpalastes. Er ließ sich in diese entsetzlichen Säle führen. Er war jetzt müde von der anstrengenden Vorführung des Mittagessens, die er hinter sich gebracht hatte. Sie war anstrengend, weil er außer Witz, Klugheit, Scharfsinn,

the morning pottering around the house in his bathrobe. He was not curious to know what the new day might bring. He rang up Wiesbaden and Zurich and then sat down at his desk.

His hand lay on the desk. It was resting on index and little fingers, the thumb lying slack alongside, with third and fourth fingers bent over. As he slowly raised his fourth finger and pushed it out, there came a moment when both bent fingers snapped forward and his hand fell flat on the desk. He waited, unanswering, until the secretary gave up knocking and retreated from the door. Thick veins across the back of narrow, rather hairy hands. The two bent fingers shot forward, and the hand lay flat, breathless as it were, on the desk. He looked at it lying there. He was not curious to know what the day might bring.

Later, colleagues needed his approval for an urgent decision. There were consultations at the chancellery over an act of clemency in which he took part by telephone. Telephoning livened him up a bit. If he pretended to be interested in the conversations long enough, the interest became real. One after the other, colleagues rang him for instructions over the internal lines. He was in no mood for any of it. No very energetic person can be enlightened. How much weakness does enlightenment take?

The middle part of the day unwound according to a plan over which he had no control except in so far as he could delay his departure from one appointment or meeting to another, and in any case these delays were partly made up again by the excellent chauffeur who piloted him through the afternoon traffic. His two juniors were waiting for him at the entrance to the law-courts. He allowed himself to be led inside the hideous rooms. By now he was tired as a result of his strenuous performance over lunch. Strenuous because apart from wit, intelligence and mental agility (qualities moreover which he

was noch dazu Eigenschaften waren, die er eigentlich nicht besaß, auch Standhaftigkeit im Trinken und Essen zeigen mußte; Gegenpol zu seiner Geschicklichkeit im Lavieren.[2] Auf diesen vorgeblichen Eigenschaften beruhte ein Teil seiner Beliebtheit. Er näherte sich mit ambivalenten Empfindungen dem Stall des Angeklagten, redete mit allen möglichen Leuten, ehe er bei seiner Bank ankam und sich zu der üblichen Begrüßung zum Angeklagten zurückwandte. Die Assessoren blätterten in den Akten. Er zog sich in die äußerste Ecke der Bank zurück, prüfte, ob hier Zugluft herrschte. Der Ange- klagte wurde befragt. Er war ein dicker, gut zahlender Kaufmann, dem Sittlichkeitsdelikte vorgeworfen wurden. Der Verteidiger wartete vor seinem Tisch, prüfte, ob ein Ein- greifen erforderlich sei. Er bewegte sich so vorsichtig, als käme es darauf an, etwas zu fangen oder zu messen. Er war müde und versprach sich, als er, halb zum Angeklagten und zur Richterbank sich wendend, etwas sagte, während er mit abgedämpften Katzenschritten, wie um keinen Gedanken zu verscheuchen oder niemand zu beleidigen oder zu treten oder zu erschrecken, auf dem gebohnerten Boden vor seinem Verteidigertisch hin- und herging. Es fiel ihm schwer, sich zu konzentrieren. Es entstand Unruhe bei den Richtern und Schöffen. Die Richter mochten ihn nicht. Es war sein Name, der sie in Subordination hielt. Er versprach sich mehrmals, und die ganze Vorführung war wohl nicht sehr gut, die Richter blätterten während seines Plädoyers in ihren Unter- lagen. Was konnten sie ihm schaden?

Als das Urteil gesprochen war, umringten ihn die Assessoren und weitere Personen wie eine Schar Verehrer und schirmten ihn ab gegen aufdringliche Fragen, die geeignet gewesen wären, ihn in Verlegenheit zu setzen. Der Angeklagte be- dankte sich. In der Vorhalle traten eine Reihe von Leuten heran, die den Anwalt zu sprechen versuchten. Er krümmte die Schultern, weil er die Zugluft in dieser Vorhalle fürchtete,

didn't in fact possess), he had also been obliged to make a show of resolution in eating and drinking; that was what it entailed, his skill in adapting himself. Part of his popular esteem was based on these ostensible characteristics. He approached the dock with mixed feelings, exchanging a word with as many people as possible before getting to his seat and turning back for the customary greeting to the accused. His juniors flicked through their documents. He edged back as far as he could go into the corner of his seat and tested the air for draughts. The accused was being questioned. He was a fat tradesman who paid well and was up on charges of offending public decency. The barrister waited at his desk gauging whether intervention was necessary. His movements were so careful it might have been a question of catching or measuring something. He was tired and tripped over his words as he half turned to the accused and the bench and spoke, all the time pacing backwards and forwards, cat-like, with muffled tread, on the polished floor in front of defence counsel's desk, as if to avoid scaring away a thought, or offending or stepping on or frightening anyone. He found it difficult to concentrate. There was a current of unrest amongst the judges and jury. The judges didn't like him; it was his name that kept them in submission. He made several slips of the tongue, and with the judges riffling through their papers as he put his case, the whole performance was doubtless fairly undistinguished. But what harm could they do him?

When judgement was given, juniors and others gathered round like a troop of worshippers to shield him from intrusive and potentially embarrassing questions. The accused expressed his thanks. In the lobby he was approached by a stream of people all trying to talk to him. He hunched his shoulders, fearing the draught there, but none the less allowed himself to be caught up in conversation by one or another of

ließ sich aber doch mit dem einen oder anderen ein, der ihn ansprach. Er hätte um diese Nachmittagsstunde mit dem Generalstaatsanwalt in die Landesheilanstalt hinausfahren müssen, da er dort einen Fall entdeckt zu haben glaubte, in dem sein Eingreifen oder aber das des Generalstaatsanwalts nötig war. Statt dessen saß er eine Zeit lang mit dem General-staatsanwalt beim Tee.

Der gutgeschützte große Mann, der nicht mehr allzu viele Jahre zu leben hatte, machte von seinem Einfluß wenig Ge-brauch. Er besaß mehr Einfluß, als er sich selbst eingestand. Er wurde um diese Abendzeit lebendig, hatte schon am Vorabend Tropfen genommen, die das Herz auf Gespräche vorbereiten und die Blutgefäße weiten. Man konnte nicht sagen, daß er in irgendeiner Hinsicht ein Spezialist war, auch nicht in seiner Eigenschaft als Anwalt, da er nirgends bereit gewesen wäre, sich sicher zu fühlen; er war aber insofern spezialisiert, als seine ganze Macht gesammelt war als Gegen-mittel gegen den eventuell jederzeit wieder ausbrechenden Pogrom. Daher ließ sich diese Macht zu nichts anderem als zur Gefahrenabwehr verwenden. Er hatte vielleicht noch fünf Jahre zu leben und brauchte sich für diese Zeitspanne nicht mehr allzusehr anzustrengen. Er kannte genügend Auswege, um auszukommen. Er konnte sich gewissermaßen im Gleit-flug bis zur endgültigen Landung in der Luft halten, wenn der Vergleich paßt. Er ging an diesem Abend früh schlafen. Er hätte noch eine Menge Einfluß ausüben können, aber er wollte gar nichts. Er wollte in den Mutterleib zurück. Er glaubte nicht an Veränderungen, war auch, solange er nicht bedroht war, gegen Veränderungen, von denen man nicht wissen konnte, ob sie nicht Bedrohungen bringen.

Schutzbedürfnis
Sehr dünne Glieder unter dem erstklassigen Anzug, sehr haarig, weil er schon in den ersten Minuten seines Lebens

his interlocutors. He should at that hour of the afternoon have driven out with the chief public prosecutor to the regional mental hospital, where he thought he had found a case requiring action either on his or the prosecutor's part. Instead he sat with the prosecutor for some time over tea.

Immune in his greatness, with not all that many years to live, he made little use of his influence; of which he possessed more than he admitted to himself. Around this time of the evening he came to life, having in the late afternoon taken drops to open up the blood vessels and stimulate the heart for conversation. In no respect could he be said to be a specialist, not even in his capacity as lawyer, since there was no area in which he would readily have felt secure. Yet in so far as all his strength was concentrated to counter the possibility of future persecution, he *had* a speciality. The application of this strength was limited to warding off danger. He had maybe five years to live and no need, in that remaining time, to take life too strenuously. He was familiar with enough ins and outs to get by. Like a glider, he was maintaining flight to the final touchdown, if the comparison holds. That evening, he went to bed early. He could have used a lot more of his influence but had absolutely no desire to. Back in the womb was where he wanted to be. He didn't believe in change and was indeed, as long as he wasn't threatened, against changes, that might, for all one knew, bring threats with them.

The need for protection
Thin, very thin limbs beneath the excellent suit, and very hairy; in the very first minutes of his life he had needed this

diesen Schutz nötig hatte; keiner glaubte damals, daß er am Leben bleibt; die Hose ist am Rückgrat aufgehängt und hängt, ohne irgendwo mit dem Körper in Berührung zu kommen, hinunter bis zu den auseinandergerichteten Füßen.

Absicherung, Heuchelei

Sitzt in Strümpfen, was aber niemand weiß, in der guten Deckung seines Schreibtischs und läßt seine Augen aufblinken, «signalisiert», als sein Besucher irgend etwas sagt, er hat nicht zugehört und heuchelt; er muß diesem Besucher gefallen, obwohl er nicht unbedingt muß. Der Besucher gehört zu den Leuten, die zwar keine Macht über ihn haben, mit denen er aber auf keinen Fall in Unfrieden sein will.

Feindin Natur

Er zieht die Schultern zusammen, nicht weil es kalt ist, sondern weil niemand etwas zu sagen weiß, das ihn erwärmt; er sucht nach Zugluft, Rechtfertigung für sein Wärmebedürfnis. Er fürchtet sich vor Erkältungen. Er kann sich eine Schwächung des Körpers nicht leisten. Er ist geschützt vor Menschen, aber verletzbar durch Eingriffe der Zugluft.

Furchtsamkeit

Die Diskussion ging über eine Stunde in die Irre, weil er, den man zum Leiter des Gesprächs gemacht hatte, sich weigerte, die Diskussionsredner zu unterbrechen, wenn sie vom Thema abkamen. Sie diskutierten zuletzt ohne Thema in der Reihenfolge der Wortmeldungen. Viele waren wütend über diese Diskussionsleitung. Die Besten waren verärgert über dieses Verfahren und warfen dem Präsidenten vor, daß er überhaupt nicht zuhöre. Er hörte auch nicht zu, was aber niemand beweisen konnte. Er nahm die Feindschaft der Guten in Kauf und weigerte sich, die Redner zu unterbrechen, was konnten

protection. No one had believed then that he would live. Trousers suspended on the vertebral column and hanging down to splayed feet, nowhere coming in contact with the body.

Prevention, pretence

He would sit, unbeknown to the world and under the excellent cover of his desk, in stockinged feet, and blink, by way of acknowledgement, when his visitor said something. Pretence was necessary since he hadn't been listening. He had to humour his visitor; and yet there was no absolute reason why he should. The visitor was one of those people with no power over him but whom he wouldn't on any account offend.

Nature's hostility

He huddled his shoulders, not for cold but because no one could find anything to say to warm him. He looked for draughts to justify his need for warmth. He was afraid of chills. He couldn't afford physical weakening. Immune from people, but vulnerable to the encroachments of draught.

Timidity

The debate meandered aimlessly for over an hour because, having been made chairman, he refused to interrupt speakers who went off the point. By the end there was no theme at all to the discussion which simply continued according to who wanted to speak next. There were many who were furious about the way the discussion was conducted. Even the best found the procedure annoying and reproached the chairman for not listening. Nor *was* he listening, although no one could prove it. The antagonism of these good people he took in his stride and refused to interrupt the speakers. What harm could

die Unzufriedenen ihm schaden? Andererseits befürchtete er Racheakte der Unterbrochenen, wenn er die Redner unterbrach, und überhaupt lag ihm so etwas nicht. (Er sagte auch in Fällen, in denen Mitarbeiter Vorschläge machten, meist ja, obwohl er ebensogut gleich nein hätte sagen können, weil er ebensogut noch morgen nein sagen konnte, niemand hätte ihm deswegen etwas tun können, und es war für seine Sicherheit ohnehin egal, ob er ja sagte oder nein; dann aber kam noch hinzu, daß er ungern nein sagte, und lieber erst ja sagte, weil die Chance bestand, daß durch den Zeitablauf die Sache sich von selbst erledigte und er vielleicht überhaupt nie nein zu sagen brauchte. Er bezahlte seine Mitarbeiter für die Vorschläge und honorierte daher auch das Recht, die Vorschläge abzulehnen. Aber er hätte ungern einen der Vorschläge, die sie ihm machten, abgelehnt, wahrscheinlich, weil er Racheakte befürchtete.)

Stimulation
Dreistündige Mittagstafel in einem Lokal in Bahnhofsnähe, wo er Gäste empfängt, denen er gefallen muß: er zeichnet die Neuangekommenen aus, indem er ihnen entgegengeht und sich auf dem Weg von der Tür, an der er sie begrüßt, zu den Tischen abfällig über die schon dasitzenden Gäste äußert. Nach Tisch redet er von seinem Tode, nicht zu allen. Die Gäste, die es hörten, waren unsicher, wie sie sich verhalten sollten. Die Ausmalung seines baldigen Todes war sein stärkstes Anregungsmittel, von dem er – wie übrigens auch von Penicillin, Chinin usf. – hemmungslos Gebrauch machte.

Verfolgung, Schützling, zwei Alternativen
Er hat einen großartigen Apparat entwickelt, der ihn im Fall von Pogromen und natürlich erst recht in Ruhezeiten schützt. Wie aber hält er den empfindlichen Apparat am Laufen, wenn keine Verfolgung da ist? Er braucht deshalb starke

the malcontents do him? But he was afraid of retaliation by the speaker if he broke in, and anyway it wasn't at all his way of doing things. (Similarly, he mostly said yes to proposals put forward by his colleagues where he might equally well have said no at once, because he could always say no the next day without anyone's being able to do anything about it, and anyway from the point of view of his own security it didn't make any difference which he said; but then there was also the fact that he disliked saying no and preferred saying yes initially, since there was always the possibility that with the passage of time the matter would sort itself out and maybe absolve him from having to say no at all. He paid his assistants for their suggestions and thus also paid for the right to turn them down. But he would have rejected any of the suggestions made to him with reluctance, probably because he was afraid of revenge.)

Stimulation
Three-hour lunch in a restaurant near the station where he was host to people by whom he had to be liked: he distinguished the new arrivals by going to meet them and, on the way from the door where he welcomed them to the tables, made derogatory remarks about those already sitting there. After the meal he talked about his own death, although not to everyone. The guests who heard him weren't sure how to react. The depiction of his own impending death was his most powerful stimulant, and he used it (as incidentally he used penicillin, quinine, etc.) extravagantly.

Persecution and someone to protect – two alternatives
He had developed a splendid defence mechanism against organized persecution – even more effective of course in times of peace. But how could he keep this sensitive apparatus working when no persecution existed? It needed strong stimuli to

Anregungsmittel, um sich am Laufen zu halten. Das stärkste Anregungsmittel wäre natürlich ein Schützling, der wirklich gefährdet ist. Aber wie soll der Schützling durch den Schutzring von Berühmtheit, Assessoren, Mitarbeitern, Büroangestellten, diese komplizierte Organisation, bis zum großen Verteidiger selbst vordringen?

6 *Das Mädchen übernachtet mit ihrem Freund in einem fremden Personenfahrzeug*

Da er nicht wissen konnte, wo er sie finden sollte, wenn sie ohne Zimmer und ohne feste Punkte war, an denen sie sich zu bestimmten Zeiten aufhielt, wartete sie in der Straße vor seiner Wohnung, bis er abends heimkam. Sie ließ ihn ins Haus gehen, da sie sich nicht aufdrängen wollte, für den Fall, daß er etwas Wichtiges vorhätte, und folgte ihm, als er wieder auf die Straße kam, aus einer gewissen Entfernung, bis sie sicher war, daß er lediglich zum Theater ging. Sie sprach ihn an. Er war überrascht und fragte, was denn passiert sei. Sie erzählte ihm irgend etwas. Sie gaben die Theaterkarte irgendeinem, der vor dem Theater wartete. Sie war so froh, ihn wiederzuhaben, daß sie zugab, daß sie ohne Unterkunft war. Sie redete davon, daß sie Geld erwarte, um seine Bedenken zu zerstreuen. Sie fand ein unverschlossenes Auto und zerstreute seine Bedenken, ein Stück damit zu fahren und es später wieder an die alte Stelle zu bringen. Er hatte Angst vor Entdeckung und Disziplinarstrafen, aber sie rechnete damit, daß dies der letzte Abend sein würde, den sie zusammen hätten, und zerstreute deshalb alles, was er sagen wollte. Es war ein sehr schwerer Fehler, den sie beging, denn er fand seine Unbefangenheit an diesem Abend nicht wieder.

Er hatte sich vorbereitet und wollte sich an diesem Tage grundsätzlich mit ihr über eine festere Verbindung aus-

keep it going. The most powerful stimulus, of course, would be someone who really was in danger and need of protection. But how was the potential ward to break through the protective shell of fame, juniors, colleagues, office staff, the whole complicated organization, to get to the defending champion himself?

6 *The girl spends a night with her friend in a stolen car*

There was no way he could find her now that she had no room, nowhere even where she would definitely be at particular times of day, so she waited in the street in front of his house until he came home in the evening. She let him go in, not wishing to impose herself on him in case he had something important to do, and when he reappeared followed him at a distance until she was sure he was only heading for the theatre. She spoke to him. He was surprised and asked what had happened. She told him something or other. They gave the ticket to someone waiting outside the theatre. She was so happy to have him back she admitted she was homeless. To calm his fears, she talked of money she was expecting. She found an unlocked car and persuaded him against his better judgement to drive around a bit before bringing it back to its original spot. He was afraid of being discovered and punished, but reckoning on its being the last evening they had together, she shrugged off everything he was trying to say. It was in fact a very bad mistake, since throughout the evening he never recovered his ease.

He had prepared himself that day to have out with her the possibility of a more permanent relationship. He couldn't find the tone the words had originally had when he thought

sprechen. Er fand den Ton nicht, den diese Worte ursprünglich in seinem Kopf gehabt hatten, aber auch die zusammenhanglosen Möglichkeiten, in denen er herumstocherte, setzten sie in eine helle Panik. Sie wollte abwehren. Es war das, was sie in den letzten Wochen mühsam angestrebt hatte; jetzt kam zu dieser Wunschvorstellung eine Flut von Gegengründen, eine Antipathie gegen jeden Gedanken einer festeren Verbindung. Ihre zerrütteten Empfindungen durchjagten eine Skala von Reaktionen, sie fand nichts zu antworten. Sie wünschte sich eine Katastrophe, aus der sie ihn befreien könnte. Oder irgendeine Macht, die jetzt eingriff und die Flucht beendete, so daß sie ihm alles aufdecken könnte – nicht einmal aufdecken: daß sie Zeit gewänne. Sie verglich sich mit einer Zauberin, die einen Kreis um den Menschen, den sie liebt, zieht und alles, was es in der Welt gibt, in diesen Kreis transportiert. Ihr Gesicht war verkrampft. Sie erschrak, da doch Liebe alles glätten sollte. Sie zweifelte einen Augenblick an ihrer Liebe und entdeckte Anzeichen dafür, daß er ihr etwas vorspiegele und sie in Wirklichkeit mit seinen Worten nur auf geschickte Art loswerden wolle.

Er hatte die Angewohnheit, alles, was er mit ihr tat, in einen offiziellen und einen inoffiziellen Teil zu zerlegen, und versuchte, sie zu entkleiden, als er mit seinen Ausführungen zu Ende war. Es kam ihr unerwartet, und sie tat, als ob sie seine Absicht nicht verstünde, da sie den letzten Abend nicht auf diese Weise fortgeben wollte. Sie klammerte sich an das Gespräch, das sie miteinander gehabt hatten, und erklärte ihm, weshalb sie gern seine Frau wäre. Sie sagte «komm», um ihn in Abstand zu halten, und redete sorgfältig kontrolliertes dummes Zeug. Es gefiel ihm gut: ob sie vom künftigen gemeinsamen Leben redete oder ihm zu gefallen suchte oder seine Hände wegbog – es bestätigte ihn nur in der Richtung, die er eingeschlagen hatte. Sie versuchte, sich zu wehren, mußte aber einfach und natürlich bleiben.

them, and added to this the incoherent eventualities he was raking around in induced in her a feeling of pure panic. She wanted to fend the whole thing off. It was what she had been painfully striving for these last weeks: now the idea of the wish's coming true was greeted by a flood of objections, an antipathy towards any thought of a firmer relationship. Her disordered feelings raced through a whole range of reactions. There was nothing she could reply. She wished there would be a catastrophe which she could use to set him free. Or some kind of power which would now intervene and end the flight, so that she could reveal everything to him, or not even that, so that she could just gain time. She likened herself to an enchantress drawing an imaginary circle round the person she loved and centring her whole world within it. Her face was rigid and set. She was shocked – love after all was supposed to smooth over all problems. For a moment she doubted her love and thought she detected signs that he was deluding her, that his words in reality were merely intended as a clever way of getting rid of her.

He had the habit of compartmentalizing everything he did with her into an official and unofficial category, and he tried to undress her when he had finished his speech. This took her unawares and, not wanting to fritter away their last evening in this way, she pretended not to understand his intentions. She clutched at their previous conversation and told him why she would like to marry him. 'Come,' she said, to keep him at a distance, and talked carefully controlled nonsense. It pleased him greatly: whether she talked of their future life together, tried to please him or pushed his hands away, it all merely confirmed him in the way he had taken. She tried to fend him off and at the same time to stay simple and natural, as she must.

Einen Augenblick rechnete sie sich aus, was geschähe, wenn sie aufdeckte: das Kind und die Fahndung, aber sie schreckte zurück. Sie fand das unfair und sagte ihm weder von dem einen noch von dem anderen etwas. Sie befreite sich aus seiner Umarmung in den engen Autositzen und kroch aus dem Wagen. Es regnete heftig. Sie ließ das Wasser auf die Haut platschen. Sie ging auf und ab. Sie duschte sich, bis er aus dem Wagen nach ihr rief. Sie war naß und schädigte die Polster, als sie wieder zu ihm hineinkroch. Es verwirrte ihn. Er schwankte zwischen den Empfindungen eines Autoeigentümers und der Empfindung ihrer Nässe.

7

Sie machte einen letzten Versuch, ihre Situation zu klären, indem sie die Eltern von Leipzig nach Bad Nauheim bestellte. Es gelang ihr aber nicht, in den zwei Tagen, die sie mit den Eltern verbrachte, die beiden auseinanderzuzerren. Sie waren eine geschlossene Phalanx der Furcht vor Strapazen. Sie brauchte Einzelkonferenzen mit ihrer Mutter und mit ihrem Vater, aber es blieb bei Plenarsitzungen. Wie nasse Bettfedern klebten die beiden aneinander, obwohl sie sich noch nie hatten leiden können und sich bei aller Gelegenheit sonst aus dem Wege gingen. Sie fürchteten sich, einen Augenblick mit der Tochter allein zu sein, und hatten sich verabredet.

Schon der Anfang war ein Fehler gewesen. Sie hatte sich in einem kleinen Café frisch machen wollen und war dort unvorbereitet von ihren Eltern entdeckt worden, die mit ihrem Wiedersehenslärm jede Bewegung abtöteten. Sie wollte sie nicht so lärmen hören, was sie ebenso abstoßend fand wie die Art, in der sie aßen oder bestimmte Dinge bemerkten und bestimmte Dinge nicht bemerkten. Sie versuchte, die geschlossene Front der beiden zu durchbrechen. Es mißlang, da das Gespräch in die schon traditionelle Fahrbahn geriet: Sie

For a second she calculated the consequences of disclosure –
the child, the police hunt – but shrank back. She found that
unfair and said nothing to him about either. She disentangled
herself from his embrace on the cramped car seats and crept
out of the car. It was raining hard. She let the water splash
down on her skin. She walked up and down. She let the rain
shower her until he called to her from the car. She was wet
and damaged the upholstery as she crawled back in beside him.
It confused him. He wavered between the qualms of a car-
owner and the feel of her wetness.

7

She made a last attempt to rectify her position by asking her
parents from Leipzig to Bad Nauheim. In the two days she
spent with them, however, she failed to prise them apart.
They formed a solid phalanx of fear of anything requiring
effort. She needed mini-conferences with her father and
mother individually, but they got no further than plenary
sessions. They stuck together like wet mattress feathers
although in fact they had never been able to stand each other
and normally lost no opportunity of keeping out of each
other's way. They were scared of spending a second on their
own with their daughter and had arranged things accordingly.

Even the start had been a mistake. She had wanted to
freshen herself up in a small café. Unprepared, she was discovered there by her parents who killed any emotion in her
with the loudness of the reunion. She disliked hearing them go
on so noisily; she found it as repellent as the way they ate or
noticed some things and failed to notice others. She tried to
break through the solid front which the two had erected. It

kritisierte die Eltern, was ihr nichts half. Sie sagte ihnen, daß sie einander haßten, was die beiden nur enger zusammenschloß, da sie Haß fürchteten. Die Eltern wiesen darauf hin, wie harmonisch das Zusammensein nach den vielen Jahren sein könnte, wenn die Tochter ihre Kritik unterließe. A. wünschte sich eine Katastrophe, die die Sperre, die sich mit jedem Wort verdichtete, beiseite gefegt hätte. Während sie das wünschte, verlor sie doch schon ihren Glauben daran, daß ihre Eltern ihr überhaupt noch helfen könnten. Sie hatte sich nicht vorgestellt, wie schwach sie waren, wenn sie gemeinsam operierten, wie sehr sie sich gegenseitig in ihrer Ehe geschwächt hatten.

Am Abend des zweiten Tages in Bad Nauheim kamen Kriminalbeamte, die den Meldezettel gelesen hatten, in das Hotel und verhafteten sie. Die Eltern erfuhren von der Verhaftung durch die Hoteldirektion. Im Laufe des folgenden Vormittags gelang es A., aus dem Polizeipräsidium zu entkommen. Sie eilte in das Hotel zurück, aber ihre Eltern waren bereits abgereist. Sie hatten Angst, in die Sache, um welche auch immer es sich handelte, hineingezogen zu werden. Sie hatten keinen Brief hinterlassen, wohl weil sie sich auf keine Fassung einigen konnten. A. vermied den Bahnhof und die Autobahn, da sie annahm, daß dort Polizei aufgestellt war, und hielt einen Wagen an auf der Reichsstraße nach FRANKFURT.

In MAINZ rannte sie in der Bahnhofsstraße direkt in die Arme der Schepp. Sie lief, ohne irgend etwas zu sehen, bis sie kurz vor ihr war, und wich entsetzt aus, über die Straße, in der Hoffnung, daß sie sie noch nicht bemerkt hätte. Sie lief in ein Auto hinein, das scharf bremsen mußte und noch weitere Fahrzeuge aus dem Kurs brachte; ein Lärm, der die Wirkung hatte, als würden Scheinwerfer auf sie konzentriert. Sie jagte

didn't work because the conversation got on to lines which had already become traditional. She criticized her parents, which didn't help. She told them they hated each other, which only pushed them closer together since hate was something they feared. Her parents pointed out how harmonious life together could be after all these years if she would just stop criticizing. A. wished some disaster would happen and sweep away the barriers, growing stronger with every word. But even as the wish was forming, she was already losing faith in her parents' ability to provide any help whatever. She had had no notion of how weak they were when they operated together, how severely they had enfeebled each other in the course of their marriage.

On the evening of the second day in Bad Nauheim, having seen the registration forms, detectives arrived at the hotel and arrested her. Her parents learned of the arrest from the hotel management. In the course of the following morning, A. succeeded in making her escape from police headquarters. She rushed back to the hotel, but her parents had already gone. Whatever the affair was about, they were frightened of getting mixed up in it. They had left no letter, doubtless because they couldn't agree over how it should be framed. Assuming that police would be posted there, A. avoided both station and motorway and stopped a car on the road to FRANKFURT.

In MAINZ she ran slap into the arms of Frau Schepp in the Bahnhofstrasse. She was running, unseeing. Suddenly she was right in front of her. A. fled in horror, across the road, hoping she still hadn't been noticed. She ran into a car which had to brake sharply, causing other vehicles in their turn to swerve. The noise they made had the same effect as if search-lights had been trained on her. She rushed up the street and

eine Straße hinauf und immer weiter, bis sie vor der Wohnung ihres Freundes stand. Sie wartete.

Sie fuhren nach WIESBADEN. Sie war gegen die Unternehmung, weil sie mit der Zeit, die noch blieb, geizte. Nach der Spur, die sie in Bad Nauheim zurückgelassen hatte, konnte es sich nur noch um Tage handeln, daß die Polizei sie aufspürte. Sie versuchte, diesen Abend zu gestalten, aber als sie kurze Zeit im «Walhalla» saßen und die Neuigkeiten ausgetauscht hatten (was sie mit Ungeduld erfüllte – die Hurengesichter, die große Leuchttraube, die sich dreht –), kam Ausweiskontrolle. Sie versuchte, die Toilettenfrau zu bereden, ihr einen Ausgang zu sagen. Während sie feststellen konnte, daß einige Prostituierte auf irgendeine Art verschwanden, hielt man sie mit halben Versprechungen hin. Wahrscheinlich hielt die Toilettenfrau sie für einen schweren Fall, der nur Unannehmlichkeiten bringt, wenn man sich auf ihn einläßt. Das Mädchen schloß sich in eine Toilette ein. Sie gab der Toilettenfrau alles Geld, das sie bei sich hatte. Die Kontrolle forderte diejenigen, die in den Kabinen saßen, auf, die Ausweise unter der Tür hervorzuschieben. Sie fingen von der linken Seite an. Es dauerte eine bestimmte Zeit, dann kam das Zeichen «danke» und Füßescharren. A. kam auf die Aufforderung hin heraus und ließ sich bis zum Ausgang der Toilette führen, wo sie sich von den Beamten losriß. Sie verbrachte die Nacht im Freien, auf halber Strecke zwischen WIESBADEN und MAINZ. Sie fürchtete, daß die Rheinbrücken nachts bewacht würden. Sie wartete am Spätnachmittag in der Straße vor der Wohnung ihres Freundes, um ihm zu erklären, weshalb sie davongelaufen sei. Er gab ihr nicht ganz hundert Mark und riet ihr, nach Nordrhein-Westfalen zu gehen. Er wußte nicht, wie er sich verhalten sollte. Er wollte sie nicht im Stich lassen. Sie ertrug das nicht und machte ein Ende.

kept on going until she found herself in front of her friend's house. She waited.

They went to WIESBADEN. She was against the idea, hoarding the time which remained like a miser. After the trail she had left behind in Bad Nauheim, it could only be a matter of days before the police tracked her down. She attempted to impose a shape on the evening, but after they had sat briefly in the Valhalla and exchanged their news (which she did impatiently – the faces of the whores, the great turning cluster of lights . . .) there was a documents check. She tried to persuade the lavatory attendant to tell her where there was a way out. She could see that several of the prostitutes were vanishing somehow or other, but she was strung along with half promises. The attendant doubtless took the view that she was a bad case and involvement with her meant trouble. The girl shut herself in one of the cubicles. She gave the attendant all the money she had on her. Those in the cubicles were required to push their papers under the door. The check began at the left. After a certain interval there was a 'thank you' signal and the shuffle of feet. On receiving the summons, A. came out and allowed herself to be led to the toilet exit, where she broke away from the police. She spent the night in the open air, halfway between WIESBADEN and MAINZ. She suspected that the Rhine bridges might be watched at night. Late in the afternoon she waited in the street in front of her friend's house to explain why she had rushed off. He gave her not quite 100 marks and counselled her to move on to North Rhine-Westphalia. He could not tell what to do. He had no desire just to dump her. She couldn't bear that and put an end to the proceedings.

8

In einer leerstehenden Villa, die Leute waren vielleicht geflohen, nistete sie sich ein. Selbst die Wasserhähne waren herausmontiert, vielleicht sollte alles abgerissen werden. Sie richtete sich in den Dachzimmern ein und hätte entkommen können, wenn sie überrascht worden wäre. Die Unruhe und Müdigkeit des Abends, an dem sie diese Unterkunft entdeckt hatte bei ihren langen Gängen durch die Straßen dieser Stadt, verwandelte sich während der Nacht in einen Druck auf der Brust, Schmerzen, wenn sie nur atmete, und schwere fiebrige Glieder, später Kopfgrippe, die etwas vom Tod hat, die Augen waren nicht mehr warm zu kriegen, schmerzhaft sehr tief in den Höhlen liegende Augen, Glieder unbeweglich, flatterig, grantig. Sie lag mit ihrer Krankheit praktisch hier wie ein Hund in dem leerstehenden Haus. Sie ging nur einmal fort und holte etwas zum Essen, nicht weil sie Hunger hatte, sondern weil sie etwas für ihr Leben tun wollte.

9

Ab zwei Uhr wurde in dieser Ecke des großen Lokals das Licht ausgeschaltet, weil der Hauptmittagsstrom der Gäste vorüber war. Als sie aufsah und die Hände, mit denen sie die Augen angewärmt hatte, wegnahm, saß sie im Dunkeln wie in einem Kellergang, aber große Balken über ihr und an den Seiten, die den Saal trugen. Sie vermutete, daß es draußen regnete, Autolärm: daß etwas geschieht. Das Blut hatte, während sie die Augen geschlossen hielt und fast schlief, an ihren Magenwänden gesessen und gesaugt, jetzt strömte es in seine Ausgangsstellungen zurück. Es funktionierte alles, Kopf, Glieder. Später verließ sie das Lokal durch einen Nebeneingang, der von der Toilette zu erreichen war und im Gegensatz zum Haupteingang nicht von der Bedienung bewacht war.

8

She moved into an empty villa; perhaps the owners had fled. Even the taps had been taken out. Maybe the whole place was about to be demolished. She made herself at home in the attic rooms from where she could have escaped if she had been surprised. During the night, the agitation and fatigue of the evening she had spent walking the streets of the town before she found her refuge became a pressure on her chest, pains at every breath, heavy, feverish limbs and later an aching head and flu which had the feel of death about it. Her eyes sank deep, deep into their sockets and they hurt: she could no longer keep them warm. Her limbs were unresponsive, shaky, sullen. Much like a dog, she lay with her illness in the empty house. Only once did she go out and get something to eat, not because she was hungry but out of a desire to do something for her life.

9

From two o'clock, the main rush of midday diners having passed, the lights in her corner of the large restaurant were switched off. When she removed the hands which had been warming her eyes and looked up, she was sitting in the dark as of some cellar passage, only with great beams holding up the room above her and on every side. She assumed it must be raining outside, that something – judging from the noise of cars – must be happening. During the time she had sat there with her eyes closed, half dozing, the blood had settled and sucked at the walls of her stomach; now it flowed back in its proper channels. Head, limbs: everything was functioning. Later she left the restaurant via a side door reached by way of the toilets. Unlike the main entrance it wasn't kept

Sie erschrak heftig, als ein Auto bis dicht an den Zebrastreifen heranfuhr. Sie ging sofort in Angriffshaltung, die Hände gegen das Auto gestreckt, das aber dann noch rechtzeitig an der äußersten Begrenzung des Zebrastreifens, bis zu der es fahren durfte, zum Halten kam.

Im Spätherbst kam A. herunter nach Garmisch, wo sie sich das Krankenhaus aussuchen wollte, in dem sie ihr Kind zur Welt bringen wollte. Sie erreichte Garmisch an einem Tag, versagte aber dann. Der Mann, der sie dorthin gefahren hatte und für alles aufgekommen wäre, wollte sie abends ausführen. Sie bekam Nasenbluten und ihr wurde übel. Es gelang ihr, die Toilette zu erreichen, wo sie erst einmal in Sicherheit war, aber es war ihr später unmöglich, dem Mann noch zu gefallen. Sie wollte ihn nicht haben.

10 *Fluchtbewegungen*

In BONN arbeitete sie als Sekretärin und Kassiererin einer Studio-Bühne. Eine Polizeistimme am Telefon verlangte, mit dem Direktor des Theaterunternehmens verbunden zu werden. Das Mädchen glaubte, der Anruf gelte ihr. Sie gab das Telefonat zum Chef durch. Sie nahm DM 200.— aus den Kassen, die sie zu verwalten hatte, und reiste nach Norddeutschland. Sie fühlte sich noch zittrig, als sie im Zug saß. Im Warteraum erster Klasse von Lüneburg konnte sie einen aufdringlichen Mann, der eine Verabredung mit ihr treffen wollte, weil er auf Grund eines Mißverständnisses glaubte, daß sie zu haben sei, nur dadurch loswerden, daß sie ihm ihren Personalausweis zur Sicherheit überließ. Sie wagte sich danach nicht mehr in den Wartesaal erster Klasse, sondern saß die Nacht über in der zweiten Klasse. Die Bahnpolizei duldete sie, da sie einen gültigen Fahrausweis vorlegen konnte; obwohl es schwer ist, von Duldung zu sprechen, wenn sie einen nur wenig abgerisseneren Mann, der auf Aufforderung sein

under surveillance by the staff. A car drove right up to the edge of the zebra crossing; she was terrified. The posture she immediately took up was one of attack, hands outstretched towards the car, which halted just in time at the nearest point to which it was permitted to come.

In late autumn A. came down to Garmisch to choose a hospital in which to have her baby. She reached Garmisch one day and then collapsed. The man who had brought her there would have seen to everything. He wanted to take her out in the evening. Her nose started to bleed and she felt awful. She managed to get to the toilet where she felt safe at last, but after that it was impossible to please him. She didn't want him.

10 *Patterns of flight*

In BONN she worked as secretary and box-office attendant at a small theatre workshop. A police voice on the telephone asked to speak to the theatre manager. The girl thought the call was about her. She put it through to her boss, took 200 marks from the cash she had charge of and went up north. She still felt shaky as she sat in the train. In the first-class waiting room at Lüneburg she was pestered for a date by a man who was under the misapprehension that she was available; she only managed to get rid of him by handing over her identity card as security. Thereafter she didn't dare go back to the first-class waiting room and sat out the night in the second-class. She was tolerated by the railway police since she could produce a valid ticket; although toleration is perhaps not quite the word, since they knocked down and ejected a man, only slightly shabbier than her, who failed to drink up his beer on the spot when ordered to do so. That was the

Bier nicht gleich austrank, zusammenschlugen und hinaus-
brachten. Das war das gute Recht der Bahn, A. nahm den
ersten Zug, der weiterführte. Sie wandte sich auf ihrer Flucht
nach ULM, AUGSBURG, DÜSSELDORF, SIEGEN, wo sie
sich jeweils nur kurz aufhielt, unter Hinterlassung kleiner
Schulden, die die Verfolgungswelle hinter ihr ankurbelten, so
daß es – wenn man die Sache ohne ihre Zusammenhänge
sieht – so aussah, als provoziere sie diese Verfolgungswelle
absichtlich, um ihre Fluchtbewegung zu motivieren.

11 *Fluchtbewegungen*

In BRAUNSCHWEIG arbeitete sie im November, bis sie, mit
der Fünf-Uhr-Welle zum Haus ihrer Wirtin kommend,
Polizei vor dem Haus sah. Sie floh nach STUTTGART.

Von STUTTGART floh sie unter Hinterlassung von Hotel-
rechnungen nach MANNHEIM, KOBLENZ, WUPPERTAL,
unter Umgehung von DÜSSELDORF, von WUPPERTAL
nach KÖLN, die Nähe von KOBLENZ schreckte sie ab und
sie wich aus nach DARMSTADT.

In der Absicht, sich einen rechtswidrigen Vermögensvorteil
zu verschaffen, mietete sie sich ein in DARMSTADT, wie schon
vorher in verschiedenen anderen Städten, unter Vor-
spiegelung eines Zahlungswillens, den sie eigentlich gar nicht
hatte.

12 *Die Ausgeplünderte*

Im Februar brauchte sie dringend einen festen Platz für die
Geburt. Sie versuchte es noch einmal im Rheinland, aber da
ihr Zustand jedem deutlich war, nahm sie keiner. Sie stellte
sich der Polizei, nachdem feststand, daß sie keine Papiere hatte
und sich definitiv nicht selbst helfen konnte. Sie wurde ein-
geliefert in die Untersuchungsstrafanstalt Dietz. Sie mußte

railway's privilege; A. took the first train out. In her flight she passed through ULM, AUGSBURG, DÜSSELDORF, SIEGEN, stopping only briefly every time and leaving in her wake modest debts which swelled the wave of pursuit behind her; so that, looking at things from outside their context, it appeared as if she was deliberately provoking the wave of pursuit to activate her flight.

11 *Patterns of flight*

She worked in BRAUNSCHWEIG in November until, coming back on the rush-hour tide to her landlady's house, she saw police outside. She fled to STUTTGART.

Leaving hotel bills behind her, she fled from STUTTGART to MANNHEIM, KOBLENZ and WUPPERTAL, with a detour round DÜSSELDORF. From WUPPERTAL to COLOGNE. The proximity of KOBLENZ frightened her off and she changed course for DARMSTADT.

She sought to raise money under false pretences. She took a room in DARMSTADT, as she had already done in various other towns, feigning a willingness to pay.

12 *Plundered*

By February she was in urgent need of a definite place for the birth. She tried the Rhinelands once again, but her condition was evident to all and no one would take her. It became clear that without papers she was finally at the end of her resources and she gave herself up to the police. She was committed to a remand institution in Dietz. There she was set to painting

dort sehr kleine Figuren anpinseln, richtete sich aber sonst in ihrer geschützten Zelle ein. Als die Zeit für die Geburt kam, wurde sie in das Anstaltshospital, zwei abgeteilte Zimmer, verlegt. Zu dem Arzt hatte sie kein Vertrauen wegen seiner holzigen Haut und seines unreinen Atems; es war genau der Typ von Friseur, zu dem sie nicht ging. Sie hatte Angst und reichte Gesuche ein, daß man sie wieder in ihre Zelle zurückbringen sollte; sie hatte eine Mitgefangene gefunden, die ihr notfalls helfen konnte. Aber noch ehe die Antwort von der Gefängnisdirektion da war, begann die Geburt. Sie mußte diesen Mann zwischen ihren Beinen hantieren lassen, aber es blieb keine Zeit. Es ging alles ganz rasch. Nach zwei Tagen wurde das Kind fortgenommen und in eine Pflegeanstalt in der Nähe von KASSEL gebracht. Die Milch in ihren Brüsten wurde abgepumpt. Sie half noch einige Tage von ihrem Bett aus, das über viele Städte verstreute Belastungsmaterial zusammenzufinden. Der Nervenzusammenbruch kam für alle überraschend. Sie wurde aus dem Anstaltshospital an die Universitätsfrauenklinik weitergeleitet, wo man vor allem mit Penicillin vorging und den Zusammenbruch nach einiger Zeit einkreiste.

tiny figures, but otherwise made herself at home in her guarded cell. When her time came she was placed in the two rooms divided off which formed the prison hospital. The doctor's wooden skin and bad breath gave her no confidence; he was exactly like the sort of hairdresser she never went to. She was overcome with anxiety and put in applications to be transferred back to her cell, having found a fellow inmate capable of helping her if the need arose. But labour began before the answer of the prison authorities arrived. She was obliged to let the man fumble around between her legs, but there was no time. Everything went very quickly. After two days, the child was taken away and put in care somewhere near KASSEL. The milk in her breasts was pumped out. From her bed, she spent a few more days helping to assemble the evidence against her which was scattered over a range of towns. The nervous collapse took everyone by surprise. She was taken from the prison hospital to the women's clinic at the university, where they treated her chiefly with penicillin and after a time brought the breakdown under control.

THE JOINER

THOMAS BERNHARD

Translated by David Horrocks

DER ZIMMERER

EINEM, im Falle des Zimmerers Winkler, mit der Plötzlichkeit, die erschüttert, aus der Haft Entlassenen, ist, wie ich immer wieder feststellen muß, nicht zu helfen. Winkler, über den die Zeitungen vor fünf Jahren, während der Dauer seines Prozesses, unglaublich viel Ordinäres und Abstoßendes, an den Wochenenden mit Bildern seines Opfers und seiner Person, vom Prozeß und vom Lokalaugenschein[1] geschrieben haben, ist am 25. Oktober in Ischl gewesen. Seine in der Vöklabrucker Gerberei beschäftigte Schwester hat mich am Nachmittag des fünfundzwanzigsten aufgesucht und mich aufgefordert, ich möge Winkler, der unten warte, empfangen, ihn auf ein paar Augenblicke ins Haus hereinlassen; er habe mit mir zu reden, mir Verschiedenes, seine Person Betreffendes mitzuteilen, Erfreuliches, ebenso Unerfreuliches, mehr Unerfreuliches als Erfreuliches. Er wolle sich, kaum entlassen, bei mir bedanken, denn daß er nur fünf von sieben Jahren habe absitzen müssen, sei doch nur mein Verdienst. Im übrigen sei ich, der ihm nach seiner Festnahme vor fünf Jahren zur Prozeßvorbereitung und zur Verteidigung zugeteilt worden war, der einzige, dem er sich jetzt, nachdem er aus Garsten[2] fort sei, anzuvertrauen nicht fürchte. Vor allen anderen fürchte er sich, umgekehrt fürchteten alle anderen ihn. Vornehmlich seine früheren Bekannten vermieden es jetzt, sich mit Winkler zu unterhalten, sie scheuten den geringfügigsten Kontakt mit ihm. Niemand grüße ihn, niemand lasse sich von ihm grüßen. Kein Mensch verliere an ihn ein Wort. Über ihn aber verlören sie ganz entsetzliche. Sie verhielten sich größtenteils so, als wenn er nicht existierte. Er selber getraue sich nicht,

THE JOINER

TIME and time again I am forced to the conclusion that
nothing can be done to help a man who, like the joiner
Winkler, has been shaken by the suddenness of his release from
prison. Winkler who, five years ago, throughout his trial, was
the object of an unbelievable amount of vulgar and offensive
comment in the newspapers, the week-end editions of which
carried pictures of him and his victim as well as of the court
proceedings and the investigation of the scene of the crime,
was in Ischl on 25 October. His sister, who worked at the
tannery in Vöklabruck, called on me on the afternoon of the
twenty-fifth and asked whether I would be so kind as to
receive Winkler, who was waiting below. Could he come
into my chambers for a few moments? There were things he
wanted to discuss with me, various matters concerning himself that he wanted to inform me of, some agreeable, some
disagreeable, the majority disagreeable. Only a short time
after his release, he wanted, she said, to come and thank me.
After all, he owed it to me that he had been obliged to serve
only five years of his original seven-year sentence. Besides, as
the lawyer appointed after his arrest five years ago to prepare
and conduct his defence, I was the only person he was not
afraid to confide in now that he was outside Garsten. He was
frightened of everyone else and everyone else feared him.
Former acquaintances, in particular, were now avoiding
all conversation with Winkler, shrinking away from the
slightest contact with him. No one greeted him; no one
was prepared to acknowledge his greeting. To his face, not a
soul uttered a word more than was necessary. Behind his back,

jemanden anzusprechen. Weiterhin würden über ihn Lügen verbreitet, ganz Ischl rede über ihn und seine Unwürdigkeit. Verleumdungen machten die Runde, das verletze ihn auf Schritt und Tritt, sie, seine Schwester, hoffe nur, daß ihr Bruder nicht die Konsequenzen aus allen diesen Fürchterlichkeiten ziehe. Alles würde ihm auf die niederträchtigste Weise erschwert. Sie bilde sich gar nichts ein, mit offenen Augen sehe sie die ihren Bruder verletzenden Vorgänge. Der Ort und seine Umgebung seien eine ständige Quelle ungerechtfertigter Gehässigkeiten gegen ihn. Komme sie nach Ischl, sei auch sie, die doch gar nichts dafür könne, davon betroffen. Daß ein Mensch einen solchen Zustand aushalten kann, glaube sie nicht, daß er weiterhin in der ihn mit allen Raffinessen zersetzenden Gegend existieren werde, könne sie sich nicht vorstellen. Winklers Schwester machte, während sie, nachmittags gegen fünf, in meiner Kanzlei vor mir stand, einen verzweifelten Eindruck auf mich. Sie habe, sagte sie, von ihrem Bruder außer Schlägen, Vorwürfen, äußeren wie inneren Verletzungen, nichts zu erwarten. Sein Charakter sei unverändert und ihr wie mir bekannt. Sie habe in ihrem ganzen Leben, in ihrer ganzen Kindheit und Jugend, vor allem während der wichtigsten Wachstumszeit, unter Winklers «fürchterlichem» Charakter zu leiden gehabt, seine ganze Umgebung, Eltern, Großeltern, sei immer von ihm unterdrückt gewesen. Die Roheit seiner plötzlichen Auftritte und Eingriffe in die Familie, in Ruhe und Ordnung, sein «Zerstörungstrieb» habe immer alle verängstigt. Eltern wie Großeltern wie Nachbarn hätten vor ihm eine fortwährende, selbst von ihren Gliedern ausgehende Angst gehabt, sie selber sei durch ihn die ganze Zeit mit dem Gericht in Beziehung gebracht und schließlich und endlich von ihm ruiniert worden. Sie gab ihm auch die Schuld am frühen Tod ihrer Eltern. Sie nannte viele Beispiele seiner unglaublichen Körperroheit, immer wieder bezog sie sich in allem, was sie jetzt hastig

however, they said all too many, absolutely appalling things. For the most part they behaved as if he did not exist. He himself did not dare address anyone. Furthermore, people were spreading lies about him; everyone in Ischl was talking about him and his disgrace. At every turn he suffered the pain of hearing some slanderous remark which was going the rounds. She, his sister, could only hope that her brother would not draw the logical conclusion from all these terrible experiences. Everything was being made difficult for him in the most despicable manner. She was not imagining any of this in the least; with her own eyes she witnessed these occurrences, so painful to her brother. Ischl and the surrounding area were a constant source of unjustifiably malicious gossip directed against him. Whenever she came to the place, she too was affected by it, although she clearly had no responsibility in the matter. She did not believe that any man was capable of enduring such a state of affairs and could not conceive of his continuing to exist in this area, where everything subtly combined to demoralize him. The impression Winkler's sister made on me as she stood before me in my office that afternoon at about five o'clock was one of desperation. Beatings, abuse, injuries both physical and mental were all she could expect from her brother, she said. He had not changed character, and I knew as well as she did what he was like. Throughout her life, throughout childhood and youth, especially during the most important formative years, she had had to suffer the effects of Winkler's 'terrible' character. Everyone around him, including parents and grandparents, had always been oppressed by him. The brutality of his sudden outbursts and intrusions into the peace and order of the family circle, his 'destructive instinct' had always intimidated everyone. Parents, grandparents and neighbours alike had lived in constant dread of him, a dread one could sense emanating from their very bones. Through him, she herself had become in-

äußerte, auf seine zu einem einzigen großen Unglück zu-
sammengeschmolzene Natur. Er habe «von seinem dummen
Kopf aus» alles um sich herum beherrscht, oft «von hoch oben
herunter» zugeschlagen, nur hätten sie, Eltern und Schwester,
immer alles vertuscht. Größere Verletzungen aber seien der
Gendarmerie bekannt geworden, und immer wieder sei er
wegen schwerer Körperverletzung in immer kürzeren
Abständen auf immer länger eingesperrt, von ihnen entfernt
gewesen. Dabei habe sie ihren Bruder immer geliebt; eine
Zuneigung, die sie sich selbst nicht erklären könne, habe sie
auch heute noch für ihren Bruder. Oft wäre er tagelang zu
Hause in der gutmütigsten Stimmung gewesen, dann aber
blitzartig zu dem Tier geworden, als das er ihr oft in der
Nacht erscheine. Sie könne über ihren jetzt fünfunddreißig-
jährigen Bruder «überhaupt nichts Gutes» berichten, wenn
sie nachdenke, zuschauen müsse in ihrem Gedächtnis, wie er
sie fortwährend auf die niedrigste Weise und schon als um
zwei Jahre jüngeres äußerst schutzloses Schulkind behandelt
habe, immer *miß*handelt habe, mit den Jahren und mit seiner
ununterbrochenen «entsetzlichen Körper- und Geistesent-
wicklung» immer gröber, immer «ungeheuerlicher», müsse
sie schweigen; sie dürfe nicht an ihre gemeinsame Schulzeit,
an ihre gemeinsame Lehrzeit, an die Zeit, in welcher sie in die
Gerberei, er in die Zimmerei gingen, denken. Aus dem Hinter-
halt seiner Unzurechnungsfähigkeit habe er ihr eine Reihe
von zum Teil ihr ganzes Leben beeinträchtigenden Körper-
und Geistesschäden zugefügt. Unter seinen Drohungen gegen
sie war sie einen Großteil ihrer Kindheit und Jugend ihrer
ganzen Umgebung gegenüber auffallend schweigsam geblieben. Wenn sie nur an «die Nacht hinter dem Bahnhof»
denke («Damals bei der Saline!») – ich verhinderte, daß sie sich
näher erklären mußte – sei es ihr unverständlich, daß sie sich
jetzt («aber vielleicht aus Angst vor ihm?») für ihn, der ihr
Leben «systematisch zertrümmert» habe, einsetze. («Uns alle

volved with the law the whole time and her reputation had
ultimately been destroyed. She also blamed him for the early
death of her parents. She cited many examples of his incredible
physical brutality and referred again and again, in support of
everything she hastily uttered, to the evidence of his nature,
all the elements of which were fused to form one single great
disaster. 'From inside that thick skull of his' he had dominated
everything around him, frequently 'raising his fist and bringing it smashing down' on people, but they, his parents and his
sister, had always contrived to cover everything up. More
serious cases of assault did however come to the attention of
the local police and, again and again, he had been away from
them, imprisoned for longer and longer periods at shorter and
shorter intervals for inflicting grievous bodily harm. And yet,
she said, she had always loved her brother; even to this day
she felt an affection for him which she was unable to explain
to herself. Often he had spent days at home in the most good-
natured of moods, only to change like a flash into the animal,
as which he frequently appeared to her in dreams. If she
thought about it, if she were asked to look into her memory,
she could find 'absolutely nothing favourable' to report about
her now thirty-five-year-old brother. She felt compelled to
remain silent about the despicable manner in which, even
when she was an utterly defenceless schoolchild, two years his
junior, he had constantly treated her, always *mal*treated her,
more and more roughly, more and more 'monstrously' as the
years went by and his 'horrifying physical and mental develop-
ment' uninterruptedly progressed. She could not bear to
think of their schooldays together, of the days when both were
apprenticed, of the days when she went to work in the tannery
and he in the joiner's shop. Under the guise of being un-
accountable for his own actions, he had inflicted a series of
physical and mental wounds on her, some of which had been
detrimental to her whole life. As a result of his threatening

hat er ruiniert!») Überhaupt komme es ihr unheimlich vor, daß sie jetzt vor mir stünde, um für ihren Bruder zu bitten; aber sie bitte «inständig», ich möge ihn jetzt, «wo er so verlassen ist», nicht abweisen. Sie sei nur vorsichtshalber zuerst zu mir heraufgekommen, ihn ankündigen; sie müsse in einer knappen Stunde wieder mit dem Postautobus nach Vöklabruck zurück, wo sie «schon seit vier Jahren», weil sie, nach Winklers Verbrechen, seiner Verhaftung und schließlich Verurteilung in Ischl «nichts mehr zu suchen, nichts mehr zu leben» gehabt habe, angestellt sei. Ich erkundigte mich, ob ihr Auskommen in Vöklabruck gut sei, und sie bejahte. Es sei ihr durch Gewaltakte Winklers, die schon mehr als zehn Jahre zurückliegen, unmöglich, ein Kind zu bekommen. Sie machte aber darüber nur eine mich sehr beunruhigende Andeutung. Jeden Abend in den letzten Tagen habe er, dem seine vorzeitige Entlassung aus Garsten selber eine Überraschung («eine unangenehme!») gewesen sei, vor der Gerberei auf sie gewartet und sie abgeholt. Sie habe den Anblick ihres Bruders, der «schmutzig und widerwärtig» tagtäglich vor fünf vor der Gerberei auf und ab ging, nicht aushalten können. «Wie ich mich geschämt habe», sagte sie. Ohne Geld («Er hat alles, was er sich erspart gehabt hat, versoffen!») sei er plötzlich, ohne Ankündigung, «keine Karte, nichts», auf einmal bei ihr erschienen. Sie wohne außerhalb von Vöklabruck, «im Graben», sagte sie, als ob das ein Begriff sei. «Er hätte oft schreiben können», meinte sie, aber er hat nicht geschrieben. Sie sprach von einem Ausbruchversuch, von einem Komplott in der Anstalt, dem er sich aber nicht angeschlossen hat, das habe seine Entlassung beschleunigt. Sie hätte ihn nicht in ihr Zimmer gelassen, wenn sie nicht Angst gehabt hätte, «er ist ja nicht allein gekommen, sie waren zu zweit», sagte sie; der zweite aber sei sofort wieder verschwunden und nicht mehr aufgetaucht. Winkler habe schon immer, «schon als Kind, seinen Fuß in der Tür gehabt». Ein paar Tage hätten sie

behaviour towards her, she had remained for much of her childhood and youth markedly reticent in her dealings with all those around her. The mere thought of 'the night behind the station' ('That time near the salt works!') – I was careful not to press for a more detailed explanation – made it seem incomprehensible to her that she should now be standing up for the brother ('unless perhaps out of fear of him?') who had 'systematically demolished' her life. ('He has wrecked all our lives!') The fact that she was now standing before me at all, in order to plead for her brother, struck her as uncanny; yet she was pleading with me 'earnestly' not to turn him away, not now, 'when he is so forsaken'. She had come up to see me first only as a precaution, to give me notice of his visit; in barely an hour she had to catch the post bus back to Vöklabruck, where she had been working 'these past four years' because ever since Winkler's crime, arrest and eventual sentence to imprisonment, people in Ischl had 'rejected her and made her life a misery'. I inquired whether she was managing in Vöklabruck and she replied in the affirmative. Because of assaults Winkler had made on her over ten years ago, it was impossible for her to have a child. But she made only one indirect reference to this, which distressed me greatly. In the last few days Winkler, who himself had been surprised ('unpleasantly!') by his premature release from Garsten, had been waiting every evening outside the tannery to meet her. The daily sight of her 'dirty and disgusting' brother, walking up and down outside the tannery before five o'clock, had been more than she could stand. 'You don't know how ashamed I've felt,' she said. Without a penny to his name ('He wasted everything he had managed to save on drink!'), without notice, 'no card, nothing', he had suddenly appeared at her home. She lived outside Vöklabruck, 'in the Graben', she said, as if that ought to mean something to me. He could in her view have written often, but he had not written. She spoke

miteinander auskommen können, dann hätte er ihr die ersten
Vorwürfe, sie täte nichts für ihn, gemacht. In der Nacht habe
sie überhaupt nicht geschlafen, nur auf sich «aufgepaßt». Er sei
immer nur auf dem Boden gesessen, «gehockt», sagte sie, oft
auch lang neben ihrem Bett auf dem Boden ausgestreckt
gewesen, so, daß er sich mit Kopf und Füßen hat zwischen
den Wänden stemmen können. Meistens habe er stundenlang
auf die Wand oder auf sie, seine Schwester, geschaut und
kaum etwas gegessen. Er sei auch, außer wenn er sie von der
Gerberei abholte, nicht fort. Sie habe ihm «alle Augenblicke
was zum Trinken» gekauft, nicht viel, aber «viel zu viel». Sein
Geruch, der Geruch, vor dem sie sich zeitlebens gefürchtet
hat, sei jetzt in ihrem Zimmer, und sie werde diesen Geruch
nicht mehr aus ihrem Zimmer hinausbringen. Vor Müdigkeit habe sie oft nicht mehr stehen können, er veranlaßte sie
aber rücksichtslos zu Wegen in verschiedene Gasthäuser um
verschiedene Schnäpse. Von dem Augenblick an, in welchem
ihr Bruder sich bei ihr niedergelassen hat, habe sie nicht mehr
geschlafen. «Seine großen Hände, Herr Doktor!» sagte sie.
Das Zusammensein und dann, wenn sie in der Gerberei
gewesen war, die Gedanken an ihn seien ihr unheimlich
gewesen. Bald habe sie keinen Einfall, wie sie sich von ihrem
Bruder wieder befreien könne, mehr gehabt. «Das war
schlimm.» In der Strafanstalt habe sich Winkler, ihrer Meinung nach, verschlimmert. Die meiste Angst habe sie vor der
Unbeweglichkeit, in welcher er immerfort auf dem Boden
«gehockt» war, gehabt. «So ein kräftiger Mensch», sagte sie. Sie
habe «aus Berechnung», wie sie, was sie sagte, erweiterte,
immer wieder ein Gespräch mit ihm anfangen wollen, um sie
beide abzulenken, er habe aber niemals ein Wort mehr als
unbedingt notwendig gesprochen, selbst das Essen und Trinken
und die Kleidungsstücke habe er sich nur mit Handbewe-
gungen, «kurzen, schlagartigen», von ihr zu sich heran-
befohlen. Ihre Ersparnisse seien, weil sie ihm einen Anzug und

of an attempted gaol-break, of a plot inside the prison, which he had not, however, been a party to. This had, she claimed, speeded his release. She would not have let him into her room, had she not been afraid. 'He didn't come alone, you know. There were two of them,' she said; but the second man had disappeared again immediately and had not turned up since. Winkler had always, 'even as a child, had the knack of getting his foot in the door'. They had been able to get on with each other for a few days, then he had begun accusing her of doing nothing to help him. At night she had not slept at all, but merely remained 'on her guard'. He had done nothing but sit on the floor the whole time, 'crouching', she said, often stretching himself out for long periods beside her bed, in such a way that he could press his head and feet hard against the walls. He had spent most of the time looking at the wall or at her, his sister, for hours on end, and had scarcely eaten a thing. Nor had he gone out, except to meet her from work at the tannery. She had kept him supplied with 'a drop to drink the whole time', not much, but 'much too much'. His smell, the smell she had dreaded for as long as she could recall, was now in her room and she would not be able to rid her room of this smell again. Although she had often been too tired to stand, he had shown no consideration, but sent her on errands to different inns in search of different kinds of schnaps. 'Herr Doktor! the size of his hands!' she said. It had made her flesh creep to be in the same room with him or, later, when at work in the tannery, just to think of him. She had soon run out of ideas as to how to rid herself of her brother again. 'That was bad.' In prison Winkler had, in her opinion, gone from bad to worse. What had frightened her more than anything was the stillness of him, as he constantly 'crouched' there on the floor. 'Such a powerful man,' she said. In order to distract both his and her attention she had over and over again attempted to start a conversation with him 'by design', as she put it, en-

einen Mantel hat kaufen müssen, Schuhe, Unterhosen («Ich hab's nicht ungern getan!»), in ein paar Tagen weggewesen. Plötzlich, es war vielleicht eine halbe Stunde vergangen, sagte sie: «Hoffentlich ist er noch unten!» Sie wollte, das sah ich, ans Fenster, getraute sich aber nicht. Was aus ihrem Bruder, der «so groß und so stumm» sei, werden würde, meinte sie, ohne dann auch nur ein Wort mehr außer «so groß und so stumm» zu sagen. Sie drehte sich um und lief, wie wenn sie sich zum Schluß noch vollständig in ihrem Mantel hätte verstecken wollen, ins Vorhaus hinunter, mit solch ungeschickten Bewegungen ihrer Beine, die auf ein, dem Geschöpf, das sie tragen müssen, zugestoßenes Unrecht hindeuten. Ich hörte, obwohl ich es hätte hören müssen, weil die Kanzleitür offen gewesen war und immer alles im Vorhaus Gesagte, auch das Leiseste, deutlich in die Kanzlei herauf zu hören ist, was sie im Vorüberlaufen zu Winkler gesagt hatte, nicht mehr, nichts mehr, nur das mich seit Jahren immer gleich und immer abstoßender erschreckende Zufallen der Haustür. Kurz darau erschien Winkler in meinem Zimmer.

Er machte denselben kräftigen Eindruck auf mich wie au seine Schwester. Es fiel mir auf, daß sich sein Gesicht während der langen Haftzeit vergröbert hatte, das Gefährliche in seinen Augen gab mir zu denken. Seine Hände waren unruhig, eine unglaubliche, mich bestürzende Unruhe ging von ihm aus. Zum Teil war er wie ein Kind, zum andern wie ein überfertiger Mensch bei der Tür hereingekommen, so plötzlich aufgetreten, daß ich annehmen mußte, er habe, während ich mich mit seiner Schwester unterhielt, hinter der Tür gehorcht. Aber es war ja nichts, das nicht auch für ihn bestimmt gewesen wäre, zwischen seiner Schwester und mir zur Sprache gekommen. Tatsächlich war ich bei dem Einfall, Winkler habe hinter der Tür gehorcht, sei unbemerkt hinter seiner Schwester ins Haus und durchs Vorhaus herauf, erschrocken; andererseits deutete aber seine Atemlosigkeit auf

larging on her account. But he had never uttered a word more than was absolutely necessary. Even when ordering her to bring him food, drink or articles of clothing he had made only 'short, abrupt' gestures with his hands. Within a few days all her savings had gone, because she had had to buy him a suit, a coat, shoes and underpants. ('Not that I minded doing it!') Suddenly, after what may have been half an hour, she said: 'I hope he is still down there!' I could see that she wanted to go the window, but could not bring herself to do it. What would become of her brother, who was 'so massive and so silent,' she began – only to break off without adding a word other than 'so massive and so silent'. She turned and ran down to the entrance hall as if, having finished, all she wanted was to hide her whole person under her coat. Her legs made those awkward movements which suggest that the creature they have to carry has suffered some wrong. I did not hear what she had said as she ran past Winkler, although I ought to have done because the office door had been open and every word spoken in the entrance hall, even the softest, can always be heard clearly up in the office. I did not hear anything more, other than the slamming of the front door, a sound which for years has had an unfailing, increasingly sickening power to terrify me. Shortly afterwards, Winkler appeared in my room.

He made the same impression of power on me as on his sister. I was struck by the way in which his facial features had coarsened during the long period in prison and the dangerous look in his eyes made me wary. His hands were restless; he exuded an unbelievable restlessness which alarmed me. He had come in and stood by the door, partly like a child, partly like an overgrown man, had appeared so suddenly that I could not help thinking that he might have been listening behind the door whilst I was talking to his sister. But then nothing had come up in the conversation between his sister

ein rasches Heraufkommen über die Stiege hin. Er wollte,
konnte aber nicht sprechen. Im ganzen schien er froh zu sein,
daß seine Schwester vor ihm bei mir gewesen war. Sein
Mantel war ihm zu eng, er hatte das Hemd offen; eine krank-
hafte Einstellung allem und jedem gegenüber hat dieser
Mensch, dachte ich. Durch dieselbe Hilflosigkeit wie vor
Gericht, ich erinnere mich, daß er hilfloser als statthaft gewesen war, vor allem immer in den entscheidenden Augen-
blicken, war ich auch jetzt wieder von ihm eingenommen.
Zwischen ihm und mir war bestimmt in den Momenten
seines Eintretens in die Kanzlei und auch später nicht, die
ganze Zeit seines Beimirseins nicht, die geringste Gefühllosigkeit gewesen. Nur waren die Verständigungsmöglichkeiten
auf beiden Seiten qualvoll eingeschränkt. Ich hatte mich,
während der Unterredung mit seiner Schwester, nicht mehr
an seine Erscheinung erinnern können. Er entstammte einem
Menschenschlag voll von der gänzlich unbewußten Substanz.
Er hatte eines der Gesichter, die man oft sieht, wenn man,
selber müde, am Abend in unseren Dörfern durch die stille,
zu keinem Aufmucken mehr fähige Müdigkeit von Men-
schenansammlungen geht, durch die aneinandergeketteten
Physiognomien der Landarbeitsmenschen. Ganz undeutlich
war mir, wie ich jetzt sah, Winkler gewesen, als seine
Schwester mir von ihm gesprochen hatte, ein anderer als der,
der jetzt vor mir stand. Nur seine Stimme hatte ich, noch
bevor er hereingekommen und ein einziges Wort gesagt
hatte, gehört; Stimmen merke ich mir ein für allemal. Wie
die aller Untergeordneten, Ausgeschlossenen, war seine
Redeweise plump, überall offen, einem Körper voller Wunden
vergleichbar, in die jeder jederzeit Salz streuen kann, aber so
eindringlich, daß es schmerzhaft ist, ihr zuzuhören. Er sei
gekommen, um mir zu danken, für was, wisse ich selber. Ich
hätte «das Beste» für ihn herausgeschlagen. Das Gericht und
die Zeit, in die sein Verbrechen gefallen sei, wären ihm von

and me which was not also fit for his ears. The sudden thought that he had been listening behind the door, having slipped into the building unnoticed behind his sister and having followed her through the hall up there, really had startled me. On the other hand, the fact that he was out of breath suggested that he had climbed the stairs rapidly. He made as if to speak, but could not. On the whole he seemed pleased that his sister had come up before him to see me. His coat was too tight for him, his shirt was unbuttoned. 'This man views everything and everyone through diseased eyes,' I thought. The same helplessness he had shown in court – I remember he had been intolerably helpless, especially at all the crucial moments – now engaged my sympathy for him again. Between him and me there had certainly not been the slightest lack of feeling, not in those first moments when he entered the office, nor later during the whole time he was in my presence. It was simply that the possibilities of communication were, on both sides, painfully limited. During my conversation with his sister I had no longer been able to recall his outward appearance. He came of a breed of men who were all substance, totally devoid of personal consciousness. He had one of those faces you often see in our villages when, feeling tired yourself, you take a walk in the evening, through silent groups of people, all too tired even to raise a whimper, through the chain-gang physiognomies of people who have spent their lives working on the land. The image I had of Winkler when his sister had been talking to me about him was, as I now realized, indistinct, and quite unlike the man now standing in front of me. I had been able to hear his voice though, even before he had come in or uttered a single word; I never forget a voice. His manner of speech, like that of all those living in subjection and exclusion, was clumsy, everywhere vulnerable, comparable to a body riddled with wounds, into which anyone at any time could rub salt, but so insistent as to be painful

Anfang an feindlich gesinnt gewesen; ein Gericht müsse anders sein; er sagte aber weder das Wort «unvoreingenommen» noch das Wort «objektiv». Er erinnerte mich augenblicklich an meine Besuche in seiner Zelle während seiner Untersuchungshaft. Vieles, an das er mich im Zusammenhang mit meinen Bemühungen um ihn, die nichts als eine Pflicht gewesen waren, erinnerte, hatte ich längst schon vergessen; er hatte sich ganze von mir vor fünf Jahren zu ihm gesprochene Sätze vollständig gemerkt. Die Anhänglichkeit Winklers, die mir aus allem, was er sagte und was er nicht sagte, deutlich wurde, bestürzte mich. Im ganzen erschien er mir übertrieben und gefährlich zugleich. Immer wieder meinte er, ich sei ihm «nützlich» gewesen. Es hatte den Anschein, als habe er den Kontakt mit mir in den ganzen fünf Jahren nicht einen einzigen Augenblick aufgegeben. Ich selber hatte Winkler schon in dem Moment, in welchem er aus dem Gerichtssaal geführt worden ist, vergessen gehabt, ein Anwalt erledigt den Fall eines Klienten kurz nach dem Schuldspruch; ich erinnerte mich: auf der Straße war auch der Fall Winkler aus meinem Kopf . . . Er habe mir im Laufe der Jahre schreiben wollen, immer wieder sei er aber davor zurückgeschreckt. «Ich bin ein dummer Mensch», sagte er; mehrere Male sagte er: «Ich bin ein dummer Mensch.» Ich forderte ihn auf, Platz zu nehmen. Er setzte sich mir gegenüber; ich rückte das Licht in die Mitte des Schreibtisches, dann aber wieder weg und löschte es schließlich ganz aus, denn er wollte kein Licht, und man sah ja auch so genug. Ich mag auch kein Zwielicht. Wie gut, daß der Schreibtisch zwischen ihm und mir ist, dachte ich, dann fing er, auf den Boden schauend, längere Zeit von besonderen Erlebnissen in der Strafanstalt zu reden an, schließlich von der Eintönigkeit und von der völligen Überraschungslosigkeit, die dort herrschen. Er redete und sinnierte und redete wieder. Ich wüßte alles, meinte er. Wie auf alles bezogen, könne man auch, was die Strafanstalt und ihre Gesetze und Gesetzlosig-

to listen to. He had come to thank me, he said. I would know what for. I had managed to get the 'best deal' for him. The court and opinion at the time when his crime had occurred had been hostile to him from the very beginning; a court ought not to be like that; but he used neither the word 'unprejudiced' nor the word 'objective'. He reminded me at once of my visits to his cell when he was being held on remand. I had long since forgotten much of what he reminded me of in connection with my efforts on his behalf. They had merely been in the line of duty. He had remembered word for word whole sentences which I had spoken to him five years previously. Winkler's affection for me, which was clear from everything he said and did not say, took me aback. All in all he seemed to me to be both larger than life and dangerous. He kept on asserting that I had been 'useful' to him. It was as if, throughout those five years, he had not for one single moment lost sight of his relationship with me. I myself had forgotten Winkler the moment he had been escorted from the courtroom. From a lawyer's point of view a client's case is closed shortly after the verdict has been given, and I remembered that then too, once out in the street, all thought of Winkler's case had vanished from my mind . . . He said he had wanted to write to me in the course of the years but had repeatedly shrunk from doing so. 'I'm a stupid oaf', he said. Several times he said: 'I'm a stupid oaf.' I invited him to take a seat. He sat down opposite me. I moved the lamp to the middle of the desk, then moved it away again before finally switching it off altogether, since he did not want it on and we could see well enough without it anyway. I don't like half-light either. It was a good thing, I thought, that the desk was between him and me. Then, staring at the floor, he began to talk for quite a while about particular experiences in prison and eventually about the prevailing monotony and total predictability of prison life. He talked, reflected, then talked

keiten betrifft, dafür und dagegen sein. Die Zeit sei ihm von
Tag zu Tag länger geworden. Über die Aufsichtsorgane, nicht
über das Essen beklagte er sich. Von seiner Zelle aus habe er
in einen Wald schauen können, manchmal auch über den
Wald hinaus auf eine Bergkette. Die Qual, mit der Zeit nicht
fertig zu werden, sei in der Unfreiheit, in Strafanstalten und
Kerkern,[3] am größten. Er habe in der Zimmerei gearbeitet.
Von Vergünstigungen war bei ihm keine Rede, die habe er
sich immer alle verscherzt. Die Fähigkeit, sich mit einem
Minimum an Spielraum, wie es in der Strafanstaltszelle sein
muß, lange Zeit nur mit seinem eigenen Körper, sonst nichts,
zu begnügen, sei ihm zugute gekommen. «Aber, was man
alles sieht!» sagte er. Er erinnerte sich an den Augenblick der
Urteilsverkündung, an die Stille im Gerichtssaal, während es
draußen zu schneien anfing. Diese Einzelheit hatte ich völlig
vergessen. Körperliche Züchtigungen hätten sich die Garstener
Aufsichtsorgane, was ihn betrifft, nicht erlaubt, er sei aber
auch nie während der ganzen fünf Jahre rabiat geworden.
«Recht und Unrecht», meinte er, darüber könne ein Mensch
wie er viel nachdenken, weniger sagen. Es waren, die Strafanstalt Garsten betreffend, einige bemerkenswerte Auffällig-
keiten, von welchen er mir Mitteilung machte. Ich fragte ihn,
was er jetzt zu tun gedenke. Obwohl ich ja wußte, daß davon
keine Rede war, fragte ich, ob er sich schon nach einer Arbeit
umgeschaut habe, und dann, er solle sich schleunigst «und
mutig», sagte ich, darum kümmern. Für einen Zimmerer sei
es nicht schwierig, eine Arbeit zu finden. In seinem Fach sei
er gut. «Überall wird gebaut», sagte ich, «je weniger Hand-
werker es gibt, desto besser für jeden einzelnen.» Aber was ich,
in einem möglicherweise viel zu belehrenden Ton sagte,
machte auf ihn keinerlei Eindruck. Ich fragte mich auf einmal,
ob der Mensch nicht verloren sei. Er sagte, für ihn sei schon
alles zu spät, es gäbe nichts mehr, das in Angriff zu nehmen
sich für ihn noch auszahlte. «Nichts. Nichts», sagte er. Auch

again. He said I knew all there was to know. Like everything else, it was possible to argue both for and against prison life with its regulations and irregularities. Each successive day had seemed longer to him. He complained of the prison authorities, but not of the food. From his cell he had been able to see into a wood; sometimes, too, he could see beyond the wood to a chain of mountains. The torment of being unable to cope with the problem of time was, he said, at its greatest in captivity, in penal institutions and gaols. He had worked in the joiner's shop. In his case there had never been any question of special privileges; he had always thrown away any right to them. His ability to make do with a minimum of room to move about in, as is inevitable in a prison cell, and to live for long periods with nothing but his own body for company, had stood him in good stead. 'But the things you see!' he said. He could remember the moment when sentence had been passed on him, the silence in the courtroom, whilst outside it was beginning to snow. I had completely forgotten this detail. As far as he was concerned, the authorities in Garsten had never resorted to corporal punishment of any kind; but then he had never, during the whole five years, turned violent. 'Right and wrong' were, he said, things a man like himself could think a lot about, but say less. He had some remarkably shocking things to say to me about Garsten prison. I asked him what he was considering doing now. Although I knew full well that it was out of the question, I asked whether he had already looked around for a job, and then said that he ought to set about it as rapidly as possible and 'like a man'. It was not difficult for a joiner to find a job. He was good at his trade. 'Buildings are going up everywhere,' I said, 'and the fewer craftsmen there are available, the better it is for each one of them.' But what I said, possibly because I adopted an all too schoolmasterly tone, had no effect on him whatsoever. All at once I began to wonder

nichts, auf das er noch einen Anspruch hätte. Er habe alle
Ansprüche längst «verwirkt». Das großstädtisch fade Wort
hatte, von ihm ausgesprochen, keinerlei Klang, es hörte sich
aber doch mystisch an und erschütterte. Schon allein der
Gedanke, sich wieder von seinem Sessel erheben zu müssen,
verursache ihm jenen Kopfschmerz, an dem er schon jahrelang
leide. Unmöglich, sich noch einmal in seinem Leben, das auch
«verhunzt» sei, bei einem der Unternehmer, Zimmerer,
Baumeister vorzustellen. «Alles viel zu spät», sagte er. Bis zu
diesem Augenblick hatte ich nicht die richtige Vorstellung
von dem Ernst der ganzen traurigen wie auch gespenstischen
Situation gehabt, und ich regulierte, was ich sagte, ganz
bewußt, in eine Richtung, in einen Begriff hinein, die ihm
zuwider waren: ich sagte jetzt immer wieder nur: Arbeit!
Dann aber sah ich die Unsinnigkeit meines Vorgehens und
retirierte. Sein Argument: in Ischl, wo jeder über jeden alles
wisse, fände er keine Arbeit und woanders hin wolle er nicht,
beruhte natürlich auf einem Irrtum, aber ich entgegnete
nichts; mir schien, als müsse ich ihn in Ruhe lassen. Er wisse,
daß er nicht mehr zu seiner Schwester zurückkehren könne,
aber andererseits . . . und dann wieder: der größte Fehler sei
es gewesen, bei ihr, «die selber nichts hat», Unterschlupf,
Beruhigung zu suchen. Immer wieder sagte er, wie sehr sie sich
vor ihm fürchte: «vor mir!» rief er aus. Er sagte: «Wohin
gehen? Vöklabruck war das nächste . . .» Den Vorwurf, er
habe seiner Schwester in ein paar Tagen, «rücksichtslos», sagte
ich, das ganze Geld abgenommen, ließ er nicht gelten; sie
bekäme, was er ihr schuldig sei, zurück. Ich wisse, sagte ich,
daß er sie täglich bedroht habe. Es war jetzt ein Menschenlärm
auf der Straße, den ich absichtlich überging. Ich würde, sagte
ich, versuchen, ihm rasch einen Arbeitsplatz zu verschaffen.
Ein guter Arbeiter, Winkler sei einer, sagte ich, habe, auch
wenn er Winkler heiße und auch in der Stadt Ischl, nichts zu
fürchten, im Gegenteil, jeder nehme ihn mit offenen Armen

whether he was not a lost cause. He said that, as far as he was concerned, it was already too late for anything. There was nothing worth-while left for him to tackle. 'Nothing, nothing,' he said. Nothing, either, which he could still expect as of right. He had long since 'forfeited' all rights. The way he pronounced it, this flat, modish, city word had no reson-ance whatsoever, and yet it had a mystical, unnerving effect on the listener. The very thought of having to get up from his seat again was, he said, enough to bring on the headache he had been suffering from for years. It was impossible for him ever again in his life – which he had 'made a hash of' anyway – to face an interview with a contractor, joiner or builder. 'Much too late for anything,' he said. Until this moment I had not correctly envisaged the seriousness of his whole situation, which was both melancholy and nightmarish, and was steering everything I said quite deliberately in a direction and towards a notion which were repugnant to him. All I was now saying, over and over again, was: Work! But then I realized the absurdity of my approach and started to retreat. His argument, that he would not find a job in Ischl, where everyone knew everything about everyone else, and that he had no desire to go anywhere else, was of course based on an error, but I said nothing in return. It seemed to me that I had to leave him in peace. He knew, he said, that he could not go back to his sister again now, but on the other hand . . . and then again, his greatest mistake had been to go seeking shelter and peace of mind from her, 'who herself has nothing'. Again and again he said how much she was afraid of him: 'Of me!' he exclaimed. 'Where else could I go?' he said. 'Vöklabruck was nearest . . .' He would not accept as valid my accusation that he had 'unscrupulously' robbed his sister of all her money within a matter of days. She would get back what he owed her, he claimed. I said I knew that he had threatened her daily. At that moment

auf. «Die Leute», sagte ich, «schauen nur auf die Hände.» Ich
bot ihm eine mir angemessen erscheinende finanzielle Unter-
stützung für die bevorstehende Nacht an, sie würde besonders
kalt werden, sagte ich, und er müsse sich ausschlafen, er lehnte
es aber ab, von mir Geld anzunehmen. In ein paar Tagen sei
er untergekommen, meinte ich, ich wollte nicht aufgeben, das
sagte ich mir: gib nicht auf! vielleicht sei er «schon morgen»
beschäftigt, dann verdiene er und könne alle Schulden zurück-
zahlen, und es ginge bergauf, rasch bergauf. Er solle sich
ausschlafen und mit klarem Kopf wiederkommen; ich stünde
ihm jederzeit zur Verfügung. Er hörte nicht zu. Er schaute auf
den Kukuruzkolben,[4] den ich, weil ich das mag, auf dem
Fensterbrett liegen hatte. Als ob ihn die fünf in die Länge
gezogenen Jahre in der Strafanstalt von der Sinnlosigkeit
jeden, auch des geringsten, des unscheinbarsten Lebens-
zeichens überzeugt hätten, ging er gar nicht auf das, was ich
gesagt hatte, ein, sondern er fragte auf einmal, und die
Beziehungslosigkeit des von ihm gesprochenen Satzes, der dann
lang zwischen ihm und mir in der Luft hing, erschreckte mich:
wieviel Geld man haben müsse, um so weit wegreisen zu können, daß man unter keinen Umständen mehr in Mitleiden-
schaft gezogen werden könne . . . Ein qualvolles Auflachen
meinerseits mußte ihn tief verletzt haben, denn er schwieg auf
diese Ungeschicklichkeit, die eine Unzucht gewesen war,
mehrere Minuten lang völlig bewegungslos. Vorsichtig ließ
ich mir dann von ihm eine Beschreibung seines Geburtsortes
geben, eines Dorfes in den Niederen Tauern, die er auf einmal, furchtlos, schien mir, mit Beschreibungen seines Schul-
wegs, seiner Lehrer, seiner Eltern und seiner Schwester
ausschmückte. Eine Vorliebe für winkelige Gassen, frisch-
geschlachtetes Fleisch seinerseits fiel mir auf; seine Einstellung
zu Verstorbenen, zu politischen Gewaltakten auf dem Land;
den Sozialismus, Parteien überhaupt, lehnte er ab. Man kann
einer solchen Art von Mensch viele Fallen stellen, und ein

I could hear the noise of people down in the street, but I deliberately ignored it. I would try, I said, to provide him with a job quickly. A good workman, and Winkler was one, I said, had nothing to fear, even if his name was Winkler and even if the town was Ischl; on the contrary, everyone would welcome him with open arms. 'People,' I said, 'don't look further than a man's hands.' I offered him what seemed to me to be adequate financial support for the coming night. It would be a particularly cold one, I said, and he must get a full night's sleep; but he refused to accept money from me. In a few days he would be settled in a job, I said, not wishing to give up trying. 'Don't give up!' I told myself. He might be taken on 'as early as tomorrow', then he would be earning something and could pay back all his debts and things would take a turn, a rapid turn, for the better. He should get a good night's sleep and come back with a clear mind; I was at his disposal at any time. He was not listening. He was looking at the corn-cob which, because I like it, I had lying on my window ledge. As if the five long-drawn-out years had convinced him of the senselessness of every sign of life, even the slightest and most insignificant, he showed no interest at all in what I had been saying but suddenly – and the unconnectedness of the sentence he uttered, which then hung for a long time in the air between him and me, startled me – he asked how much money one would need to be able to go so far away that one could no longer, under any circumstances, get involved in anything . . . An outburst of pained laughter on my part must have hurt him deeply since for several minutes after this tactlessness – it was an obscenity – he remained silent and completely motionless. Then, treading cautiously, I got him to give me a description of his birthplace, a village in the Lower Tauern, which, suddenly, and, so it seemed to me, undaunted, he embellished with descriptions of the route he had taken to school, his teachers, his

solcher Mensch tritt hinein. Mit großer Anteilnahme sprach
er auf einmal wieder über die verschiedensten traurigen Vorfälle in seinem Leben, er malte, je mehr sich diese Vorfälle
seiner am Ende nur noch grausamen Hilflosigkeit zu nähern
schienen, nur graue Bilder. Alles, was er sagte, war von einem
gleichmäßig von seinem seltsamen Unglück beherrschten
Grau, oder Grauschwarz, oder Schwarzgrau. Seine Stimme
war weder leise noch laut, sie gehörte nicht eigentlich ihm,
sondern war aus seinen Zuständen und Zusammenhängen; es
ließe sich höchstens ein solcher Urvergleich⁵ ziehen wie in
Betrachtung eines noch nicht und schon nicht mehr lebenden,
aber doch existierenden Wesens, das doch kein bloßer Gegenstand ist. Er machte das Gesprochene in der eng zusammen-
gezogenen späten, plötzlich völligen Nachmittagsstille der
Kanzlei, vor allem, weil es schon beinahe finster war, un-
gemein anschaulich. Ich hatte an diesem Nachmittag, das ist
außergewöhnlich, und auch an dem darauffolgenden Abend,
keine meiner sonst so dringenden Arbeiten zu erledigen, und
ich war froh, das Haus nicht mehr verlassen zu müssen, und so
überließ ich es Winkler, fortzugehen oder zu bleiben. Es
schien mir einen Augenblick lang, als hätte er sich bei mir nur
aufwärmen wollen. Seine Schwester war gewiß längst wieder
in Vöklabruck. Ich dachte: die Kinderlosigkeit zweier wie der
beiden Winklerschen Menschen, wodurch sie auch immer in
jedem von ihnen beiden ein nicht mehr rückgängig zu
machender Dauerzustand geworden ist, kann hinaufführen,
in die höchsten und in die schwindelerregendsten Höhen
führen und in die grauenerregende Ohnmacht hinunter. – Ich
fragte ihn, ob er schon ein Nachtmahl gegessen habe, die
Leute auf dem oberösterreichischen Land essen immer schon
früh ihr Nachtmahl, obgleich ich ja schon gewußt habe, daß
sein Magen leer gewesen ist, auch zu Mittag hatte er sicher
nichts gegessen, denn da waren Bruder und Schwester mit
dem Postomnibus von Vöklabruck in die Stadt Ischl herein-

parents and his sister. I was struck by a liking on his part for narrow crooked streets and for freshly slaughtered meat; his attitude to the dead, to acts of political violence in country areas; socialism, indeed any form of political party, he rejected. You can set any number of traps for a man of his kind, knowing that such a man will walk right into them. All at once he was talking again with great involvement about the most diverse unhappy incidents in his life. The pictures he painted, the nearer these incidents seemed to get to his ulti- mate, unrelievedly cruel state of helplessness, were exclusively grey. His peculiar misfortune coloured everything he said uniformly grey, or greyish-black, or blackish-grey. His voice was neither soft nor loud; it did not really belong to him but was a product of the conditions and contexts in which he lived. At the very best, one could draw a comparison with the way one looks upon some primitive entity which is both not yet living and no longer living, but which none the less exists and is for all that not simply an object. In the intensely concentrated, suddenly total afternoon silence of the office, he managed, especially as it was almost dark already, to make what he said appear extraordinarily vivid. That afternoon, and the ensuing evening as well, I had none of my usual urgent business to attend to and, happy for once not to have to leave the house, I left it to Winkler's discretion whether he went or stayed. For a moment I had the feeling that his only motive in coming to see me had been to get warm. His sister must have been back in Vöklabruck long ago. Being permanently, irremediably in a state of childlessness, as were both the Winklers, whatever the cause may have been in each case, can,' I thought, 'enhance a person, raise him up to the most lofty and dizzy heights or reduce him to an awesome level of impotence.' – I asked him whether he had already eaten his evening meal – in Upper Austria the country folk always eat early in the evening – although I knew quite well

gehetzt; auch das ein Grund seiner Müdigkeit. Er lehnte es ab, mit mir etwas, «etwas Warmes», hatte ich gesagt, das in der an die Kanzlei angeschlossenen Küche zu finden gewesen wäre, zu essen. Auch zu trinken wollte er nichts. Im Grunde beherrschte mich dieser Mensch, der mir einerseits so fremd war wie keiner, andererseits alles andere als fremd. Ein Verbrecher ist zweifellos ein armer Mensch, der für seine Armut bestraft wird. Ich dachte das hoch über der Grenze sogar der höheren Wissenschaftlichkeit. Er könne, meinte er, über die besonders krassen Vorfälle in der Strafanstalt, die er mir ganz bewußt verschweige und die ihn immer wieder beschäftigen, nichts sagen, aus nicht erklärbaren Gründen, auch aus «Kopflosigkeit». Er fühle alles nur und die Folgen davon seien tödlich. Eine Existenz wie die seine schwäche, das Eingesperrtsein ruiniere im Menschen jedes brauchbare Gefühl für die Außenwelt, es verstopfe die Zugänge zu ihr. Bessern, wie man das immer von ihm verlangt habe, könne einer wie er sich nicht. Er habe keinerlei Besserungs- und Verbesserungsmöglichkeiten mehr, er habe sie nie gehabt. Er wolle sich auch gar nicht verbessern. Was heißt das? Seine Kindheit und seine Jugend seien von der Aussichtslosigkeit verfinstert gewesen, sich jemals bessern oder verbessern zu können. Es hätten ihm eigentlich alle Voraussetzungen für ein Leben, das unauffällig vor sich geht und niemandem weh tut, immer gefehlt. Seiner Anlage nach sei er von vornherein eine einzige finstere Fundgrube für Grausamkeiten und Schmerz gewesen. Eine von Grund auf falsche, weil nicht einmal in Ansätzen vorhandene Erziehung habe seine Anlagen in das Verbrecherische hinein- und hinunterentwickelt. Seine Schmerzen, schon die allerfrühesten, seien mit Gefühllosigkeit behandelt worden, die Eltern hätten ihn, anstatt in Leintücher, in ihre leibliche und seelische Kälte gewickelt. Nur mit seinen Körperkräften konnte er eines Tages, sie waren ihm ganz plötzlich bewußt geworden, seiner familiären Unterdrücker Herr werden: er

that his stomach was empty. I was sure that he had not eaten
at lunchtime either because at that time brother and sister had
come rushing into Ischl in the post bus from Völklabruck; that
too was a reason for his tiredness. He refused to join me in
'something warm' which, I had said, we could get in the
kitchen adjacent to my office. Nor did he want anything to
drink. At bottom I was dominated by this man who on the
one hand was as foreign to me as anyone could be, on the
other hand anything but foreign. A criminal is without doubt
a poor man who gets punished for his poverty. I imagined
that to be way beyond the ingenuity of even a higher
scientific mind. For reasons he could not explain and also
because 'his head was in a whirl', he could not, he main-
tained, say anything about the particularly flagrant occurrences in prison; they were constantly on his mind but he
was deliberately withholding them from me. He merely felt
everything and the consequences of that were fatal. An
existence such as his weakened, and being locked up ruined
every useful feeling a man had for the outside world and
blocked every approach to it. For a man like him to improve,
which was what people had always demanded of him, was an
impossibility. He no longer had any chances of improving or
of bettering himself, indeed he had never had any. Nor had
he any desire at all to better himself. What was the meaning
of that anyway? The absence of any prospect of ever being
able to better himself or to improve had clouded his childhood
and his youth. As a matter of fact he had always lacked all the
necessary conditions for a life lived without attracting undue
attention and without causing pain to anyone. By disposition
he had been from the very first nothing but a dark source of
atrocities and pain. An upbringing which was wrong from
first to last, since even the most rudimentary elements were
lacking, had caused his innate tendencies to evolve in the
direction of and deteriorate into criminality. His suffering,

schlug, wenn man ihn reizte, einfach zu. Diese für ihn einzige
Methode, sich über Wasser zu halten, sich Gehör, ja sogar
Respekt zu verschaffen, führte ihn schon nach kurzer Zeit in
die Gefängnisse. Das Eingesperrtsein, sagte er, vergrößere
Furcht und Überdruß. Es gäbe heute eine hochentwickelte
Justiz, aber keinerlei Fortschritt in der Justiz. Der moderne
Strafvollzug habe seine «gerissenen» Eigenheiten. Er sprach das
Wort «Einsamkeitshysterie» aus, das er gehört oder gelesen
haben mußte, es war nicht von ihm. Nicht mehr ins Körperliche des Sträflings ginge die moderne Bestrafung, sondern
ausschließlich nurmehr noch tief ins Seelische, sie dringe da-
hinein, wohinein früher, vor fünfzig Jahren noch, nichts
gedrungen sei. Erklären könne er, was er meine, nicht.
Menschenverstörend arbeite die heutige Justiz, und ich dachte:
als eine Wissenschaft für sich. Der Anblick seiner neuein-
gekauften Kleider brachte mich wieder auf den Gedanken,
wie Winkler so rasch wie möglich zu Geld kommen könne.
Die Gefahr, daß er sich von der Außenwelt völlig abschließt,
abschließen mußte, wenn er sich nicht schon von ihr ab-
geschlossen, aus ihr, bei der ersten Berührung mit ihr, zurückgezogen hat, war zu offensichtlich, als daß ich ihn hätte sich
selbst überlassen können. Ich stellte mir vor, wie der Ankauf
seiner Kleider, in welchen er wie zum Hohn steckte, in
einem Vöklabrucker Geschäft am Vormittag – und vielleicht
hatte er sie sich nur meinetwegen gekauft? – vor sich gegangen
war, wie er, Winkler, wohl auf die Schwester hörte, aber
doch, während des Anprobierens, wieder nicht auf sie hörte,
fürchterliche Kleiderankaufentscheidungen fällte, wie seine
Schwester viele seiner Schimpfwörter hat einstecken müssen
(sie hätte sehen müssen, daß ihm der Mantel an den Schultern
zu groß war, im ganzen aber doch wieder zu eng); das
Zusammenlaufen der im Kleiderhaus Angestellten in der
Mantelabteilung; Winklers Befehlston den bleichgesichtigen
dummen Mädchen gegenüber, dann wieder seine jedes

even the very earliest, had been treated with callousness. Instead of in linen sheets, he had been wrapped in the physical and mental coldness of his parents. Only his physical strength, which he had suddenly become aware of, had enabled him eventually to get the better of his oppressors within the family. When roused, he had simply hit out. This, the only means available to him of keeping his head above water, of gaining people's attention or even their respect, had led in no time at all to prison. Being locked away made a man more afraid and more weary of life, he said. Our judicial system nowadays was highly sophisticated but there was no improvement in the system whatsoever. Modern penal practice was not without 'cunning' devices. He used the term 'isolation hysteria' which he must have heard or read somewhere. They were not his words. Modern methods of punishment were now no longer aimed at a convict's body but exclusively at his deep subconscious, probing into regions which earlier, even fifty years ago, nothing had been able to penetrate. He could not, he said, explain what he meant. The administration of justice today had an unbalancing effect on people, he said, and I thought: Yes, it's a science in its own right. The sight of his newly purchased clothes made me think again of ways in which Winkler might come by some money as quickly as possible. The risk that he might cut himself off totally from the outside world, might be compelled to cut himself off, if, that is, he had not already cut himself off from it, had not withdrawn from it at the first contact, was too evident for me to consider leaving him to his own devices. I pictured how, that morning in a shop in Vöklabruck, he had set about buying his clothes, in which he looked an object of derision – perhaps he had only bought them for my benefit? – how he, Winkler, probably listened to his sister's advice but then again, during the trying on, did not listen to her as he made those terrible decisions you have to make in a clothes shop; the

Frauen- und Mädchenherz aus der Fassung bringende naiv-
rustikale Männlichkeit, Angeberei. Wieder getraute ich mich,
weil ich ihn genügend abgelenkt wußte, ihm den Vorschlag
zu machen, er solle sich, auf eine Nacht nur, in eines der
verhältnismäßig gut ausgestatteten und billigen Gasthäuser an
der unteren Traun legen und anderntags zu mir kommen, ich
hätte Zeit für ihn, meine Geschäfte seien jetzt überraschend
ein wenig zum Stillstand gekommen; ja, ich hatte die Absicht,
ihn am nächsten Morgen einzuladen, sprach diese Absicht aber
nicht aus. «Inzwischen», sagte ich, aber ich belästigte ihn nur
mit dem, was ich sagte, «habe ich ein paar Adressen, ein
qualifizierter Arbeiter . . .» Ich schwieg und nahm mir vor,
nachdem Winkler fort wäre, bei einer oder der anderen
Zimmerei anzufragen, ob sie Interesse an Winkler hätte. Ich
sah in der Stellungssuche für ihn keine Schwierigkeit. Er solle
sich den Kopf nicht zerbrechen, sagte ich, und ich entdeckte,
daß ich, wenn mich nicht alles täuschte, schon wieder die
ganze Zeit zu einem Menschen redete, der mir, auch wenn er
so tat, als höre er zu, aus Höflichkeit, gar nicht zuhörte,
dessen Gedanken überall, nur nicht bei mir waren. Nur sein
Körper sitzt da, dachte ich, Winkler ist zwar in meiner
Kanzlei, aber seine Gedanken sind nicht in meiner Kanzlei. In
den ersten Nächten nach seiner Entlassung, er habe sich zuerst,
«in einem besseren Zustand», nicht entschließen können, in
einem Gasthaus zu übernachten, er hatte sich keinem Haus in
die Nähe getraut, geschweige denn einem Menschen, habe er
entsetzlich gefroren; es sei ihm einfach nicht möglich gewesen, irgend jemanden anzusprechen und so sei er die ganzen
Tage und Nächte fast ausnahmslos im Freien umhergegangen,
nach Möglichkeit in den Wäldern, wo er annehmen mußte,
daß ihm niemand begegnet. In manchen Wäldern sei Wärme,
sagte er, in anderen nicht. Völlig entkräftet habe er dann doch
ein Gasthaus aufgesucht, gegen Mitternacht, «da wird man
nicht so genau kontrolliert», sagte er. Ohne Rücksicht auf sein

amount of bad language his sister had to put up with from him (she ought to have noticed that the coat was too big for him round the shoulders and yet too tight overall); how the staff of the clothes shop congregated in the coat department; Winkler's domineering tone of voice to the pale-faced, stupid shop-girls and also that naïvely rustic masculinity of his, that big talk which was enough to give any woman or girl palpitations. Knowing him to be sufficiently distracted, I ventured yet again to suggest that he should take a bed, for the one night only, in one of the relatively well-appointed but cheap hotels on the banks of the Lower Traun and come and see me the next day. I could spare him the time as my affairs were, surprisingly, rather stagnant at the moment. Indeed, I intended to invite him for the following morning, but did not say so. 'Meanwhile,' I said, although I could see that what I was saying was annoying him, 'I've got a few addresses, a qualified worker . . .' I stopped, making up my mind to inquire, once Winkler had gone, at one firm of joiners or another, to see whether they might be interested in him. I saw no difficulty in finding a job for him. I said he ought not to make himself sick with worrying; and then I realized that, unless my eyes were deceiving me, I was yet again talking the whole time to a man who, even if he pretended to listen out of politeness, was not listening to me at all, and whose thoughts were anywhere but with me. 'That is only his body sitting there,' I thought. 'Winkler may well be sitting in my office, but his thoughts are not in my office.' He said that during the first few nights after his release he had been frozen stiff. Initially, when feeling 'in better condition', he had been unable to make up his mind to stay the night in a hotel and had not been confident enough to approach any house in the vicinity, much less any human being. He had simply been incapable of speaking to anyone and so he had, almost without exception, spent every day and night wandering around in

Geld sei er nurmehr darauf bedacht gewesen, nicht mehr frieren zu müssen. «*Wie* ich gefroren habe!» sagte er. Die ihm zuletzt verbliebene Hälfte seines Geldes habe ihm ein Kirchtagsordner[6] aus Lambach, den er vor einem Gasthaus in Stadl Paura getroffen hatte, während Winkler eingenickt war, aus der Manteltasche gezogen, er habe «den Kerln» aber noch im letzten Augenblick stellen können. Er sprach auch von dem Glück, das es für ihn gewesen sei, mehrere große Zeitungen zu besitzen, mit welchen er sich in einem Hohlweg bei Wimsbach habe zudecken können. Zum Trinken, meinte er, hätten ihn die Gasthäuser wohl in ihre Wärme hineingelassen, zum Schlafen nicht; sein Aussehen sei zu schäbig gewesen. Zwölf Tage lang habe er es auf diese Weise aushalten können, keinen Tag länger. Schließlich sei er, ohne einen Groschen, nach Vöklabruck, und zwar gegen die ganz natürlichen Widerstände in ihm, zu Fuß, über Wiesen und durch Wälder, zu seiner Schwester. Die sei bei seinem Anblick erschrocken und habe ihn nicht zu sich ins Zimmer hineinlassen wollen. Er sei wieder fort und habe sich einem in einer ähnlichen Lage wie er Befindlichen angeschlossen; beide seien sie, von seiner Schwester auf die vielen entsetzlichen Wege in Kälte und Finsternis zurückgezwungen, schließlich wieder in mehrere Gasthäuser und dann, auf Anraten des ihm völlig unbekannt Gebliebenen, der einen Schlosseranzug angehabt hatte («Ich habe mir nicht einmal seinen Namen gemerkt!»), wieder zur Schwester zurück. Sie habe, sagte der Zimmerer, von Anfang an vor ihm Angst gehabt, dieselbe Angst wie *vor* seiner Haftzeit, an dieser ihrer Angst ihm gegenüber habe sich seit ihrer Kindheit nichts geändert gehabt, diese ganz bestimmte, nur mit ihm und seinem Unglück zusammenhängende Angst. Sie glaubte, er würde ihr Zimmer in Unordnung bringen, ihre Hausfrau könne ihr unter dem Eindruck des plötzlichen Auftauchen Winklers kündigen. Sie habe auch um ihre Stellung in der Gerberei gebangt. Um fünf habe er sie tag-

the open, whenever possible in woods, where the likelihood was that no one would come across him. There was warmth in some woods, he said, but not in others. Then, in a state of complete collapse, he had gone to a hotel after all, towards midnight. 'They are not so strict at checking up on you then,' he said. Intent now only on escaping the freezing cold he had disregarded the expense. 'You don't know I froze!' he said. The remaining half of his money had been stolen from his coat pocket, when he had nodded off, by a fairground steward from Lambach whom Winkler had met up with outside a hotel in Stadl Paura. But he had just managed to collar 'the bloke' at the last moment. He talked too of his joy at getting hold of several large newspapers which he had been able to use as blankets in a sunken lane near Wimsbach. He would probably, he thought, have been allowed to enter the warmth of the hotels for a drink, but not to sleep, since he had looked too shabby. He had managed to stand living like this for twelve days, not a day longer. Finally, without a farthing, and overcoming the natural resistance he felt, he had walked across meadows and through woods to his sister's in Vöcklabruck. At the sight of him, she had been alarmed and had refused to let him into her room. He had gone away again and had joined company with a man in a similar situation to his own. Because of his sister they were forced to journey again along all those terrible paths in the cold and the dark and had finished up, as before, in several hotels. Then, on the advice of the man in the boiler suit, who had remained a complete stranger to Winkler ('I didn't even find out his name!'), they had returned to his sister's. From the beginning, the joiner said, she had been afraid of him. Her fear was just the same as *before* his time in prison. This fear of hers with regard to him had not changed at all since her childhood. It was a quite distinct fear, which attached only to him and his misfortune. She thought he would mess up her room and that

täglich von der Gerberei abgeholt; ihre Arbeit dort be-
zeichnete er selbst als «schwer». Auf dem Heimweg habe sie
sich für ihn geschämt, und der Gedanke, ihn neu einzukleiden
– was er angehabt hatte, war schon über zehn Jahre alt gewesen! –, war ursprünglich sogar von ihr ausgegangen. Als
sie dann aber eingesehen hatte, daß sie, wenn sie ihm neue
Kleider kaufte, ihre ganzen Ersparnisse verlieren würde,
wollte sie zurückziehen. Es war aber zu spät: Winkler zwang
sie am fünfundzwanzigsten vormittags, kurz bevor mich die
beiden aufsuchten, zur Herausgabe ihres Geldes und in das
Kleidergeschäft. Sie selber hat von einer jetzt langsam fortschreitenden Beschmutzung ihres Wesens durch Winkler
gesprochen. Den ersten Abend habe sie sich geweigert, ihn
neben sich auf dem Fußboden schlafen zu lassen, aber eine
andere Möglichkeit bestand nicht. Er habe sich «wie ein
Hund» neben sie auf den Boden gelegt. Da keine Decke vor-
handen war, hatte er mit ein paar alten Ausgaben des ‹Linzer
Volksblattes› vorlieb nehmen müssen. In der ersten gemeinsamen Nacht hatte keiner von ihnen geschlafen. Wortlos
sinnierten sie in der kleinen Kammer unter dem Dach des
Hauses ‹Im Graben›. Wieder dachte ich, Winkler war auffallend ruhig geworden, daß seine einzige Rettung ein Arbeitsplatz sei. Aber die Schwierigkeiten, ihm das klar zu machen,
hatten sich zu diesem Zeitpunkt schon schmerzhaft vergrößert gehabt. Noch während die Leute in Haft sind, gehört,
von seiten der Justiz, für sie ein Arbeitsplatz und ein Quartier
beschafft, sonst werden die Männer gleich wieder straffällig;
die Schuld trifft den Staat, die Gesellschaft; die Behörden
verschaffen den Haftentlassenen nichts als das Fürchterliche
der plötzlichen Freiheit, immer wieder Ursache zahlloser
Rückfälle durchaus Besserungsfähiger. Die Behörde begeht
dadurch immer wieder diese hundsgemeine Nachlässigkeit.
Die Justizbehörde ist, unter Außerachtlassung ihrer Obsor-
gepflicht gegenüber den Ärmsten, ausgesprochen verbre-

her landlady might, because of Winkler's suddenly turning up like this, give her notice to quit. She had been anxious too about losing her job in the tannery. Every day at five he had gone to meet her from the tannery. He himself described her work there as 'hard'. On the way home she had felt ashamed of him and the idea of buying him a new outfit of clothes – those he had been wearing were already over ten years old! – had actually come from her in the beginning. But then, when she realized that she would lose all her savings if she bought him new clothes, she had wanted to go back on it. But it was too late: on the morning of the twenty-fifth, shortly before the two of them came to see me, Winkler had forced her to hand over her money and go to the clothes shop. She herself spoke of the way in which Winkler was now slowly, progressively, defiling her whole being. The first evening, she had refused to allow Winkler to sleep next to her on the floor, she said, but there was no alternative. He had lain down 'like a dog' near her on the floor. As there was no blanket available, he had had to make do with a few old copies of the *Linzer Volksblatt*. That first night together, neither of them had slept. Without exchanging a word they had spent the night deep in thought in the small attic room of the house 'in the Graben'. Again I thought – Winkler had become strikingly calm – that his only salvation lay in finding a job. But by this time, the difficulty of making him understand had become even more painful. The law ought to provide people with a job and a place to stay before they even come out of prison, otherwise men return immediately to crime. The state is guilty, society is guilty. All that the authorities provide for ex-prisoners is the terrifying shock of sudden liberty, which again and again is the cause of recidivism in countless cases of men who are perfectly capable of reform. In this way, again and again, authority is guilty of the same gross neglect, which is beneath contempt. Judicial authority is, if it disregards its

cherisch. Allein die Justiz hat von seiner vorzeitigen Entlassung schon mindestens vierzehn Tage vor dem Termin gewußt. Sie hätte ihm eine Arbeit verschaffen müssen. So halst der Staat sich immer wieder selbst die abzuschaffenden, abschaffbaren Übel auf! Ich selber bin von Winklers plötzlicher Entlassung völlig überrascht worden, wenngleich ich auch, ungefähr vor einem Jahr, einen Antrag auf seine «Entlassung vor der Zeit» an das Justizministerium gestellt habe. Aber diese Anträge sind obligatorisch und führen meistens auch nur in Fällen, in welchen es sich um fügsame, «nicht gemeingefährliche» Häftlinge handelt, zum Erfolg. Winkler hatte meiner Meinung nach nicht die geringste Aussicht, vorzeitig entlassen zu werden; dem widerspricht auch ganz seine Häftlingsbeschreibung, die ich erst kürzlich studiert habe. Solche überraschende Entlassungen führen in fast allen Fällen unweigerlich zu Komplikationen, meistens in die Katastrophe. Winkler hat, außer seiner Schwester, keinerlei Verwandtschaft mehr. Möglicherweise stand seine Entlassung in Zusammenhang mit dem im März in Garsten in Angriff genommenen Umbau des straßenseitig gelegenen Strafanstalttraktes, in welchem Winkler untergebracht gewesen war. Bei solcher Gelegenheit werden oft Entlassungen, die gar nicht geplant gewesen waren, überraschend schnell durchgeführt. Ich ersuchte Winkler, der jetzt einen besonders niedergeschlagenen Eindruck machte, auf seine, mir ausgesprochen kränklich erscheinende Schwester Rücksicht zu nehmen. Sie sei in dem Glauben, er kehre jetzt, nach dieser Unterredung mit mir, zu ihr zurück. Das dürfe er nicht. Davor fürchte sie sich. In Anbetracht des schon weit überbeanspruchten Verhältnisses zwischen ihnen beiden hielte ich es für besser, er bleibe in Ischl. An seinem entsetzlichen, ihm auswegslos erscheinenden Zustand sei auch das Wetter schuld, sagte ich, der naßkalte, finstere Tag. Anstrengungen, Opfer blieben ihm naturgemäß, gleichgültig, was er jetzt unter-

responsibility for the welfare of the poorest, positively criminal. Only the authorities knew of his premature release, and they knew about it at least a fortnight before the date fixed. They ought to have provided him with a job. That is how the state, of its own accord, constantly saddles itself with the kind of evil which it ought to be abolishing and which it is in its power to abolish! I myself was completely surprised by Winkler's sudden release, even though, about a year ago, I had entered a petition with the Ministry of Justice for his 'release ahead of time'. But these petitions are obligatory and lead to success for the most part only in cases where prisoners are noted for good behaviour or are not 'a public danger'. In my opinion Winkler did not have the slightest hope of being prematurely released. All the evidence of his prison record, which I have only recently studied, also runs counter to it. Being abruptly released in this way leads inevitably, in almost all cases, to complications and is for the most part catastrophic. Apart from his sister, Winkler no longer has any relations whatsoever. It was possible that his release was connected with the building operations begun in Garsten in March, when alterations were being made to the prison wing nearest the road, in which Winkler had been quartered. On such an occasion releases which have not been planned at all are often carried out with astonishing haste. I entreated Winkler, who now gave me the impression of being particularly downcast, to show some consideration for his sister who looked, I said, decidedly unwell to me. She was under the impression that he would be going back to her now, after this conversation with me. He must not do that. That was what she was afraid of. In view of the already highly overstrained relationship between them both, I thought it better for him to stay in Ischl. The weather too, on this cold, wet, gloomy day, was, I said, to blame for his terrible condition, which appeared to him to be so hopeless. Irrespective of what he now undertook, he would not be

nehmen werde, nicht erspart. Sein Verbrechen sei als eines
von Hunderten und Tausenden von Jugendverbrechen,
meinte ich, verzeihlich. Die ganze Welt eine Welt von Ausgeschlossenen, die Gesellschaft an sich existiere nicht, jeder sei
allein, keiner sei im Vorteil. Er hörte sich, was ich sagte, nur
scheinbar an. Lange Zeit schaute er auf die Uhr an der Wand,
ein Geschenk meiner Schwägerin. Ich verzichte natürlich auf
die Verteidigungskostenrückzahlung. Die im Gesetz vor-
geschriebene Verteidigungskostenrückzahlung ist eine un-
gerechtfertigte Härte. Alle Erschwernisse würden ihm aus
dem Weg geräumt, darauf könne er sich verlassen. Ich würde
mich verschiedenenorts für ihn einsetzen. Er sei nicht allein
mit seinen Verbrechen, wiederholte ich, jeder beginge Verbrechen, die größten, aber die meisten Verbrechen blieben
unaufgedeckt, unerkannt, unbestraft. Verbrechen seien Krank-
heitserscheinungen; die Natur bringe unaufhörlich alle
möglichen Verbrechen, darunter die Menschenverbrechen,
hervor; die Natur verschaffe sich ihre Verbrechen rechtmäßig.
Alles sei immer in der Natur und aus der Natur, die Natur
sei von Natur aus verbrecherisch. Weil er einen so kläglichen
Eindruck machte, fragte ich ihn, ob er nicht augenblicklich,
was doch möglich sei, die Kraft dazu habe, sein Leben zu
überschauen, mit der ganzen Welt hinter sich und dann vor
sich, zu einem Anschauen seiner doch unerhörten Entwick-
lung, er fände darin, auch das sei gesetzmäßig in der Natur,
nicht nur Finsternisse. Die Welt sei nicht nur entsetzlich. Die
Materie ungeheuer exakt und voll Schönheit. Unabhängig
von Ort und Zeit sei der Einzelne immerfort zu den erstaun-
lichsten Entdeckungen, derentwillen das Leben sich auszahlt,
fähig. Aber Winkler antwortete nichts, er reagierte auf nichts.
Er schien sich mehr und mehr in sich selber, und zwar in eine
grauenhafte Vorstellung von sich selber, einzuschließen. Wenn
einmal, bemerkte ich, und ich dachte dabei mehr an mich als
an ihn, die Spaziergänge, die man macht, nicht mehr in den

spared those strains and sacrifices which were a part of nature.
His crime was, I said, as one of hundreds and thousands of
juvenile crimes, forgivable. The whole world was a world of
outsiders, society as such did not exist, each one of us was
alone, no one was at an advantage. He only *seemed* to be listening to what I was saying. For a long time he stared at the clock
on the wall, a present from my sister-in-law. I am, of course,
waiving my claim to the repayment of defence costs. The
legally prescribed payment of defence costs is an unjustifiable
hardship. He could rest assured, I said, that all obstacles would
be removed from his path. I would use my influence on his
behalf in various quarters. He was not alone with his crimes, I
repeated. Everyone committed crimes, of a most serious
nature, but the majority of crimes remained undiscovered,
unidentified, unpunished. Crimes were symptoms of disease;
nature was incessantly giving birth to every possible manner
of crime, including human crime; nature came by her crimes
legitimately. Everything was always a part of nature and born
of nature; nature was by nature criminal. I asked him, since
he looked so pitiful to me, whether at this minute, which was
quite possible, he had the strength to survey his life with the
whole world both behind and ahead of him. If he could bring
himself to contemplate his whole evolution, which was after
all a scandal, he would find – that too was part of the laws of
nature – that it contained not only darkness. The world was
not only terrible. Matter was tremendously exact and full of
beauty. Independently of place and time, the individual was
constantly capable of making the most astounding dis-
coveries, for the sake of which life was worth living. But
Winkler said nothing in reply, showed no reaction to anything. He appeared to shut himself up more and more within
himself, that is, in his own hideous conception of himself. I
remarked, and in doing so I was thinking more of myself than

Wald oder an den Fluß oder in das doch warme und pulsierende Gehäuse einer Stadt oder zu den allgemein Menschlichen und zurück führen, sondern nurmehr noch, wenn auch in den Wald und an den Fluß und in die Stadt und zu den allgemein Menschlichen, in die Finsternis und in nichts als in Finsternis, dann ist man verloren. Es war mir klar, daß Winkler, hätte er Geld genommen, ins Gasthaus gegangen wäre, nicht um zu schlafen . . . und er wäre am andern Tag nicht fähig gewesen, sich einem der Zimmerermeister vorzustellen. Wie schwach war der große Mensch, der riesige! Wenn er aufspränge und mich zusammenschlüge! Die Schläger und die Totschläger springen urplötzlich aus ihrer entsetzlichen Schwäche auf. Winkler erinnerte mich an ein Tier, das in mehreren wilden und zahmen Tieren zugleich ist, existiert, in Feindschaft, in der Natur der Feindschaft. Ich hätte mich über seine Kindheit nicht zu informieren brauchen: der Zimmerergehilfenbrief war ihm mehr ein nicht von ihm, sondern von seinen Eltern in höchster Höhe angebrachtes Sprungbrett, um sich davon, von ihm aus, dem für seinesgleichen oft unerreichbaren, in das Abgrundtiefe ja -tiefste fallen zu lassen, gewesen. Ich verzichtete an dem so unerwartet traurig gewordenen Abend darauf, einen Rundgang zu machen, wie das meine Gewohnheit ist. Winkler sagte nichts mehr und blieb bewegungslos mit geschlossenem Mantel; schließlich mit den Händen in seinen Manteltaschen im Sessel sitzen. Sein Kopf war dann, für mich hinter meinen Büchern verborgen, auf seinen Knien. Ich blätterte in den verschiedensten Aktenstücken, während Winkler, eingeschlafen, wie ich feststelle, einen nurmehr noch entsetzlichen Eindruck machte. Ich überlegte, ob ich ihn, der den für Magen- und Leberkranke und Strafanstalten charakteristischen Geruch in meinem Zimmer verbreitete, nicht aufwecken und vor die Haustür hinunterbegleiten sollte. Es war ein kalter und nasser Abend. Ich bin erschrocken, als Winkler

of him, that once the walks you take no longer lead to the
wood or to the river or to the warm, pulsating nest of a town
or to the fold of common humanity and back again, but only –
even if to the wood and the river and the town and to the
fold of common humanity – into darkness and nothing but
darkness, then you are lost. It was clear to me that Winkler,
if he had accepted money, would not have gone to a hotel
for the purpose of sleeping . . . and on the next day he would
have been in no state to go for an interview with the foreman
of a joinery firm. How weak this great giant of a man was!
What if he were to pounce on me and beat me up? Thugs and
murderers pounce all of a sudden out of a sense of their own
terrible weakness. Winkler reminded me of the animal which
is present in and exists inside several animals, wild and tame
ones alike, in hostility, in the nature of hostility. There would
have been no need for me to make inquiries about his childhood; his joiner's apprenticeship certificate had been like a
springboard to him, mounted at the highest of heights, not so
much by him as by his parents, for him to drop from; a
starting point, often beyond the reach of his sort, from which
to plunge into the depths, the very lowest depths of the abyss.
That evening, which had turned out so unexpectedly sad, I
refrained from going for my customary walk round. Winkler
said nothing more, but remained sitting motionlessly in his
chair, his coat fastened and, eventually, his hands in his coat
pockets. Then his head was down on his knees, hidden from
me behind my books. Whilst I flicked through all sorts of
documents, Winkler had, I discovered, fallen asleep; the sole
impression he made on me now was terrifying. His smell
typical of prisons and of people suffering from stomach or
liver complaints, was spreading round my room. I considered
whether I ought to wake him and show him down to the
front door. It was a cold and wet evening. Winkler startled

zu sich kam und, ohne nur ein einziges Wort zu sagen, und zwar mit dem Rücken zuerst, aus dem Zimmer ging; abrupt, kam mir vor. Sein Fall war schwierig. Ich habe von dem Menschen bis heute nichts mehr gesehen und nichts mehr gehört.

me when he came to and, without saying even a single word, walked, or rather backed out of the room; abruptly, so it seemed to me. His was a difficult case. To this day I have neither seen anything more nor heard anything more of the man.

NOTES ON GERMAN TEXTS

THE DOLPHIN (*Penzoldt*)

1. '*Heut bedarf's der kleinsten Reise . . .*': *Faust II*, ll. 8067–9.
2. *Davidsbündler*: a friendly and musical association formed by Schumann in 1834 to combat the Philistines of his day.
3. *delphinisch*, *Delphinios* (p. 48): epithet of Apollo as god of seafarers – in the form of a dolphin he led the Cretan colonists to Delphi.
4. *Frankfurter Zeitung*: a prestigious newspaper to which Penzoldt himself contributed until its suppression by Hitler in 1943.
5. '*Er ist neugierig wie ein Fisch*': *Faust II*, l. 8232 – said of Proteus. In the form of a dolphin he carries Homunculus into the sea. Proteus – 'the old storyteller', Goethe calls him (*Faust II*, l. 8225) – is behind the transformations Penzoldt's stranger recounts: satyr, dolphin, god. (cf. p. 44.)

   Pliny discusses the nature of dolphins in Book IX, 20–34 of his *Natural History*. 'For a voice they have a moan like a human being . . . they answer to the name of Simo (snub-nose).' The dolphin's love for the boy and its death on dry land are told by Pliny.
6. '*Jünglingsknabe*': *Faust II*, l. 9157.
7. '*sie duften Jugend*': *Faust II*, l. 9046.

FEDEZEEN (*de Bruyn*)

1. *Kreuzberg* is the name of an elevation of some 200 ft above sea level, lying just to the south of the old city centre. The district named after it was, in the years prior to the Second World War, the most densely populated working-class area of Berlin. Gneisenau St, which is also mentioned later on, is one of the main roads of the district.
2. *Rosinchen*, translated literally, means little sultana.
3. The block-warden was a post created by the National Socialist Party, in readiness no doubt for future hostilities. Other references

to the influence of Nazi ideology are the 'duty' to which the other boys report, the uniforms of the Party, and the stay at camp – which all suggest the activities of the Hitler Youth movement in its official capacity, while the 'unofficial' activities of the movement are suggested by the constant threat of violence and ambush in dark streets.
4. *Kajot* is the name of a large clothes store.

THE RENUNCIATION (*Lenz*)

1. *Masuren:* a district of East Prussia, Lenz's own homeland.
2. *Domäne:* state-owned land and forest.

THE DOGS (*Bachmann*)

1. *Hietzing:* the 13th district of Vienna, an area of villas and parkland, on the western side.
2. *Meinl:* a large Viennese grocery and delicatessen chain.
3. *Semmering:* a Viennese resort, to the south-west of the city.

LOBELLEN GROVE (*Bobrowski*)

1. *Zollbichs: Bichs* is a dialect word meaning 'fellow' or 'friend'.
2. *Lützows wilde, verwegene Jagd:* a song celebrating the volunteer force raised by Freiherr von Lützow against the French. Words by Th. Körner, music by K. M. Weber (1814).
3. *Afrikanisches:* from Meyerbeer's *The African Maid*.
4. *Szeszupe* etc.: to the east of Tilsit, now U.S.S.R., Bobrowski's own homeland. The border referred to later is that between what was before the war Germany (East Prussia) and Lithuania.
5. *Lindenbaum:* words by Wilhelm Müller, set to music by Schubert in his *Winterreise*.
6. 'O *Täler weit . . .*': words by Eichendorff, music by Mendelssohn.
7. *koppschellern:* cf. *kaufschlagen* – to shake hands at the conclusion of a deal.
8. *Müde bin ich, geh' zur Ruh:* a nineteenth-century bedtime prayer.

NOTES ON GERMAN TEXTS

ANITA G. (*Kluge*)

1. *Theresienstadt:* now Terezín, Czechoslovakia, from 1941–5 a concentration camp for Jews. Anita is Jewish, as is the lawyer, with his fear of renewed pogroms.
2. *Lavieren:* literally, 'to tack', 'to shift one's course'.

THE JOINER (*Bernhard*)

1. *Lokalaugenschein:* Austrian legal term for the official investigation of the scene of a crime or accident.
2. *Garsten:* on the river Enns, formerly a monastery, since 1851 a prison.
3. *Kerker:* the word is now old-fashioned, but is still used in Austria for prisons where harsher sentences are served.
4. *Kukuruzkolben:* used in Austria and East Middle Germany instead of *Maiskolben*. The word is Romanian in origin.
5. *Urvergleich:* literally, a comparison of a primitive, primordial kind. The equivalent prefix in English would be 'proto-', but as 'proto-comparison' is too bold the epithet has been transferred to *Wesen*.
6. *Kirchtagsordner: Kirchtag* is in Austria what the Germans call *Kirchweih*, i.e. a fair, originally held on the anniversary of the consecration of a church.

refresh yourself at penguin.co.uk

Visit penguin.co.uk for exclusive information and interviews with
bestselling authors, fantastic give-aways and the
inside track on all our books, from the Penguin Classics
to the latest bestsellers.

BE FIRST

first chapters, first editions, first novels

EXCLUSIVES

author chats, video interviews, biographies, special
features

EVERYONE'S A WINNER

give-aways, competitions, quizzes, ecards

READERS GROUPS

exciting features to support existing groups and
create new ones

NEWS

author events, bestsellers, awards, what's new

EBOOKS

books that click – download an ePenguin today

BROWSE AND BUY

thousands of books to investigate – search, try
and buy the perfect gift online – or treat yourself!

ABOUT US

job vacancies, advice for writers and company
history

Get Closer To Penguin ... www.penguin.co.uk